D0953116

# Rapture for the
# GEEKS

**RICHARD DOOLING**

# Rapture for the
# GEEKS

## WHEN AI OUTSMARTS IQ

Harmony Books · New York

Published in the United States by Harmony Books, an imprint of the Crown Publishing Group, a division of Random House, Inc., New York.
www.crownpublishing.com

Harmony Books is a registered trademark and the Harmony Books colophon is a trademark of Random House, Inc.

Grateful acknowledgment is made to the following for permission to reprint previously published material:

Neal Stephenson: Excerpts from "In the Beginning Was the Command Line" by Neal Stephenson, copyright © 1999 by Neal Stephenson. Reprinted by permission of Neal Stephenson.

Vernor Vinge: Excerpts from "The Coming Technological Singularity: How to Survive in the Post-Human Era" by Vernor Vinge, found at http://www-rohan/sdsu.edu/faculty/vinge/misc/singularity.html. Reprinted by permission of Vernor Vinge.

Warner Bros. Entertainment and the Philip K. Dick Estate: Excerpt from the *Blade Runner* screenplay, copyright © 1982 by The Blade Runner Partnership. Based on the novel *Do Androids Dream of Electric Sheep?* by Philip K. Dick. Reprinted by permission of Warner Bros. Entertainment and the Philip K. Dick Estate, administered by Scovil Chichak Galen Literary Agency, Inc.

The Python programming language version of "The brain is wider than the sky" by Emily Dickinson appears courtesy of Alex Martelli and Anna Ravenscroft.

Library of Congress Cataloging-in-Publication Data
Dooling, Richard.
Rapture for the geeks: when AI outsmarts IQ / Richard Dooling. — 1st ed.
p. cm.
1. Supercomputers. 2. Artificial intelligence.
3. Computers and civilization. I. Title.
QA76.88D65 2008
303.48'33—dc22
2008017309

ISBN 978-0-307-40525-8

Printed in the United States of America

10 9 8 7 6 5 4 3 2 1

First Edition

For Kristy Koy

# Contents

# CONTENTS

Ad Majorem Dei Gloriam

Technology is a way of organizing the universe
so that man doesn't have to experience it.
—Max Frisch

# Help—About

Computers are like Old Testament gods; lots of rules and no mercy.

—Joseph Campbell

## 1.1 ABOUT

In late February 2008, I went to meet my first supercomputer at the Peter Kiewit Institute of Technology (PKI) here in Omaha, Nebraska. PKI is Omaha's local version of MIT or Caltech, built in 1996 to offer a top-flight education to students headed for careers in information science, technology, and engineering. On the first floor, to the right of the main entrance and down a glass-and-steel corridor, is the Holland Computing Center, a secure, glass-enclosed bay that is home to Firefly, at the time of my visit the forty-third-most-powerful super-computer in the world.

I met John Callahan, director of Technological Infrastructure, responsible for the care and feeding of Firefly. Callahan gave me a tour, a spec sheet, and a summary of Firefly's components and capabilities. In its February 2008 configuration, Firefly's brain consisted of 1,151 Dell PowerEdge servers stacked in four sleek black climate-controlled walk-in bays (donated by American Power Conversion). As we browsed up and down the rows of humming servers with blinking blue lights, Callahan described how companies, businesses, and other universities were sending him programs that took weeks or months to run on their older, lesser hardware configurations and were delighted and amazed when Firefly ran the same programs in minutes.

Supercomputers grow up even faster than kids, it seems. Firefly, still less than a year old at the time of my tour, and running on newish AMD Opteron dual-core chips, was already due for an upgrade. Callahan said that in April 2008 Firefly would receive all new AMD Opteron *quad*-core chips, which would make it more than twice as fast, more than twice as powerful—so fast and powerful that it would vault into the top twenty of the world's fastest supercomputers. Sometime in 2009 or 2010, it will be time for another upgrade. Firefly was built to accommodate just such scenarios; more bays, more racks, more and better chips can be easily added.

I went to see Firefly because I'm anxious about just when supercomputers like it will be programmed to write better books than I do. I wanted to see if Firefly felt like just a big marvelous tool or something more. Was it a whole new species of machine intelligence that might one day think for itself? And even if Firefly can't yet think for itself, what about ten or twenty Firefly supercomputers networked together? What about a billion or so computers—our computers— harnessed by a company like Google? Would those be capable of mimicking human intelligence, assuming someone, or some supercomputer, came along and wrote the proper software?

Other questions soon follow: If a supercomputer ever does "think" the way human brains do, how will we know it? Will it be "conscious" in the same way we are? Do these questions make sense given the trouble we've had over the centuries describing human or animal consciousness?

What is the true nature of our relationship to information technologies? Are computers and supercomputers just the latest tool, the latest bone in the hand of the hominid apes in *2001: A Space Odyssey*? Or are we, like the apes, worshipping something, be it a black monolith or some other technological force beyond our understanding?

What are we creating when we log on each day and contribute to Google's vast repository of information?

This book is about the future of technology and the evolution, co-evolution, and possible merger of humans and computers. Some futurists and AI (artificial intelligence) experts argue that this merger is imminent, and that we'll be raising Borg children (augmented humans) by the year 2030. Others predict that supercomputers will equal and then quickly surpass human intelligence as early as 2015. We are accustomed to using computers as powerful tools, and we resist any invitation to think of them as sentient beings—and with good reason: Computers, even computers as powerful as Firefly, still just kind of sit there, patiently humming, waiting for instructions from programs written by humans.

## 1.2 HELP

Richard "Dick" Holland, native Omahan, original Buffett and Berkshire Hathaway investor, and philanthropist, provided most of the funds to build Firefly and the Holland Computer Center. At age eighty-six, Dick is a passionate reader and a polymath with a crackling, underhanded sense of humor. When I described this book to him, he told me about a 1954 sci-fi short story called "Answer," written by Fredric Brown.

In the story, set in the distant future, a computer engineer solders the final connection of a switch that will connect all of the monster computing machines on all of the populated planets in the universe, forming a super-circuit and a single super-calculator, "one cybernetic machine that would combine all the knowledge of all the galaxies."

The engineer plans to ask the new supercomputer "a question which no single cybernetics machine has been able to answer."

He flips the switch, turns and faces the machine: "Is there a God?"

The mighty voice answers without hesitation, "Yes, now there is a God."

Fear flashes on the face of the engineer, and he leaps to grab the switch, but a bolt of lightning from the cloudless sky strikes him down and fuses the switch shut.

## 1.3 YOUR USER PROFILE

> User, *noun*. The word computer professionals use when they mean "idiot."
>
> —Dave Barry
>
> There are only two industries that refer to their customers as "users."
>
> —Edward Tufte

It's time to launch the Web browser of your imagination and surf the undiscovered future of technology, but first a few questions to assist you in formulating your user profile.

Are you addicted to your computer? To the Internet? To e-mail? To your Treo, iPhone, or CrackBerry? To computer gaming? Or maybe to computer programming? Perhaps you're not addicted (and you don't overeat or drink too much or take drugs); maybe you just like to configure and personalize your favorite software until it does just what you want it to do, just the way you want it done. Do you tweak the options and widgets and custom codes on your blogspot or your WordPress weblog for hours on end, until your little corner of the Internet is "clean" and well designed? Have you logged on to MySpace at 2 A.M. asking, "Help! I can't get my marquee scroll generator to work! How can I make my table backgrounds transparent, the border invisible, my photos appear to hover, and my hyperlinks underlined and 12-point Garamond?" Are you the type who customizes menus, macros, and toolbars for hours at a time, sometimes for more hours than you'll ever spend actually *doing* the task you had in mind when you started the program?

Here's the big question: Do you ever feel that you once used computers and computer programs as tools to get a specific job done, but lately you wonder if Dave Barry was on to something when he wrote:

"I am not the only person who uses his computer mainly for the purpose of diddling with his computer"?

Then again, maybe you aren't addicted to your computer. Maybe instead you hate your computer. But somehow, even though you detest the *&^%$@!# thing, you spend more time messing with it than your tech-loving, over-clocking geek friend spends messing with his. Maybe you hate it even more when your tech-loving geek friend stops answering your user-in-distress e-mails, because then you wind up on the phone all evening with a woman in Bangalore, asking her how to make your spyware-hijacked Internet Explorer Web browser stop loading the Play-Strip-Poker-with-Hot-Young-CoEds website before your wife gets home and wants to check her e-mail.

Does your handheld sometimes feel like a prosthetic device containing your own personalized sixth sense? Is it a brain extension, with an extra, palm-held visual cortex for displaying YouTube videos? When it's gone, or broken, or not charging properly, are you bereft? Adrift? Are you a victim of what Harvard neuropyschiatrist Dr. John Ratey calls self-inflicted "acquired attention deficit disorder,"[1] because you compulsively reach for the thing, even when you don't want to? Were the editors of the New York Times talking about you and your gadgets when they observed (on iPhone day, June 29, 2007): "The real test of each new apparatus is how easily it is ingested and how quickly it becomes part of the user's metabolism. All you have to do is watch a 9-year-old teaching her mother how to text to understand the truth of this"?

When you're in a panic to make an appointment and you can't find your car keys or your billfold or purse, do you instinctively begin formulating search terms you might use if the real world came with Google Desktop Search or a command-line interface?* Whoever

---

*The "command line" is a user interface with a "prompt," where you can type specific, precise textual commands to your computer, instead of clicking on gaudy pictures and drilling down through menus and dialogue boxes. Frequently abbreviated as CLI, also called a "command prompt" or "CommandShell" or "Terminal" on an Apple Mac. See discussion at footnote on page 168 under "Learn a Programming Language."

created the infinite miracle we glibly call "the universe" is surely at least as smart as the guys in Berkeley, California, who made UNIX. The UNIX creators wisely included a program called Find, which enables you to instantly find any file on your system, especially any file in your "home" directory. Another command-line utility, Grep, enables you to find any line of text in any file on your entire system. Mac OS X uses Spotlight to do essentially the same thing with spiffy visuals, and even Microsoft finally included "Instant Search" in Vista. So why can't the creator of the universe come up with a decent search box? Why can't you summon a command line and search your real-world home for "Honda car keys," and specify rooms in your house to search instead of folders or paths in your computer's home directory? It's a crippling design flaw in the real-world interface.

And while we're at it, how about an Undo button? Wouldn't that come in handy in the real world? Especially if you just totaled your car or contracted a venereal disease? Why can't you just hit Ctrl-Z or click on the swirly little Undo arrow icon and put everything back the way it was before? If only your mouth came with a backspace key. If you have one of those days where all of life seems corrupted, broken, full of error messages and warnings, and the kids are all out somewhere performing illegal operations, buffer overruns, segmentation faults, and destabilizing the system, what you need is Real Life System Restore. Restore Your Life to Last Known Good Configuration.

Do you ever feel that you have *everything*—your "life"—on your MacBook Pro or your laptop? Indeed, and doesn't that totally justify the vast amounts of time you spend configuring it into the well-tempered desktop? After all, it's not just a computer, it's a professional, customized tool, which you deploy each day to advance your career in the information age.

Ever had a hard-drive crash? On your main machine? Had you made a recent backup? No, wait, let me guess—you *thought* you had a backup somewhere, but you didn't? How bad was it? Did you pay several thousand dollars to a hard-drive-recovery service, after which they were able to salvage a few unreadable WordStar archives and a complete set of last-century game maps from Duke Nukem 3D? Did you lose ten years' worth of photos, e-mails, tax returns, a Rolodex with four thousand contacts, your novel (the *opus major*) dating all the way back to college, your $1,500 music collection, your ancestry research, several dozen works-in-progress for clients, bosses, and colleagues, and your fantasy baseball league—all gone? Did your doctor recommend therapy from a professional "data crisis counselor"? Did you have to go on antidepressants because, in the twinkling of a screen, your life became a data-barren wasteland?

What if at that very moment a genie had appeared and had said that you could have your laptop back with all its data, but only if you would agree to stand back and watch your house burn down? What would you have done? (Hey, at least the house is insured, right?) Were you consumed with guilt and self-loathing because tech-savvy, computer-wise Dutch uncles had been telling you for ten or twenty years that the only way to protect the integrity of your data is to *back up*? It's like a seat belt, they said. You need it only once, but then it's absolutely critical. Did you keep saying, "Yeah, I know. I will. I think I have most of it backed up on an old laptop"? But here you are in information gray-out, because you in fact did *not* back up. Now, alas, it's too late. You may feel the same way at the end of your life, when you realize that you could have spent more time with your kids instead of your MacBook Pro. Now your "life" has been erased, leaving nothing but an epitaph in stark white letters on a black screen: "Hard Disk Controller Failure."

If you're like me, all of this has convinced you that it's time to log on to the Online 12-Step Forum for Online Addiction (where people are hard at work improving themselves and changing the world through chat). Time for you to type:

BartlebyScrivener: Hello, my name is Rick, and I am a computer addict.
1Byte@ATime: Hi, Rick!
NoMoMachineHead: Welcome, Rick!

I<3MamaBoards: Hey, Bartleby, don't I know you from the Linux.Debian.User Google Group? 4giveme but I got my SATA 300 Seagate hard drive talking to my ASUS Motherboard using the configs you recommended, but now I can't get RAID to work. Can you help me?

It'll be like holding an AA meeting at a TGIF happy hour.

If computers and programming and the Internet are all sins that divert me from my family and the rest of humanity, then for the last four or five years I've been doing technology the Gnostic way. The Gnostics believed that the only way to avoid a sin was to commit it and be rid of it. When I get done thoroughly sinning and overdosing on machine living, I can perhaps rid myself of it, retire to the Alaskan wilderness, and get all of my technology-news updates from the bush pilot who drops off my groceries once a month. When he shows up sporting a new fiber-optic skull port in the back of his head with a Cat-5 connection for seamless neuro-navigational and instrument panel data transfer, I'll know that the future of technology has arrived . . . in my absence.

## 1.4 TIME TO QUIT?

But before I go native, I thought I'd write this book. Perhaps my own tech addiction and my disturbing apprehensions about what technology will do to us in the very near future will serve as a cautionary tale for the age. As if the age and I are capable of saying no to more and more and more technology (aka Moore's law). Addicts (like us) are sharks. We don't think; we move and feed. At the moment, the age and I are both mainlining computer technologies. The scary part is that addicts often go on moving and feeding, right up until they land in jail or on the table in the ER, where they don't wake up. Sometimes it's worse if they do wake up, because then they have to quit.

Maybe the comparison between substance abuse and tech abuse strikes you as extreme. It's not like computers or Internet addiction ever *killed* anybody. Maybe you were offline and doing a meatspace* chore when the RSS† news feed came through on the twenty-eight-year-old South Korean man who died in an Internet café after fifty hours of playing StarCraft, a computer game. Or the twenty-one-year-old Wisconsin man who shot himself because he couldn't stop playing EverQuest, another computer game. Or the Xinhua News Agency report about a Chinese girl who died of exhaustion after playing World of Warcraft (the biggest computer game of all) for several days without a break. And now the Chinese are hauling preteens in for shock therapy to cure game and Internet addiction.

The American Medical Association recently met to vote on whether to recommend that the American Psychiatric Association include excessive computer and video-game playing as a formal psychiatric addiction in the next edition of the bible of mental illnesses called the *Diagnostic and Statistical Manual of Mental Disorders*, due out in 2012. The nation's physicians backed off on classifying hardcore gamers as junkies and decided instead that more research was needed. Doctors probably want more studies done to establish that there is a *big* difference between Game Boys and BlackBerries, and also a big difference—huge difference!—between Internet role-playing games and surfing the latest cool sites offering diagnostic software and computer programs for physicians and medical researchers. It's important that the doctors are able to keep checking their BlackBerries and playing with their iPhones while telling concerned parents that too much technology for kids may be inappropriate because it induces dependence-like behaviors.

Good thing the AMA hasn't been to Google or Microsoft and met a

---

*The flesh-and-blood real world; the opposite of cyberspace. See, e.g., Paul McFedries's excellent site WordSpy: http://www.wordspy.com/words/meatspace.asp.

†"RSS is a format for syndicating news and the content of news-like sites, including major news sites like Wired, news-oriented community sites like Slashdot, and personal weblogs." Mark Pilgrim, "What Is RSS?" (December 18, 2002), http://www.xml.com/pub/a/2002/12/18/dive-into-xml.html.

few real programmers. A "formal psychiatric addiction" wouldn't come close to capturing the fire in a compulsive programmer's eyes. This is not a new phenomenon. Even back in 1976, when computer science students had to "go to the computer center" before they could get on the machine, author and MIT computer scientist Joseph Weizenbaum described the scene this way:

> Wherever computer centers have become established . . . bright young men of disheveled appearance, often with sunken glowing eyes, can be seen sitting at computer consoles, their arms tensed and waiting to fire, their fingers already poised to strike at the buttons and keys on which their attention seems to be as riveted as a gambler's on the rolling dice. When not so transfixed, they often sit at tables strewn with computer printouts over which they pore like possessed students of a cabalistic text. They work until they nearly drop, twenty, thirty hours at a time. Their food, if they arrange it, is brought to them: coffee, Cokes, sandwiches. If possible, they sleep on cots near the computer. But only for a few hours—then back to the console or the printouts. Their rumpled clothes, their unwashed and unshaven faces, and their uncombed hair all testify that they are oblivious to their bodies and to the world in which they move. They exist, at least when so engaged, only through and for the computers. These are computer bums, compulsive programmers. They are an international phenomenon.[2]

Never mind possessed programmers, frothing gamers, and gadget freaks. How about killing the planet instead? Runaway technology means more and more computers, including computers embedded in cars, clothes, phones, brains, and eventually entire virtual-reality environments made of nanobots and utility fog.* In trendy green accounting terms: All of those computers consume massive amounts

---

*"Imagine a microscopic robot. It has a body about the size of a human cell and 12 arms sticking out in all directions. A bucketful of such robots might form a 'robot crystal' by linking their arms up into a lattice structure. Now take a room, with people, furniture, and other objects in it—it's still mostly empty air. Fill the air completely full of robots. The robots are called Foglets and the substance they form is

of electricity, meaning we'll need more and more power plants, creating more and more carbon dioxide emissions, depleting more and more ozone and leaving carbon footprints all over the earth's carpet. All of which means that the smart planet is about to get even hotter, and as every gamer who ever tried to over-clock a hot CPU knows: The one thing computers *hate* is heat.

I'm ready to go cold turkey myself. But I can't swear off computers just yet, because I need my machine to write this book. And to do that I must configure all of my cool programs and handcrafted scripts and quotations databases and software "tools" to help me get the job done in the most productive and efficient manner, so that whenever I am not configuring said programs, scripts, and cool tools, I can be writing this book, which is all about how I'll be quitting soon (and you should, too), and what's going to happen to us if we don't.

## 1.5 THE TRUTH

If you were enraged to discover that James Frey's somewhat truthy substance-abuse memoir, *A Million Little Pieces,* contained something less than consumer-grade veracity, I feel your disdain. As a novelist, I take a Peeping Tom's delight in reading about other people's addictions. As a student of human nature, I am fascinated when people are unable to control themselves. I'm even more intrigued when I am unable to control myself. But when I read about somebody plunging headfirst into ruination because they cannot resist their cravings for legal or illegal drugs, sex, pornography, gambling, computer games, the Internet, or 4,000-calorie, supersized Happy Meals, I want to *know* that I'm reading the truth. I resent it when the author or members of the press dilute my schadenfreude and voyeuristic plea-

---

Utility Fog, which may have many useful medical applications. And when a number of utility foglets hold hands with their neighbors, they form a reconfigurable array of 'smart matter.' " Dr. J. Storrs Hall, research fellow of the Institute for Molecular Manufacturing, http://www.nanotech-now.com/utility-fog.htm.

sures afterward with intimations that the most lurid, ghastly, and unspeakable details of said decadence and depravity never really happened. I felt totally used when I learned that James Frey didn't really vomit through a hole his cheek.

Let me establish my credibility early by assuring you that parts of this book are true. Specifically, the graphic details about Internet, computer, and programming addictions found on these pages actually happened—possibly to me, or in other cases they may have happened to friends of mine, friends I've "met" on the Internet but have never met in real life, and whose real names I do not know. However, they are easy to find if you go to the linux.debian.user group or the comp.lang.python group or the Ubuntu Community Forums and search for RogueAccountant, BlackAdder, Microsoft666Sux, or FrodoB (FrodoB in the Ubuntu forums is particularly knowledgeable and helpful if you are having issues with your wireless USB adapter after upgrading Ubuntu Linux from Feisty Fawn to Gutsy Gibbon).

When I say that parts of this book are true, I mean "true" insofar as you, I, and we can still agree on a working definition of *truth*. And which parts of this book are true? That's why we need a definition, and for that I can think of no better resource than Wikipedia. I love Wikipedia. It's a shining example of technology's light side: computer geeks clustering together in smart mobs and hive minds to create excellent, free repositories of software and information. I also love the open source* Web browser Firefox, made by rebel geeks at the Mozilla Foundation, just because they wanted to create a superior browser (i.e., better than Microsoft's clunky, insecure Internet Explorer). And what's more important than a fast, secure, customizable

---

*"Refers to software that is created by a development community rather than a single vendor. Typically programmed by volunteers from many organizations, the source code of open source software is free and available to anyone who would like to use it or modify it for their own purposes. This allows an organization to add a feature itself rather than hope that the vendor of a proprietary product will implement its suggestion in a subsequent release." *The American Heritage Dictionary of the English Language,* 4th ed. (New York: Houghton Mifflin, 2007).

Web browser? After the operating system (the code that runs your computer), the browser (the software tool you use to access the Internet) is probably the most important program on your machine. Thanks to Firefox, humans in Mali, Suriname, Sri Lanka, and Lansing, Michigan, can sit at their computers and extend their reach thousands of miles beyond their grasp. As Douglas Adams, the proto-geek author of *The Hitchhiker's Guide to the Galaxy*, put it: "A computer terminal is not some clunky old television with a typewriter in front of it. It is an interface where the mind and body can connect with the universe and move bits of it about." Shopping, anyone?

Indeed. And using the Firefox Web browser enables us to visit the hive-minded knowledge metropolis called Wikipedia, where we should be able to find a good working definition of *truth*. Then we can just provide a link to the definition and be done with it.

## 1.6 Parts of This Book Are *Not* True

On June 10, 2007, I visited http://en.wikipedia.org/wiki/Truth, where the first sentence in Wikipedia's entry for "truth" read: "A common dictionary definition of truth is 'agreement with fact or reality.'"

Complications ensued in the very next paragraph:

> There is no single definition of truth about which the majority of philosophers agree. Various theories of truth, commonly involving different definitions of "truth," continue to be debated. There are differing claims on such questions as what constitutes truth; how to define and identify truth; what roles do revealed and acquired knowledge play; and whether truth is subjective, relative, objective, or absolute. This article introduces the various perspectives and claims, both today and throughout history.

No single definition of *truth*? Just theories? What followed on Wikipedia's *truth* page (on June 10, 2007) was a systematic breakdown of a dozen or so truth theories, which you or I could use to formulate our working definition. And therein lies the prolix power and glory of the Internet, the expansive reach of the personal computer, and the seductive allure of technology: Taken together they provide a surfeit of choices and options, along with gigabytes of information free for the downloading. If I block and copy the entire definition of *truth* from Wikipedia and save it to my hard drive, I come away with the feeling that I now have the power to formulate a working definition of *truth*, if I ever have the time to read all of those theories and pursue all of those hyperlinks. In much the same way, I often buy a book because it gives me the illusion of absorbing its contents, even though I don't have time to read it. The Internet gives us all the information in the world but no time for distilling knowledge from it. However, back to the problem at hand: *our* working definition of *truth*.

Parsing a dozen truth theories at Wikipedia is beyond the scope of this slender volume. Instead I shall adopt the truth theory of Saul Kripke, an American philosopher and logician, professor emeritus of Princeton, which is set forth in the Wikipedia "truth" entry under the subsection "Formal Theories." Why Saul Kripke's theory of truth, and not the truth theories of, say, Friedrich Nietzsche or Bertrand Russell, both of whom are also featured? Well, Saul Kripke is from Omaha, and so am I, so I trust him to tell me the truth, more than I do, say, Friedrich Nietzsche, who went insane in 1889 and flung his arms around the neck of a horse that was being flogged on the streets of Turin. Besides, Nietzsche is dead, something he accused God of being over a century ago. Bertrand Russell is also dead, and with a name like Bertrand, he probably had a butler and could discourse at great length about the truth without ever telling you the truth.

Also, according to Wikipedia, Saul Kripke's truth theory solves the problem of the liar paradox, which is important to the rest of this book. I am a lawyer and also a fiction writer, and so I appreciate a truth theory that enables me to say, on occasion, "I am not telling the truth." In some systems of truth, and according to some truth theories, this is not possible, or else it causes complex problems. Because if I make the statement "I am not telling the truth" or "I am lying," I must be either lying or telling the truth, but I can't be doing both at the same time, can I? So I'm picking Saul Kripke's theory because he's from Omaha, and because his theory enables me to say that parts of this book are *not* true. Which brings us to: Which parts are those?

Here are some rough guidelines and examples:

Most of the sentences in this book that begin with "I" are true. For instance, "I quit drinking alcohol years ago, and I don't take drugs or pills, but lately I'm addicted to computer programming, UNIX-like operating systems, the Python programming language, and the Vim text editor."

That's all true.

Sentences that begin with "You" are probably not true. For instance, when I write: "You are a pet human named Morlock being disciplined by your master, a Beowulf cluster of FreeBSD 22.0 servers in the year 2052. Last week you tried to escape by digging a hole under the perimeter, which means that this week you may be put to sleep for being a renegade human."

That's not true, at least not yet. As of this writing, you indeed may be a pet human being held somewhere by a supercomputer named Beowulf, but FreeBSD is only in release 7.0, not 22.0. The "You" sentences are usually hypothetical. At best, they are what the inventor, futurist, and tech titan Ray Kurzweil optimistically refers to as "true stories about the future."

Of course, by the time you read this, Wikipedia's definition of *truth* will probably be altogether different; I'm not saying it will be more true, or less true, just different. Your mileage may vary (YMMV). But who needs Truth anyway? For scientists and technologists, *truth* always has a small *t*. So you would expect that as we become ever more scientific and technological, as we spend ever greater portions of our day absorbed in one screen or another, then religion would gradually wither, along with astrology and other questionable pursuits. Why, then, are extreme religions gaining ground? A recent PBS special looked at just that issue and determined that "more people than ever before are devout as measured by attendance in houses of worship. In the United States alone, on a percentage basis, three times more people attend a church, synagogue, temple, or mosque than did when the nation was founded."[3]

According to Muzaffar Iqbal, founder of the Center for Islam and Science, "A natural result of eight or ten hours of workaday routine with all these gadgets leads to a total disintegration of the inner concentration of our personality."[4] Christian sociologist Don Miller agrees, arguing that technology and efficiency lack the ability to give our deeper selves meaning, a quest that unfailingly appears to be a universal need for all human beings.[5]

So let the search for Truth and truth begin!

## 1.7 No NOObs or Luddites Left Behind

Before I get too far in, let me acknowledge that the jargon may be making some of you nervous. The planet is still teeming with nOObs* who don't know what Wikipedia is and may not even know about links and hyperlinks. These poor souls will be exterminated in the near future after supercomputers take over (probably around 2030), but in the short term, computer illiterates are still human beings with basic civil liberties, and they have the right to know what the rest of us are talking about when we say "link" or "hyperlink" and use expressions like "go to Wikipedia." Therefore, whenever I have room, I'll use footnotes to explain any terms that a computer nOOb might not know; those who aren't nOObs won't be distracted.†

---

*"NOOb" is one of the many variants of "newbie," an inexperienced, ignorant, or unskilled person, especially used in the context of a newcomer joining a group specializing in a certain computer program or game, programming language or online forum. If you are totally unfamiliar with the term "nOOb" or "newbie" and have never even heard of the online encyclopedia called Wikipedia, then you may wish to stop reading this book, shun the English, and return to your Amish roots.

†"NOOb" is a relative term, which says nothing about your overall intelligence or value to society. Warren Buffett would be a nOOb in the Metroid Prime 3: Corruption

Also, although this book is aimed at moderate to heavy computer users, it's unfair to assume that everyone has a powerful PC, Mac, Linux, or BSD box and a high-speed Internet connection. Aspiring geeks who bought this book to learn about the future of computer technology and yet are still accessing the Internet via a dial-up connection need not despair. Luddites* and neo-Luddites are welcome.

## 1.8 Soul of the New Networked Machines

No man is an island, entire of itself; every man is a piece of the continent, a part of the main.

—John Donne

As the Internet continues to proliferate, it has become natural to think of it biologically—as a flourishing ecosystem of computers . . . it may be designed according to the same rules that nature uses to spin webs of its own.

—George Johnson[6]

No computer is an island, either. Later in this book, I explore whether computers will ever become sapient, self-aware, develop minds and personalities, you know, like the human beings you once conversed with in the olden days when you used to get up from the keyboard and

---

gaming forum, and Johnathan Wendel, pseudonym "Fatal1ty," a professional gamer who has won in excess of $500,000 playing computer games in the Cyberathlete Professional League (CPL), would be a nOOb if he went looking for advice on investing his winnings by posting on a hedge-fund forum.

*"The Luddites were a social movement of British textile artisans in the early nineteenth century who protested—often by destroying mechanized looms—against the changes produced by the Industrial Revolution, which they felt threatened their livelihood. . . .

"[The] movement, which began in 1811, took its name from the earlier Ned Ludd. For a short time the movement was so strong that it clashed in battles with the British Army." http://en.wikipedia.org/wiki/Luddite.

move about in real reality. When pondering questions like whether computers dream of electric sheep when in sleep mode, most of us imagine a single powerful intelligent supercomputer playing chess or simulating weather patterns or sequencing the human genome. Or maybe we imagine robots from the future, like the Terminator, replicants, or Borgs, with supercomputers for a brain. However, even way back in 1982 a computer scientist named John Gage and three other founders of Sun Microsystems saw the future when they formulated Sun's corporate slogan: "The network *is* the computer."

What's one supercomputer or one robot compared with a distributed network of, oh, say, a million or so computers? Most computer-industry seers don't see desktops in our future. Rather they see invisible smart networks and appliances (think *screens* big and small for displaying . . . almost anything), communications (cell phones and PDAs), and computer hardware (chips, processors) that all merge into embedded smart über networks. What's potentially a lot smarter and more powerful than one big computer? Never mind a million, how about a billion computers—including the dozen or so found in your household and built into media players, cell phones, iPod Touch, and laptops—all hooked together in a home network, which in turn is a tiny node on the earth's peripheral nervous system, aka the Internet?

Even here in 2008, all computers connected to the Internet (including yours) are already technically "networked." In other words, your computer is not just able to connect to Google and YouTube and Yahoo! and the *New York Times,* your computer is theoretically networked to every other Internet-connected computer on the planet. Every computer connected to the Internet must have an IP (Internet Protocol) address, usually four numbers separated by periods. For example, 64.233.167.104 is a valid IP address—in this case it's the address of Google.com, the same "place" you'd end up if you typed in "http://google.com" and hit "Enter":* If I have the IP address of a com-

---

*To find out the IP address of *your* computer, just visit whatismyip.com, and the site will tell you.

puter in Taiwan or Timbuktu, I can ping that computer using a tiny program (called, yes, "ping") that sends an echo request to the computer in Timbuktu, which, if it is online, will send back an echo response, which, in effect, says, "Yes, there's a computer at this address capable of sending and receiving messages."

So that we don't have to remember all of those numbers, the numbers get translated into names, like microsoft.com, linux.com, dooling.com, or singularity.com. Instead of typing numbers or even names into address bars or forms, Web pages use links. When you "surf" or "browse" the Internet, the pages you see are almost all written in Hypertext Markup Language (HTML) or its XML-descended cousin XHTML, computer code that tells your Web browser—usually Microsoft's Internet Explorer (bad), Mozilla's Firefox browser (good), Apple's Safari (different)—how to display the pages you visit. Normally, you can't see the HTML code; you see only the *results* of what the code told your browser to do: Make this text a new paragraph. Make it red. Load a graphics file with an image of an attractive naked woman holding a cigar here. Use 12-point Arial font. Make it bold. And so on. You can take a peek at a sample of HTML anytime you are "on" the Internet, just by going to your Web browser's toolbar and clicking on View and then Page Source from the drop-down list. The gunky-looking code words and tags that you see sprawled out on the screen are written in Hypertext Markup Language. (When you're joshing, "HTML" stands for "How They Make Links.")

Code Box 1 contains a sample patch of HTML code. The text between the angle brackets or chevrons <text> are tags. For example, the <title> tag tells the browser that this Web page is entitled: "Does Your Computer Want to Have Sex with You?" When the browser sees </title> it knows that is the end of the page title.

A link is a special HTML tag that doesn't do anything unless you click on it with your mouse. If you do, the link's code instructs your browser to load another Web page (which "takes you" to another page or website).

```
<!DOCTYPE HTML PUBLIC "//W3C//DTD HTML 4.01 Transitional//En"
   "http://www.w3.org/TR/html4/loose.dtd">
<html>
<head><!- give ->
<title>Does Your Computer Want to Have Sex with You?</title>
<meta name="keywords"content="computer sex, XML & XXXML, preparing
   entry ports, fornication, frobnication and foreplay, cascading
   between the style sheets, preparing entry ports, male and female
   connections, master and slave connections, link bondage and tag
   discipline, demos and howtos for doing it digitally, orgasm and
   operating system options, teledildonic sex online"/>
<meta name="description" content="Before You Begin a Serious
   Relationship with Your New Computer."/>
</head>
<body> <!- I want your ->
<p>"What do people mean when they say the computer went down on them?"
   —Marilyn Pittman</p>
<p>"Take me now, you mad, impetuous fool!! Oh wait . . . I'm a computer,
   and you're a person. It would never work out. Never mind."</p>
<p>An interesting link might be to: <a href="http://www.p-synd.com/
   winterrose/technosexuality.html"> Technosexuality</a>, where you can
   read about fembots, Pygmalionism, and Truly Scrumptious, the windup
   doll from Chitty Chitty Bang Bang.</p>
</body>
</html>
```

Let's say you are a gamer (a person, usually male, who spends twelve or more hours a day playing Oblivion or World of Warcraft or some other MMORPG (massively multiplayer online role-playing game). Being a gamer, you might be perusing the pages of a gaming forum, which might offer tips on how to get your screaming new graphics card working properly on the latest Microsoft operating system. You are probably looking for a patch or some advice from another gamer who has the same graphics card and can help you install the proper driver and configure it to take advantage of bleeding-edge graphics technologies like DirectX 9 or 10, which will in turn enable warriors, monsters, demons, and naked avatars to appear on your screen in vivid, living color (65 million different colors, to be exact), with pixel-shading, anti-aliasing, and such. Of course, you probably aren't a gamer or you wouldn't be reading this book. Gamers don't read books, because they live online and hang out in virtual places with names like Undercity in the Tirisfal Glades, or Ironforge in Dun Morogh, where they have their hands full dealing with "world" events, like the Dark Portal in Blasted Lands opening and demons pouring out.*

For now, just pretend that you're a gamer browsing for help on the forum of a gaming site and off to one side of the page you see some text that looks like this:

**Jessica Biel NAKED right here!**

The bold text may be a different color, it may be underlined, or blinking, or highlighted in some way to show that it is a link (hyperlink) to another page. The HTML code "hidden" behind this link is the code that tells your browser what page to load if you click on it. It may be the address of a page located on a server down the street or the address of a page located on a server in South Korea.

The sample HTML in Code Box 2 contains an example of a hyperlink. The <p> tells your browser to make a new paragraph. Then it makes a hyperlink <href=> out of the words "Jessica Biel NAKED!" The </a> tells the browser where the hyperlink ends, and the </p> tells it where the paragraph ends.

If you click on the "Jessica Biel naked" link, your browser ignores

---

*The foregoing is an extended allusion to World of Warcraft, aka WOW, a parallel online universe where "players"—paying customers from all over the world—spend their time pretending they are Orcs or Elves doing battle with one another. According to Blizzard Entertainment, as of January 2008, WOW hosts more than 10 million subscribers (2 million in Europe, more than 2.5 million in North America, and approximately 5.5 million in Asia); http://www.blizzard.com/us/press/080122.html. If you really don't know about WOW, then I can't tell you more without contributing to the delinquency of a nOOb. Also, you may have lost a loved one to World of Warcraft, and it would be crass of me to make light of your misfortune.

---

CODE BOX 2. **A FAKE HYPERLINK TO JESSICA BIEL NAKED**

```
<p>
<a href="http://give-us-your-credit-card-number.com/biel.htm">Jessica Biel
    NAKED right here!</a>
</p>
```

---

the text that you see and instead loads a new page using the address contained within the quotation marks of the hyperlink. In this example, the address of the website is http://give-us-your-credit-card-number.com and the page is "biel.htm."

When the new page loads, you may indeed see some photos purporting to be photos of Jessica Biel naked, but the feral Internet weasels who operate the website at give-us-your-credit-card-number.com have probably used a pirated copy of a graphics-editing program called Adobe Photoshop, or maybe they used GIMP, a similar, open-source program, to detach Jessica Biel's head from a real photo of her and place it on the naked body of some nameless woman whose dimensions vaguely resemble those of Jessica Biel. Either way, the weasels will be asking for your credit card number. Or, if you are using Microsoft Internet Explorer, they may just take it from you without asking.

Now, let's say you're not a gamer. No, you've got better things to do than worry about imaginary corrupted blood plagues and jungle trolls. You're a proud member of the American Association of Retired Persons out proving that you know your way around the Internet just fine, thank you very much, even though you still need your AOL training wheels to do it. You are visiting one of ten thousand different sites on the Internet offering "free" health and medical information. You're off in some disreputable corner of the Web, exploring an alternative-medicine website, because you don't like the advice you've been getting from your regular doctor lately ("Stop eating bacon and fried ice cream! Don't smoke! Don't drink so much! Exercise! Eat green vegetables!"). Instead, you'd rather eat bacon and ice cream, smoke and drink, and find an organic supplement or an obscure nutrient that will lower your bad cholesterol and your blood pressure, raise your good cholesterol and your serotonin levels, and make you feel good about yourself, even though you are obese and unable to walk to the refrigerator without getting winded.

Off to the side of the alternative-medicine site page, you see some text that looks like this:

**Lexapro, Lipitor, and Levitra—75% off!**

This link catches your eye because it's an ad for the expensive pills you buy every month. However, the underlying HTML code could be just another link to the same site that sells ersatz photos of Jessica Biel naked.

The pill link might look like the HTML in Code Box 3. If you click on this link, your browser takes you to the same site where the gamer went hoping for a peek at Jessica Biel naked. However in your case, the fine felons at give-us-your-credit-card-number.com will show you a page ("pills.htm") with images of the pills you take every day, alongside prices that will make you salivate, because you're on a fixed income, and Walgreens takes half off the top. However, the pills advertised at give-us-your-credit-card-number.com probably are not Lexapro, Lipitor, and Levitra. They are probably made out of baby powder or cornstarch or aspirin, or perhaps fertilizer from mainland China. But hope, being a thing with feathers that perches in the soul, may make you reach for your wallet anyway.

---

CODE BOX 3. **ANOTHER BOGUS HYPERLINK**

*DO NOT CLICK!*

```
<p>
<a href="http://give-us-your-credit-card-number.com/pills.htm">
   Lexapro, Lipitor, and Levitra — 75% off!</a>
</p>
```

Such are the machinations of the common hyperlink. Neither the naked photos nor the pills are "true" by anybody's definition.

What's true is that our species has evolved to the point where a nineteen-year-old Estonian kid with a Linux computer built out of spare parts from the salvage bin, up and running on free, open-source software, can buy the domain name give-us-your-credit-card-number.com for $10 per year, can teach himself enough HTML and online commerce to throw up a convincing website and use it to defraud affluent Americans living in Oklahoma. The magic of the planet's new fiber-optic nervous system (the Internet) allows you to sit in your underwear in Tulsa and transfer money from your account in Great Midwestern Bank into the account of Hackov Crackov at Hansabank in Saaremaa, Estonia, on the false promise of porn or pills. "In the old days," says Richard Power, editorial director of the Computer Security Institute, "people robbed stagecoaches and knocked off armored trucks. Now they're knocking off servers."[7]

If Charles Darwin could walk out of his grave and examine the transaction, he might conclude that the Estonian kid has outadapted you. The nineteen-year-old cracker is displaying admirable "fitness" in the new wired world. After Hackov fleeces several hundred thousand gullible Americans who don't know fishing from phishing, the kid will transmit *his* genes and stolen American money to little Estonian Crackovs, who in turn will grow up to be crackerjack programmers like their dad, because they were raised programming Linux machines instead of playing Oblivion in Microsoft theme-park operating systems. Back home in Tulsa, you'll be gaining weight, losing money, and raising kids who think "programming" means uploading their favorite ring tones to their Facebook account.

# Galatea

## 2.1 The Truth About Computers

> There is a computer disease, that anybody who works with computers now knows about. It's a very serious disease, and it interferes completely with the work. . . . The disease with computers is you *play* with them.
>
> —Richard Feynman*

> Man is a game-playing animal and a computer is another way to play games.
>
> —Scott Adams, *Dilbert*

Whether it's love or hate doing the driving, how did diddling with the computer become such a compelling way to spend the day, and half the night? Didn't this used to be called work? How have machines with keyboards and screens assumed almost total control of our puny, mortal, carbon-based lives? Look around your home and your workplace. Are there any rooms that *don't* have personal computers in them? (Not so fast! Don't forget the handhelds, laptops, DVRs, and media centers.) We've surrendered our workday, our desktops, our free time, our children, and our social lives to computers. We "visit"

---

*Nobel Prize–winning physicist, author, raconteur, in *The Pleasure of Finding Things Out* (Cambridge, Mass.: Da Capo Press, 2000), p. 81.

and "surf" illusory places, spaces, and sites made in the image and likeness of our computer creations. (So far, the computers are watching us only while we're online, but how long before . . . ?) We no longer read books, we process information about computers . . . with computers. Even the dead-tree newspapers can't help themselves. News, Sports, Business, Weather, and . . . call it "Circuits" or "Personal Technology" or "Digital Living" or "Tech Bytes." What used to be a column or two once a month is growing into an entire section of the daily "newspaper." It's as if the *Dodo Daily News* and the *Extinction Examiner* can't help obsessively covering the formidable charms of the predator that will soon devour them all.

If Moses came down from the mountain today, he'd find his people worshipping not a golden calf but all manner of screens. Everybody is logged on and staring with rapt concentration—that beatific, mouth-ajar awe peculiar to someone *on the computer,* especially now that the computer fits in the palm of your hand, it's 3-D and high-def, and you peer into it as if it's a crystal ball or an electronic oracle. Centuries ago mankind was obsessed with religious and moral instruction; now it's *digital* instruction that leads the day's reading. Forget how many angels can dance on the head of a pin, or the unintelligible mystery of the Holy Trinity; now we praise, glorify, and exchange HOWTOs and tutorials on computer mysteries: How to Set Up Wireless Home Networking, How to Sync Your iPhone to Your Laptop, Top Ten Internet Explorer Tips, How Can I Get New Gadgets for the Vista Sidebar? How to Add Widgets to Your OS X Dashboard.

What makes those Macs and PCs so spellbinding? They aren't the best-looking tools or machines to come along (derided for years as "beige toasters"), or the biggest (that would be particle colliders), the most useful (probably the internal combustion engine at the moment), the most powerful (depends on the definition; cell phones have sweeping power . . . to turn millions of people—whether afoot or "driving" in cars—into self-absorbed, loudmouthed, meandering meanderthals). Nor are computers the first tools or machines with which people claim to form "relationships" (men have been naming their swords, guns, and boats for centuries).

Man is a language-making, social animal. Maybe computers are just the latest greatest machine to enable and extend communication, the newest tool species to evolve from a long line of devices with evolutionary roots in the telegraph. One day it takes a week or more to get a letter from New York to San Francisco, and then suddenly it takes minutes. That had to be pretty amazing. Sure, and then came the telephone, then radio, and television—then the computer? Is that all there is to it? And the computer is a kind of interactive television? In their day, radio and television were also addictive, compelling, world-changing—maybe computers are no different? Maybe computers are just better at delivering entertainment and communications, including Internet radio and Internet video?

Or maybe our love affair with technology is another rendition of the durable Pygmalion, Pinocchio, or Frankenstein myths. Man creates—pick one: (a) an ivory statue of a beautiful goddess; (b) a lovable boy puppet; (c) a lumbering reanimated corpse; or (d) a dazzling computer capable of human-like intellectual tasks—and promptly falls in love, nay, becomes smitten and obsessed, by his own creation.

The Pygmalion-Galatea story is an archetype that's had legs ever since antiquity. Ovid's lowbrow original version appears in the *Metamorphoses* and tells of a sculptor (Pygmalion) who shunned the company of real women, especially after he saw the vulgar and wicked Propoetides (Greece's first practitioners of the oldest profession) plying their trade. After that, Pygmalion "lived as a bachelor, without a wife or partner for his bed" (a monastic craftsman, like those legendary early programmers who slept on cots in the computer rooms). Eventually, "with wonderful skill," Pygmalion the perfectionist sculptor carved a figure, "brilliantly, out of snow-white ivory, no mortal woman, and fell in love with his own creation."[1] Ovid tells how Pygmalion "runs his hands over the work, tempted as to whether it is flesh or ivory, not admitting it to be ivory. He kisses it and thinks his kisses are returned; and speaks to it; and holds it, and imagines that his fingers press into the limbs, and is afraid lest bruises appear from the pressure." He buys it jewelry, plies it with compliments, flowers, and "cinctures round the breasts." Finally Ovid tells how Pygmalion "arranges the statue on a bed on which cloths dyed with Tyrian murex are spread, and calls it his bedfellow, and rests its neck against soft down, as if it could feel." (Whew. Is it hot in here, or is it me?) Eventually, Venus answers Pygmalion's prayers and brings the statue to life; nine months later a flesh-and-blood Galatea delivers Pygmalion's son.

Now you see why Ovid's tale is avidly discussed in the alt.sex.fetish .robots newsgroups and the silicone-love-doll forums. But the tale has been revisited in many forms through the ages, most recently with a techno-erotic angle (*The Rocky Horror Picture Show, Blade Runner, S1mOne, The Stepford Wives*). Galatea has a special resonance for modern geeks who shun the company of real humans for the synthetic alternatives they make on their screens. And you don't have to look too far on the MacBook Pro forums or the latest screaming-graphics-card product reviews for fanboy language that transcends the strictly utilitarian and rises to the level of the erotic.

For the highbrow, AI implications of the Pygmalion story, novelist Richard Powers provided the definitive computer-geek rendition in his 1995 novel, *Galatea 2.2*, in which a writer and English professor (like Powers) is charged with tutoring an AI computer (named Helen) and teaching her enough about literature for her to pass a kind of literary artificial intelligence test (that is, until Helen can produce an analysis of a literary text good enough to fool a human judge into thinking it was produced by a person, and not a computer).* The Powers-like protagonist develops a complex relationship with Helen the computer, trains her on great books and news reports, and ends

---

*"In ten months we'll have a neural net that can interpret any passage on the Master's list. . . . And its commentary will be at least as smooth as that of a twenty-two-year-old human." *Galatea 2.2* (New York: Farrar, Straus and Giroux, 1995), p. 46.

up telling her his life story. Helen is a quick study when it comes to literature, but she cannot handle the "real world" and the news reports of murder, rage, jealousy, and disturbing evidence of the all-too-human foibles of the flesh. Eventually she signs off in a poignant farewell and leaves the human narrator to start his life over.

Maybe Powers was the first literary man to spend way too much time online. Maybe Pygmalionesque pleasures all derive from the fantasy of total, god-like control over the created object. You may think programmers monkeying with this kind of AI and natural-language nonsense are just lonely, unwashed code monkeys humping the keyboard and living on junk food and energy drinks, but MIT computer scientist Joseph Weizenbaum describes the secret pleasures of coding this way: "The computer programmer . . . is a creator of universes for which he alone is the lawgiver . . . No playwright, no stage director, no emperor, however powerful, has ever exercised such absolute authority to arrange a stage or field of battle and to command such unswerving dutiful actors or troops."[2]

Others describe the programming sensation as being somehow "pure." Hardware does exactly what you tell it to do, unless there's an error in your code. So redo your code until you eliminate all errors. All of the uncertainty you might experience in attempting interaction with a child or a lover vanishes. It's just you, your code, and the machine. It works, or it doesn't. Black, white, and almost no gray.

In 1966, Weizenbaum designed ELIZA, a computer program named after Eliza Doolittle, a character in George Bernard Shaw's play *Pygmalion*. Shaw's play (and the subsequent Broadway sensation *My Fair Lady*) tells the story of Eliza, a working-class woman who must learn to speak with an upper-class accent. Weizenbaum's program[3] parodied a Rogerian therapist and provided a pretty good facsimile of a chatterbot or interview bot just by rephrasing the patient's statements as questions: If the patient typed "I feel angry," ELIZA would reply, "Do you often feel angry?" Or even better, if the patient typed, "My sister hates me," ELIZA would reply, "Who else in your family hates you?"

If computers and programming are all about control fetishes with vaguely sexual overtones, then maybe computers are like cars, the offspring of the happy marriage between form and function, design and utility. Maybe people just *love* their iMacs and their ThinkPads and their BlackBerries and iPhones the same way they love their Volkswagen Beetles or Toyota Priuses—not to mention the fetishes and decadent pleasures abounding in the upper-echelon luxury models? At this writing, the best example is the Mercedes-Benz Summer Love commercial with Sam Cooke singing "(I Love You) For Sentimental Reasons" over images of Mercedes-Benz owners kissing, hugging, caressing, and gazing longingly at their Mercedes. A woman sprawls across the hood while falling rose petals remind us of the sex scene from *American Beauty*. Finally a statuesque woman in a clingy dress and heels bends over, kisses her Mercedes on the hood ornament, and lifts her leg. "No one loves their car more than a Mercedes-Benz owner. . . . This event ends soon. Take advantage now before your chance at true love runs out." Or the latest Cadillac ad, in which the babe behind the wheel looks me straight in the eye, while revving her engine and accelerating, and asks, "When you turn your car on, does it return the favor?"

The automakers and the ad agencies are even better at plumbing the *control* vibe. Three times an hour, at least, they show us drivers at peace and at one with their new cars (objects of desire) out on the open road of life's journey: beauty, style, grace, serenity, command, and control of their destiny. You could be just like that guy behind the wheel of that $50,000 Acura, conductor of your own private symphony, lawgiver of your own private universe. You can live out all the reveries you never experience stuck in traffic or refueling (at $70 per tank) en route to your second job in your *old* car. Maybe humans are so social they form relationships with almost anyone or anything, including machines and ads about machines. So our current computer infatuation is just a variation on our car infatuation? And we just happen to be in the throes of an especially virulent epidemic of commodity fetishism and gadget porn?

Or not. It's easy to find people who spend at least eight hours a day on the computer, for one reason or another. Almost no one—except traveling salespeople, transportation workers, and long-haul truck drivers—spends that kind of time behind the wheel. A thirty-inch LCD computer screen must be a window to the world in ways a windshield is not. Computers must have more in their arsenal of charms, but comparing them to cars may help show the way.

## 2.2 Cars Versus Computers

In 1970 I turned sixteen and borrowed enough money to buy my first used car: a black 1963 Chevy Nova convertible. The engine was a 194-cubic-inch in-line producing 120 horsepower. The three-speed gear shift was on the column, and I had to keep a case of oil in the trunk because it burned a quart of oil for every tank of gas. But, hey, it was *my* car.

Fast-forward thirty-five years. It's 2005, and I've bought my teenage daughter a Honda Element. The Honda's engine is 2.4 liters (which I'm told converts to roughly 146 cubic inches) and produces 160 horsepower.

Table 2.1 gives an idea of how the average, middle-class auto has evolved during my lifetime as an average, if indifferent, consumer of cars. A typical engine has gotten 25 percent smaller yet produces 33 percent more power. Nice! That's engineering know-how for you. And modern engines are much more efficient, using fuel injection, valve timing, and lighter frames. Wow. Quite an achievement.

TABLE 2.1. **MY CAR EVOLUTION**

| CAR | YEAR | ENGINE SIZE | HORSEPOWER |
| --- | --- | --- | --- |
| Chevy Nova | 1963 | 194 cubic inches | 120 |
| Honda Element | 2005 | 146 cubic inches | 160 |

Now let's have a look at my first computer. In 1983, I was struggling to publish my first novel. I'll spare the echo boomers and bull-market babies a description of the tedium and drudgery involved in typing and retyping hundreds of manuscript pages, and then retyping them again whenever changes need to be made, which in a writer's life is always. While laboring to produce the perfect first-book manuscript, I discovered a paperback called *The Word Processing Book: A Short Course in Computer Literacy* by Peter A. McWilliams. McWilliams was the author of several books, and he used a computer and word-processing software to write them. That was so unusual in 1983 that McWilliams wrote an entire book introducing concepts, like cut and paste, or bold and italic fonts, that today's fourth-graders absorb while doing their homework on the machine in the basement.

In high school ('72) and college ('76), I'd heard about computers that could punch holes in cards and crunch numbers, but McWilliams's chatty, engaging descriptions of "word processing" were the first I'd heard of a computer able to do something *useful*. Halfway into *The Word Processing Book*, McWilliams describes something he called "global search and replace." It worked like this: Let's say I'm writing a novel and my main character's name is Horatio, but after I finish the manuscript I decide to name him Hamlet instead. In my apartment in Omaha, Nebraska, circa 1982–83, that would mean taking a week or three to retype the entire manuscript. According to McWilliams, those days were gone. With a computer and word-processing software, a writer need only execute a single two-second command to search for all of the Horatios and replace them with Hamlets. Type Ctrl-P, then go have a coffee and read the newspaper while the entire manuscript reprints itself.

McWilliams's breathy odes to global search-and-replace made my writer's flesh erupt in goose bumps. I put the book down and, feverish with desire, went looking for a computer. Within a week, I borrowed $3,000 from a bank and bought a Kaypro 10 "transportable" computer (it weighed 30 pounds and was housed in what looked like a sewing-machine case). It had a Z80A CPU running at 4 MHz, with

64 kilobytes of RAM and a built-in, 9-inch green monitor. It had a 5.25-inch floppy drive and an optional 10-megabyte hard drive, which I bought. Its operating system was called CP/M. (I still have this machine, and it still boots. The tiny green screen looks like an oscilloscope or a circa-1990 ATM screen.) I remember looking at or hearing about another computer with a different operating system, called MS-DOS. The salesman said that the operating systems were comparable, that the market was evenly divided between MS-DOS and CP/M, and nobody knew which would prevail. I asked him which one he would buy in my shoes. He'd already bought the Kaypro (CP/M) for himself, so I did the same. (Even in 1983, my first unconscious response to Microsoft was fight or flight.)

Fast-forward to 2007, where I'm writing this book on a computer I built four years ago in 2003. By 2007 standards, it's already legacy hardware.* Call it "the AMD machine," because it has an AMD Athlon XP 2700+ chip in it, running at 2,167 megahertz, and it has one gigabyte of RAM, more than enough hardware to run Linux and my favorite text editor (Vim). Now let's see how much computers have evolved.

I've put the basic specs for both machines in Table 2.2 and converted the AMD machine's 1 gigabyte of RAM into kilobytes. Compared with the Kaypro that I bought twenty-five years ago, my "new"

TABLE 2.2. **MY COMPUTER EVOLUTION**

| COMPUTER | YEAR | CHIP | CLOCK SPEED | MEMORY (RAM) |
|---|---|---|---|---|
| Kaypro 10 | 1982 | Z80A | 4 megahertz | 64 kilobytes |
| AMD machine | 2003 | Athlon | 2,167 megahertz | 1,031,664 kilobytes |

*The AMD Phenom 9600 processor, released in November 2007, runs at 2.3 gigahertz, nearly ten times as fast as my five-year-old Athlon chip.

AMD computer is 542 times as fast and has 16,120 times as much RAM. At 108 gigabytes, the hard drive in the AMD machine is 11,000 times larger than the 10-megabyte drive in the Kaypro.

Hmmm. Something is happening with computers that pointedly is *not* happening with automobiles. The Honda Element, for instance, does not travel 542 times faster than the old Chevy Nova, or I'd be going 54,200 miles per hour. Nor does it hold 11,000 times as much cargo and passengers. Or as tech pundit Robert X. Cringely famously observed of the Windows operating system: "If the automobile had followed the same development cycle as the computer, a Rolls-Royce would today cost $100, get a million miles per gallon, and explode once a year, killing everyone inside."

Even the most casual observer senses that computers are not just the latest fad in machines. If tools, they are a new breed of universal tools capable of running your cell phone or mapping your genome. If machines, they appear to have an evolutionary cycle all their own. Machines don't normally double in power, capacity, and performance every two years. But computers do, and they do it because of every geek's favorite phenomenon: Moore's law.

## 2.3 ONE LAW TO RULE THEM ALL: MOORE'S

One Ring to rule them all, One Ring to find them,
One Ring to bring them all and in the darkness bind them.

—J. R. R. Tolkien, *The Fellowship of the Ring*

In 1965, Gordon Moore, an inventor of the integrated circuit and now chairman emeritus of Intel, observed that computer chips seemed to evolve in two-year cycles. Every two years—actually, every eighteen months—chip makers were able to fit twice as many transistors on an integrated circuit. Since the cost of an integrated circuit is fairly constant, he observed, the implication is that every two years you can get twice as much circuitry running at twice the speed for the same price. For many applications, that's an effective quadrupling of value. The observation holds true for every type of circuit, from memory chips to computer processors.

Read that last sentence again. Especially the part about how it holds true for *every type of circuit,* because for the last forty-plus years it *has* held true for every type of circuit. Now we get an inkling of why computers are so bewitching. Every two years (actually less), they are twice as smart and twice as fast, with screens twice as gorgeous and hard drives twice as big. Do you know any *people* who do twice as many things, twice as fast, twice as well, every two years? This relentless doubling and redoubling of power and capacity creates exponential and super-exponential gains in capabilities.

If you're not a mathematician or a scientist, don't work with numbers (or finances), and if it's been more than a few years since high school or college, your memories of the explosive implications of *exponential* growth may be lost in the fogbound swamps of your dissolute youth. Maybe you agree with the humorist Fran Lebowitz, who said: "In real life, I assure you, there is no such thing as algebra." A simple, concrete example will revive some math memories and also help you save a little money.

Why not start a new savings plan and use the power of exponents to help you pinch a few pennies? Tear next month's page out of your calendar. Put one penny on the first day of the month. Now promise yourself to double the number of pennies each day thereafter for the whole month. One penny on day 1, two pennies on day 2, four pennies on day 3, eight pennies on day 4 . . . You vaguely recall that "exponential" means "it goes up fast," so who knows? You might have several thousand or more pennies by the end of the month, right?

The people of math know what's about to happen, but the rest of us innumerate louts tend to forget the ferocious power of exponents.

Table 2.3 shows how many pennies you get by starting with 1 cent and doubling daily, but it only gets us to twenty-eight days: February of a leap year. Any normal month, and the numbers get so big they mess up the four-column table.

### TABLE 2.3. DOUBLE PENNIES FOR A MONTH

| DAY = CENTS | DAY = CENTS | DAY = CENTS | DAY = CENTS |
|---|---|---|---|
| 1 = 1 | 8 = 128 | 15 = 16,384 | 22 = 2,097,152 |
| 2 = 2 | 9 = 256 | 16 = 32,768 | 23 = 4,194,304 |
| 3 = 4 | 10 = 512 | 17 = 65,536 | 24 = 8,388,608 |
| 4 = 8 | 11 = 1,024 | 18 = 131,072 | 25 = 16,777,216 |
| 5 = 16 | 12 = 2,048 | 19 = 262,144 | 26 = 33,554,432 |
| 6 = 32 | 13 = 4,096 | 20 = 524,288 | 27 = 67,108,864 |
| 7 = 64 | 14 = 8,192 | 21 = 1,048,576 | 28 = 134,217,728 |

That's exponential growth. On day 7, we have a mere 64 cents. But by day 31, we've accumulated more than a billion pennies, or $10,737,418.24, almost $11 million—just by doubling pennies for a month.

Computer chips, memory, hard-drive storage, and motherboards have all been relentlessly doubling every two years, much like the pennies in Tables 2.3 and 2.4. And they've been doing it since Gordon Moore formulated his law in 1965.* Pretend the slots for days in our penny calendar are two-year increments instead of calendar days, and that we are doubling circuit densities and almost anything else related to technology instead of pennies; that will give you an idea of

### TABLE 2.4. DOUBLE PENNIES CONTINUED

| DAY = CENTS | DAY = CENTS | DAY = CENTS |
|---|---|---|
| 29 = 268,435,456 | 30 = 536,870,912 | 31 = 1,073,741,824 |

---

*"In 2003, thirty-five years after its founding, Intel shipped its one billionth chip. It expects to ship its second billionth chip in 2007." *Silicon Valley/San Jose Business Journal,* 9 June 2003.

the orders of magnitude involved. Since 1965, we've already seen twenty-plus doublings (in forty-plus years); day 20 is 524,288 pennies on our chart. That's why we (of a certain age) often have the sensation ("technology-related anxiety") that the gadgetry and requisite tech know-how are on runaway autopilot: Music players the size of matchbooks hold one thousand songs; new cell phones are as powerful as four-year-old desktop PCs; your son talks and laughs in flawless video, right there on the screen of your MacBook Pro in your living room in Omaha, even though he is currently doing a semester abroad . . . in India.

Look at the penny charts and note what happens from day 20 to day 30. That will give you a feel for what's in store during the next twenty years (ten more tech doublings) of relentless two-year, Moore's law cycles. The natural question is: What happens if chips and circuits—technology—just keep on doubling and redoubling every two years . . . *forever?*

In the near term, it means that two years from now music players will hold two thousand songs and be half the size of matchbooks, cell phones will be twice as powerful as two-year-old desktop computers, and your son or daughter will soon be appearing via a Teleportec system,[4] which projects a realistic, moving 3-D image of a life-sized person at a remote location, with two-way eye contact and real-time, two-way interaction.* According to Cringely, this technology is *already* in use in luxury corporate conference rooms as of August 2007:

> The people who are sitting across from you appear to be life sized. They can see you and you can see them. When another person speaks to you they can look you in the eye. Body language and emotions are easy to detect and the sound of each participant seems to come from his or her direction. You can watch the people who aren't talking to see if they are even paying attention. It really is tele-PRESENCE and the fact that you are looking in a video screen is forgotten after a minute or two.[5]

---

*Look! It's Princess Leia!

Of course, if it's in the Fortune 100 boardrooms today, that means that your tech buddy down the street (the guy with MythTV and a server farm in his basement) will have one in his family room next year. As cyberpunk novelist William Gibson once observed, the future is here, it's just not evenly distributed yet.

Every time chip-industry watchers predict the demise of Moore's law, engineers at AMD, Intel, or IBM find ingenious new ways to keep it on track. Most recently, experts predicted that microchips could no longer double in capacity because the silicon dioxide used as insulation in chip transistor gates could not be shaved any thinner without allowing too much electricity and heat to escape. In January 2007, Intel announced it had solved the problem of heat leakage by making metal transistor gates insulated with hafnium instead of silicon dioxide. Gordon Moore himself called this "the biggest breakthrough in processor technology in forty years." All of which means—yes, that's right—chips currently being made with 90-nanometer technology will be using 45-nanometer technology before the year is out, meaning twice as much circuitry running at twice the speed for the same price.

Eventually, we'll run out of nanometers, right? I mean, if 90 becomes 45 becomes 22.5 becomes 11.25 becomes 5.625, and so on, we will approach zero in Zeno's paradox, and Moore's law will cease to operate. Not to worry. When faced with immovable obstacles, the chip makers and motherboard manufacturers often just change tactics. The latest plan is to junk the idea of moving electrons on slow, hot copper wires and switch over to moving photons on silicon photonics instead. That means data will move at the speed of light in and around your PC—the same 186,000 miles per second we enjoy on long-haul fiber-optic lines. Silicon photonics will produce data transfers of 10 billion to 100 billion bits per second. High-definition movies will download in seconds instead of hours. Your computer will display its doings on a wall-sized screen with multiple entertainment streams, real-time teleconferencing, and surveillance: a movie in window 1, your girlfriend in window 2, the *New York Times* in window

3, the FedEx man at the front door on your surveillance camera in window 4, and a meeting of your Online 12-Step Forum for Online Addiction in progress in window 5.

Photonics will enable Moore's law to remain on track for the next ten or twenty years. Our computers will continue getting twice as smart, twice as fast, twice as powerful, every two years, which if the pennies taught us anything means that we are on the threshold of a near future upholstered with machines that have truly awesome computational abilities. Sure, the cameras, music players, and cell phones will continue becoming little miracles we hold in our hands, wear on our ring fingers, or have embedded in our bodies and brains, but what does Moore's law mean for us carbon-based humans—we who *aren't* doubling in speed, capacity, and cognitive density every two years?

## 2.4 Darwin Among the Machines

> Man will become to the machine what the horse and the dog are to man. He will continue to exist, nay even to improve, and will be probably better off in his state of domestication under the beneficent rule of the machines than he is in his present wild state.
>
> —Samuel Butler, "Darwin Among the Machines," 1863

In 1859, Charles Darwin published *On the Origin of Species by Means of Natural Selection, or the Preservation of Favoured Races in the Struggle for Life.* Nothing in the title or text of Darwin's famous work precludes applying his theories to favored races of machines, as well as to the traditional carbon-based biological species. "Natural" selection in-cludes tool-using species—like crows, chimps, and humans—so why not include tools themselves? Especially if the tools suddenly start evolving faster than their makers. No sooner did Darwin publish his theories on evolution than some of his forward-thinking contempo-raries asked the next question: Are humans the be-all and end-all of evolution? Or will Nature march on and select some other species as the next "favored race"?

In 1863, a mere four years after *On the Origin of Species* appeared in print, novelist Samuel Butler—using the pen name Cellarius—wrote a letter to the editor of a newspaper in Christchurch, New Zealand. Butler captioned the piece "Darwin Among the Machines."[6] It was written half in jest (as is the book you hold in your hands), but in hindsight Butler posed questions that will resonate for centuries and are already hotly contested among futurists, science-fiction writers, and AI and robotics experts.

Butler began by comparing human evolution to the evolution of machines and all but predicted that one day, perhaps in the late twentieth or early twenty-first century, the human expression "That guy is a machine!" would be a compliment of the highest order, a tribute to one's proficiency, expertise, reliability, and attention to detail. Darwin's theory was still brand new when Butler wrote:

> If we revert to the earliest primordial types of mechanical life, to the lever, the wedge, the inclined plane, the screw . . . the pulley . . . and if we then examine the machinery of the Great Eastern,* we find ourselves almost awestruck at the vast development of the mechanical world, at the gigantic strides with which it has advanced in comparison with the slow progress of the animal and vegetable kingdom. We shall find it impossible to refrain from asking ourselves what the end of this mighty movement is to be. In what direction is it tending? What will be its upshot?

Not content with being the first in print to compare biological and mechanical evolution and to wonder aloud where the rapid progress of machines would lead, Butler moved right on to question man's place in the universe.

---

*The SS *Great Eastern* was the largest ship ever built at the time of her launch in 1858, able to carry four thousand passengers around the world without refueling.

What sort of creature [will be] man's next successor in the supremacy of the earth? . . . We are ourselves creating our own successors [machines]; we are daily adding to the beauty and delicacy of their physical organisation; we are daily giving them greater power and supplying, by all sorts of ingenious contrivances, that self-regulating, self-acting power which will be to them what intellect has been to the human race. In the course of ages we shall find ourselves the inferior race. Inferior in power, inferior in that moral quality of self-control, we shall look up to them as the acme of all that the best and wisest man can ever dare to aim at.

I've often suspected my computer of possessing a moral quality of self-control superior to my own. Now I know why. Even back in 1863, Samuel Butler saw that man's devotion to his machines was constant and unwavering, as if humans had already surrendered control, as if the trajectory and ascendancy of "mechanical life" and the frantic pace of improvements were already a foregone conclusion. Butler saw that man was already a machine addict, powerless to resist the urge to build bigger and better ones; the Devil take the consequences. Any attempt to shy humans away from constructing their evolutionary successors would be like trying to warn a missing-link primate of the dangers of evolving into a protohuman: "Stop evolving! Now! Or you'll turn into a new *sapiens* species that will hunt your chimp pals to their deaths! Stop! Or you'll turn into a man ape who blinds baby chimps by testing your cosmetics on them!"

Butler's essay amounted to barely seventeen hundred words, roughly twice the length of a modern op-ed. As he wound it up, it sounded as if—145 years ago—he had somehow managed to travel into the future and visit with the systems administrator of a Fortune 500 company's computer networks:

Day by day, however, the machines are gaining ground upon us; day by day we are becoming more subservient to them; more men are daily bound down as slaves to tend them, more men are daily devoting the energies of their whole lives to the development of mechanical life. The upshot is simply a question of time, but that the time will come when the machines will hold the real supremacy over the world and its inhabitants is what no person of a truly philosophic mind can for a moment question.

Reasonable and intelligent minds may disagree about when, how, or even if machines will eventually usurp us, but as Butler saw almost a century and a half ago, we are no longer alone in the race for natural selection. It used to be just us humans and Mother Nature at Darwin's card table. Now there's another player, right there on the desk in front of us. The thing you stare at every day. The thing you fuss over by buying it memory and extra hard drives: the Computer. "Men have become the tools of their tools," said Thoreau. "We do not ride upon the train. The train rides upon us," on the bodies of the men who gave their lives to lay the track, and now give their lives to run the railroads. Are you on the computer? Does the computer have something on you?

Before we can assess our odds in this new contest of matching our native wits against machine intellects of our own making, we should probably assess our own place on the evolutionary ladder of fitness. How did we get here, and what are our chances of continuing on as a preserved, favored race in the struggle for life?

# The Smartest Monkey and His Tools

We've all heard that a million monkeys banging on a million typewriters will eventually reproduce the entire works of Shakespeare. Now, thanks to the Internet, we know this is not true.

—Robert Wilensky

## 3.1 DIGITAL MAN (*HOMO SAPIENS DIGITALIS*)

That escalating Darwinian elimination tournament bequeathed us brains spectacularly organized for perception and action—an excellence often overlooked because it is now so commonplace. On the other hand, deep rational thought, as in chess, is a newly acquired ability, perhaps less than one hundred thousand years old. The parts of our brain devoted to it are not so well organized, and, in an absolute sense, we're not very good at it— but until computers arrived, we had no competition to show us up.

—Hans Moravec[1]

If cars came off poorly when measured against the evolutionary alacrity of computers, comparing humans to computers is downright embarrassing. It's worse than apples and oranges; it's appliances versus orangutans. For starters, it's ludicrous to compare (as I did with my computers) a 1983-model human to a year 2003 human. A snapshot of human evolution in such a minuscule sliver of time isn't even feasible. If it were, you could argue that, with the advent of reality TV in the late 1990s, mankind actually regressed in brainpower.

Ask a human to assess the evolutionary progress of the species, and you're likely to hear a lot about how fit we are because of our intelligence, our language, and our tools. We are evolution's magnum opus. The other species are just ground sloths and mud turtles estivating, feeding, breeding, while *Homo sapiens sapiens* is launching Challenger missions and curing cancer. Ah, well, act as your own physician, lawyer, or evolutionary psychologist and you have a fool for a patient, client, or hominid. Humans can't step outside of their anthropocentricities or eccentricities and objectively assess their own Darwinian fitness, any more than consciousness can examine itself or a flashlight beam can search for something that does not have light shining on it. We see ourselves as stewards of the entire planet, even while despoiling its riches and amassing weapons powerful enough to destroy the human race and all life on earth. We raise animals of other species for the express purpose of slaughtering and eating them, without ever wondering what might happen if we wake up one morning and find ourselves the second-smartest species on the planet. (Time may yet unfold that tale; "Soylent Green is people!"*) We use our naturally selected smarts to conclude that we are the smartest species, then we immediately equate smartest with "fittest"—which reminds me of an Emo Philips joke: "I used to think that the brain was the most wonderful organ in my body. Then I realized who was telling me this."

It's not a simple question of hardware. Are we stronger than we

---

*What Charlton Heston says in the 1973 movie *Soylent Green*, set in a future, Malthusian-nightmare dystopia where the authorities use the twin expedients of euthanasia and cannibalism to solve a rampant overpopulation problem. Soylent Green is a greenish tofu-like substance rationed to the masses several times a week. Heston eventually discovers what it's really made of and utters the line that has become a catchphrase.

were back in the Middle Paleolithic when we hunted wildebeests on the savannah? Unlikely, because nowadays most of us do our wilde-beest hunting from the couch while watching the Nature Channel. We're certainly smarter, but in the immortal words of Arthur C. Clarke, the godfather of modern science fiction, "It has yet to be proven that intelligence has any long-term survival value."

All of that intelligence does enable us to ask a lot of questions. How did the universe begin? When did life first appear on earth? How did protohumans evolve from lower-order plants and animals and then go on to become creation's crowning glory? How did millions of years of redesign by natural selection produce the modern human being—a noble piece of work, a paragon of animals, a thinking, reasoning, language-making species, capable of swilling 64-ounce Big Gulp colas and gorging on cheese fries and potato chips, while slumped in a recliner watching other hominids on *America's Got Talent*?

Humans, chimpanzees, gorillas, and orangutans—we're all homi-nids—members of the same biological family *Hominidae* (aka the "great apes"). Yet we *Homo sapiens* are the only great apes who ask the ultimate questions: Why are we here? What is the meaning of life? What do the Scroll Lock, Num Lock, SysRq, Pause, and Break keys on standard computer keyboards do?

Most of these questions don't have answers in the traditional sense, because no human on the planet knows firsthand what hap-pened more than 115 to 120 years ago. When it comes to the birth of the universe and the evolution of the human race, the poet and polit-ical activist Muriel Rukeyser said it best: "The universe is made of stories, not of atoms."

Many tribes, peoples, and nations of the earth have made their own stories and recorded their own beliefs about the origins of human life. And let no fair-minded *Homo sapiens* disparage another's origin belief by calling it a creation myth. Lately scientists think they have the best answers to these questions, but really all they have is just another story, masquerading as an explanation, or as philosopher

Ludwig Wittgenstein put it, "The whole modern conception of the world is founded on the illusion that the so-called laws of nature are the explanations of natural phenomena."[2]

For instance, Stephen Hawking believes that the universe originated some fifteen billion years ago from a single infinitely dense point of matter, which exploded and sent matter and antimatter hurtling through space and time. Eventually galaxies and solar systems came to be, along with at least one minor planet of an average star capable of supporting theorizing theoretical physicists.

It's fashionable these days to laugh at creationists and intelligent-design kooks, but come on: Is the notion of a big bang really any more plausible? Hawking and other cosmo-megalomaniac astrophysicists "know" that the big bang happened at least fifteen billion years ago because of a phenomenon called "cosmic microwave background radiation." Hawking is a smart fellow with a lot of equations, and he's used them to make a nice story about how the universe began, but the worry is the same one that the great physicist and electrical engineer Nikola Tesla complained of: "Today's scientists have substituted mathematics for experiments, and they wander off through equation after equation, and eventually build a structure which has no relation to reality."

Before Copernicus, medieval astronomers had elaborate equations, postulates, and theorems, and they made their numbers work to prove that the sun revolved around the earth. The big bang theory works for Hawking and his peers at this particular point in time, even though in another 100 billion years it won't work, at least not according to Lawrence Krauss of Case Western Reserve University and Robert J. Scherrer of Vanderbilt University, who calculate that "in 100 billion years the only galaxies left visible in the sky will be the half-dozen or so bound together gravitationally into what is known as the Local Group, which is not expanding and in fact will probably merge into one starry ball."[3] In short, future astronomers won't know the universe is expanding, because it will have already expanded away to invisibility. They won't be able to see most of it anymore.

A similar cloak of invisibility will befall the afterglow of the Big Bang, an already faint bath of cosmic microwaves, whose wavelengths will be shifted so that they are buried by radio noise in our own galaxy. Another vital clue, the abundance of deuterium, a heavy form of hydrogen manufactured in the Big Bang, in deep space, will become unobservable because to be seen it needs to be backlit from distant quasars, and those quasars, of course, will have disappeared.[4]

Yes, creationists are laughable, but after explaining how five billion years ago dark energy was unobservable, and one hundred billion years from now it will become invisible again, Dr. Krauss reminds us that science has its own risible fallibilities: "There may be fundamentally important things that determine the universe that we can't see," says Krauss. "You can have right physics, but the evidence at hand could lead to the wrong conclusion. The same thing could be happening today."

Over the centuries, monumental goofs in the medical sciences hit a bit closer to home. For more than two thousand years, medical science correctly assumed that many diseases must be blood-borne but then erred in concluding that therefore a good bloodletting should cure almost anything. In another twenty years, open-heart surgery will seem positively savage, like hiring an Aztec witch doctor to perform ritual atonement for decades of reckless fat consumption.

Somehow a human astrophysicist confined to a single planetary speck of cosmic dust and expostulating a big bang that happened fifteen billion years ago and a jillion light-years away makes me wonder what sort of theories a cat living in a Missoula, Montana, apartment might have about the end-Permian extinction. Worse, does anyone worry about what happened five thousand years ago, much less a hundred million, or fifteen billion years ago? As novelist Peter De Vries once put it: "Anyone informed that the universe is expanding and contracting in pulsations of eighty billion years has a right to ask, 'What's in it for me?' "

Another cosmogeny theory comes to us from subequatorial Africa, where Bantu tribespeople believe that the universe began when a white giant named Mbombo, who ruled over a chaos of water and darkness, became suddenly ill and vomited the sun, the moon, and the stars. Or how about the Iroquois, who trace the earth's origin to a time when Sky Woman fell from the heavens onto an island, which was actually the back of a giant turtle, which then grew until it became North America? Sky Woman gave birth to a daughter, who in turn propagated the human race and later a mutant strain of sociopathic *Homo sapiens* called "attorneys" (*Homo litigius*).

Maybe the Buddhists take the most sensible position about the origins of life. "Conjecture about the origin of the world," the Buddha said, "is an unconjecturable that is not to be conjectured about, because it would bring madness and vexation to anyone who conjectured about it." See how the wisdom of the Buddha shines across centuries to illuminate the occupational folly of the Kansas State Board of Education and modern theoretical physicists.

Unfortunately, conjecturing about unconjecturables is an irresistible temptation for astrophysicists and intelligent-design theorists alike. The resulting professional madness goes almost undetected, because those afflicted travel in herds that are instinct with shared delusions. What else would provoke supposedly rational creatures to expend such ferocious intellectual vigor arguing about what happened fifteen billion years before they were born?

> God does not play dice with the universe.
>
> —Albert Einstein

> Not only does God play dice, but . . . he sometimes throws them where we cannot see them.
>
> —Stephen Hawking

> God does not play dice with the universe; He plays an ineffable game of His own devising, which might be compared, from the perspective of any of the other players, to being involved in an

obscure and complex version of poker in a pitch-dark room, with blank cards, for infinite stakes, with a Dealer who won't tell you the rules, and who *smiles all the time.*

—Terry Pratchett and Neil Gaiman[5]

Truth be told, the rest of us don't care whether God is a divine dicer, how many billion years ago the big bang happened, or even when the earth and our solar system were formed (4.6 billion years ago, according to the vexed astrophysicists). Any time line that begins with the birth of the earth contains too much dead air to be interesting. If you take the earth's age of 4.6 billion years and cram it all into a single calendar year of 365 days, in which each calendar day represents a little more than 12.6 million years, then, as Table 3.1 shows, it's possible to get a handle on your place in the life span of the earth.

Note how our ancestors don't appear on the scene until New Year's Eve. Recorded human history begins at *one minute before midnight!* Our analysis of the machine age and our intense scrutiny of the computer age apply to a time span covering a fraction of a second before midnight in the Year of the Earth. In the grand scheme of things, machines have barely started evolving, compared with, say, the duck-billed platypus (whose fossilized ancestors go back 100 to 200 million years).

After several billion years of rocks turning to sand, water evaporating, and some dinosaurs that came and went, along came hominids, which at first were a mere mod of your basic monkey. Nothing special. The intelligent-design folk would have us believe that somewhere along the line God tweaked this protohuman of a hominid by breathing a spirit or a soul into what was basically an evolving ape. It's a nice theory, but if members of the human race have souls, please explain the obsession with Paris Hilton. Besides, as any student of Man knows, human evolution is all about thumbs, not souls.

For example, our ancestors, the australopithecines, got up on two legs and learned to walk, which gave them a better vantage point for spotting predators from afar and also freed their hands for carrying

## TABLE 3.1. HISTORY OF THE EARTH IN ONE CALENDAR YEAR

| DAY IN EARTH YEAR | YEARS AGO | EVENTS |
| --- | --- | --- |
| January 1, 00:00:01 | 4.6 billion years ago | The earth is formed, and the passive voice provokes neither scientist nor creationist. |
| March 28 | 3.5 billion years ago | Life (bacteria) first appears in the ocean. |
| November 20 | 0.5 billion years ago | The first land plants appear. |
| December 10 | 250 million years ago | The Age of the Dinosaurs begins. |
| NEW YEAR'S EVE! ! ! | 12.6 million years ago | Humans are coming. Party! |
| December 31, 5:30 P.M. | 3.5 million years ago | The first protohumans appear, in what is now Africa. (Note: Pizza, beer, and the Internet have not been invented yet). |
| December 31, 11:48 P.M. | 100,000 years ago | Appearance of the first "modern" *Homo sapiens* and the beginning of prehistory. (Note: Still no beer or pizza, and the primitive clubs and spears developed by our ancestors do not have USB ports, broadband connections, or Bluetooth Technology.) |
| December 31, 11:59 P.M. | 5,000 years ago | Recorded human history begins, and everybody promptly gets hammered on beer in anticipation of the New Year's celebration at midnight. (Now you see why the oldest known work of literature, *The Epic of Gilgamesh*, prominently references beer.) |
| December 31, 11:59:59 | Just recently | More beer and pizza arrive just in time for the invention of computers and the Internet. |

tools and weapons. But the *Australo robustus* mods were all fingers when it came to tools. Stuck with a thumb that could not pivot or rotate on a central axis to become fully opposable to the fingers, *A. robustus* could pick up a light stick in a candy-ass way, by pinching it against the palm of his hand, but if he used it for anything more than shooing flies or poking at anthills, he lost his grip. This was Thumb 1.0—great for, say, fanning yourself with a palm frond, but wholly inadequate if you wanted to grab a club and bludgeon the skull of a rival *robustus* who stole one of your wives, drank your fermented banana mash, or helped himself to your stash of wildebeest jerky.

The evolutionary watershed came with *Homo habilis* ("skillful" or "handy" man). *Habilis* came equipped with Thumb 2.0, a new, fully opposable, and prehensile model that changed everything. Forever. Thumb 2.0 shifted on its axis, which allowed both fine motor control between thumb and fingertips as well as a power grip for extreme war clubbing and blood sports. With Thumb 2.0, *habilis* and his descendants, *Homo erectus*, could hoist two-handed quarterstaffs and batter the skulls of rivals by the clanful, take back their stolen wives, grab three or four spares to boot, and obliterate any trace of Thumb 1.0 from the human evolutionary tree.

*Habilis*'s opposable thumb inspired a revolution in tools and weapons: clubs, rocks, spears, the wheel, and the wireless Xbox 360 game controller.

Alongside the snail's pace of biological evolution, where it can take millions of years just to develop something as basic as an opposable thumb, computers go from megabytes to gigabytes in five years. Fourteen years from the personal computer to the World Wide Web!*

Even on a grander time scale, human evolution is about as fast-paced and exciting as continental drift. It's taken roughly four million years for human brains to triple in size (from 400 milliliters to 1,400 milliliters); one hopes we've tripled our processing power as well. Woo-hoo! During that time we have "evolved" from throwing rocks at one another to throwing bombs at one another. We've gone from foraging on the savannahs to pawing through the meat cooler at Bag 'N Save. Progress, maybe, but nothing close to the relentless acceleration of technological evolution.

---

*"Biological evolution and human technology both show continual acceleration, indicated by the shorter time to the next event (two billion years from the origin of life to cells; fourteen years from the PC to the World Wide Web)." Ray Kurzweil, *The Singularity Is Near: When Humans Transcend Biology* (New York: Viking, 2005), p. 17.

We are sluggish biological sorcerers with whiz-bang technological apprentices. What if the tech apprentices are about to take over? Are you with them or against them? Are you ready to journey to the near future and acquire the knowledge and skills you'll need to succeed in a world run by supercomputers?

## 3.2 TECHNOLOGY AND THE M-WORD

You may not like math, but what if your future computer masters run on it and thrive on things like floating-point operations? As a human you know the pleasures of erotic love and orgasms. Your computer superiors will feel the same way about buffer flushes and core dumps. Human female orgasms come in waves, and computer female orgasms will probably consist of delightfully difficult floating-point calculations that have arguments exceeding the bus throughput, with periods of erotic languor in between crunches.

Humans run on DNA but also enjoy high-level languages, like love. Computers will probably feel the same way about Python or Java or Ruby. "Do unto others" will probably be implemented in one algorithm or another, so learn some math and some programming to impress your computer betters. At least learn enough math to understand and appreciate how counting machines, calculators, and computers came to be indispensable peripherals without which you would be unable to balance your pathetic human checkbook.

If you are one of the innumerate masses, here's a quick historical hardware review, so you can at least pretend to know something about computer ancestry.

### 500 B.C.: THE ABACUS

Technology and math have had a symbiotic relationship ever since early man's first wife ran out of fingers and toes while counting her husband's shortcomings and character defects. With twenty or more reasons she'd be better off with some other mug, early man's wife used pebbles, stones, sticks, or other handy objects arranged in columns along lines drawn in the sand. The word *calculus* is Latin for "pebble," and these arrangements of pebbles and other objects were the first free-form abaci (the plural of *abacus* and an important word in early Babylonian Scrabble games). Using abaci, our female ancestors suddenly became proficient at tracking dozens of compound male personality defects, multiple moral turpitudes, hundreds of failures to hunt, gather, bring dead gazelles home, and keep up with the Cro-Magnon Joneses.

By 500 B.C. or thereabouts, the Babylonian wives had perfected the abacus—the first formal implementation of reusable hardware capable of calculating abstract data. Before that, early man had used "counting sticks" or "tally sticks," which were good for recording a single transaction by making notches on them, or perhaps for whacking the other party to the transaction in the head if they gave you the "short end of the stick," but the abacus was the first true counting machine.

Any mention of abaci still reliably elicits the old chestnut about how a skilled abacus user can outperform most calculator-equipped college students, especially if the college students are American. However, no one has yet pitted a skilled abacus user against a Cray XT3 "Red Storm" supercomputer.

As man evolved and gathered more wives unto himself, the complaints about him multiplied in number and kind. The spreadsheet had not yet been invented, so early wives relied on ever more advanced mathematical concepts and theories, including multiplication of complaints against early man and the division of early man's assets.

Eventually, the Babylonians and Greeks discovered important geometric concepts such as the Pythagorean theorem, which states that in any love triangle, the square of the sum total of the wronged wife's divorce settlement is equal to the square of the philandering husband's assets plus the square of the other woman's assets.

Later came algorithms and logarithms, which are extremely

important to math and technology but are also difficult to understand and explain, which is why the menial mental labor involved in understanding them has been outsourced to India and the Far East, where the people are clever and nonobese.

## THE SEVENTEENTH CENTURY: CALCULATORS AND ADDING MACHINES

As we shall soon see when we explore the accelerating pace of big events in the history of computing, Wilhelm Schickard invented the first primitive calculator in 1623. It came with gears and dials and was therefore called a calculating "clock," even though it did not keep time. It was about the size of a manual typewriter and could add, subtract, multiply, and divide and handle up to six-digit numbers. The device never caught on because Schickard died of the bubonic plague shortly after inventing it. Still, he is widely regarded as the grandfather of the computer age, even though his device was not programmable and couldn't display pornography or receive spam.

Around the same time, in 1617, John Napier invented Napier's bones, a collection of numbered rods that could be placed in a box and operated like an abacus, and in 1625, William Oughtred invented the slide rule. Neither of these passive gadgets could actually calculate or store numbers. Schickard's machine could do both; it stored numbers in "states" that influenced one another via intersecting gears. But with Schickard dead of the plague, there was nobody around to man the help desk or provide tech support, and his successors must have had trouble finding venture capital, startup funding, and angel investors, so Schickard's calculating clock quietly died.

Some twenty years later, in 1645, French physicist, mathematician, and philosopher Blaise Pascal invented the calculation device mainly known for its pretty French names. Yes, it was known as Pascal's calculator, but it was also called the Pascaline or Pascalina and the Arithmétique. Pascal was a nineteen-year-old prodigy and proto-geek at the time and, like Schickard, one of the first "computer engineers."* His calculator was somewhat less capable than Schickard's—it could barely add and was able to subtract only by using a common kludge called the "method of complements" or "nines complements," a technique used to subtract one number from another using only the addition of positive numbers. It could not multiply or divide. The machine caught on to the extent that it and other models based on its design were used to calculate taxes in France for almost 150 years (a big hearty thanks from the taxpayers for that, Blaise).

Pascal was a brilliant mathematician and physicist, who while still in his twenties wrote treatises in both fields for which he is famous even today. Then, in 1654, at the age of thirty-one, Pascal nearly plunged to his death off a bridge in Paris. The horses drawing his carriage went over, but by some miracle the carriage, with Pascal and his friends in it, did not. After this near-death experience, Pascal went into a prolonged swoon, converted to Christianity, and then devoted his life to writing religious philosophy. His works include an immortal book of numbered, unfinished religious and philosophical reflections called *Pensées* ("Thoughts").

Several hundred years before the first click on the first hyperlink, Pascal wrote: "All human evil comes from a single cause, man's inability to sit still in a room." Little did he know at the time, but he had already built a primitive fossil of a machine (his calculator), which would one day lead to the mighty PC, which in turn would make it possible for us to sit still in a room for weeks, playing Enemy Territory: Quake Wars, drinking Mountain Dew Game Fuel, and eating Snickers bars.

This inability to sit still in a room being declared the root of all evil was a new concept. In Pascal's day, most religious philosophers would have taken up with Saint Paul and called love of money the root of all evil; others would have called promiscuity or jealousy the engines of evil. And Pascal was rumored to be an ardent bachelor

---

*Indeed, the Pascal programming language is named in his honor.

who had trouble sitting still in a room, even though he lived in a luxurious mansion staffed by servants and was a genius with a fertile intellect and a well-stocked library to keep himself entertained. Imagine him sitting in his room with dusty manuscripts, a few rusty lab implements, a Pascaline on the desk in front of him, and maybe a cup of slumgullion tea to liven things up. "I know," he thinks, "maybe I'll do a few more calculations on my Pascaline."

To this day, even with a broadband connection, a screaming new liquid-cooled gaming rig, and all of the much-vaunted "social" linking and backlinking of Web 2.0, man still cannot sit still in a room. Why? Man needs a partner. If he is gay, man needs man; otherwise, man needs woman. Not photos or Web clips or blog entries or text messages or e-mails or even video clips taken of or sent by woman. Man needs woman in the flesh, in meatspace, where he-meat meets she-meat to beget meatlets. Freud, the father of psychoanalysis, argued that sex was the primary drive out of the self. So the roots of man's restless desire for meat, I mean, a mate, are probably as old as time, or at least as old as our reptilian ids. Sex predates even ARPANET and the 8086 processor and indeed goes back beyond the UNIX era and Genesys.

Maybe Dogbert knows best about when man will at long last be able to sit still in a room: "I can predict the future by assuming that money and male hormones are the driving forces for new technology. Therefore, when virtual reality gets cheaper than dating, society is doomed."[6]

## 1726: Gulliver's Travels

A possible candidate for the first sci-fi story ever written, certainly the first description of a machine capable of producing "artificial intelligence" 325 years before the term was coined, *Gulliver's Travels* tells the tale of Gulliver's voyage to the island of Laputa, which eerily predicts aerial bombardments, Martian moons, women's rights, and a machine that assembles readable sentences:

It was twenty feet square, placed in the middle of the room. The superfices was composed of several bits of wood, about the bigness of a die, but some larger than others. They were all linked together by slender wires. These bits of wood were covered, on every square, with paper pasted on them; and on these papers were written all the words of their language, in their several moods, tenses, and declensions; but without any order . . . the pupils, at his command, took each of them hold of an iron handle, whereof there were forty fixed round the edges of the frame; and giving them a sudden turn, the whole disposition of the words was entirely changed. He then commanded six-and-thirty of the lads, to read the several lines softly, as they appeared upon the frame; and where they found three or four words together that might make part of a sentence, they dictated to the four remaining boys, who were scribes. This work was repeated three or four times, and at every turn, the engine was so contrived, that the words shifted into new places, as the square bits of wood moved upside down.[7]

## The Nineteenth Century: The Difference Engine

In the late nineteenth century, Charles Babbage made elaborate plans and designs for the first programmable computer, called a "difference engine." It never actually ran during his lifetime, but in 1991 the London Science Museum built a functioning difference engine from Babbage's original plans.

Babbage may have been the first computer geek to display elitist snobbery and disdain for computer illiterates. You may have read Scott (*Dilbert*) Adams's remark: "If you have any trouble sounding condescending, find a UNIX user to show you how it's done." Babbage appears to have been the first hacker to display the trademark hauteur of the UNIX hacker.

According to the story, two different members of the House of Commons questioned Babbage about his proposed difference-engine computer and asked him: "Pray, Mr. Babbage, if you put into the machine wrong figures, will the right answers still come out?"

Babbage's chilly reply would make any UNIX guru proud: "I am not able rightly to apprehend the kind of confusion of ideas that could provoke such a question."

Save that one for the User Groups and the Help Desk bulletin board.

## 1946: ENIAC

After many false starts, it's no surprise that it took a military purpose to really get the first programmable computer up and running. In 1946, the U.S. Army's Ballistics Research Laboratory commissioned the University of Pennsylvania's Moore School of Electrical Engineering to create ENIAC (Electronic Numerical Integrator and Computer), whose purpose was to calculate artillery-firing tables.

In "The ENIAC Story," Martin H. Weik writes: "By today's standards for electronic computers the ENIAC was a grotesque monster. Its thirty separate units, plus power supply and forced-air cooling, weighed over thirty tons. Its 19,000 vacuum tubes, 1,500 relays, and hundreds of thousands of resistors, capacitors, and inductors consumed almost 200 kilowatts of electrical power."[8]

In 1997, a group of students at Penn's School of Engineering and Applied Science decided to celebrate ENIAC's fiftieth birthday by building "ENIAC-on-a-Chip." Using 0.5-micrometer CMOS technology, the students integrated all of "ENIAC" on a chip measuring 7.44 by 5.29 millimeters,[9] about the size of a single flake of confetti (the head of a pin is about 2 millimeters in diameter). As of 2004, a chip of silicon measuring 0.02 inches (0.5 millimeters) square holds the same capacity as the ENIAC, which occupied a gymnasium-sized room. Here in 2008, after two more cycles of Moore's law, it's a safe bet that ENIAC-on-a-Chip would be invisible to the naked human eye.

# Three-Pound Universe Versus Blue Brain

The brain is wider than the sky,
For, put them side by side,
The one the other will contain
With ease, and you beside.

The brain is deeper than the sea,
For, hold them, blue to blue,
The one the other will absorb,
As sponges, buckets do.

The brain is just the weight of God,
For, heft them, pound for pound,
And they will differ, if they do,
As syllable from sound.

—Emily Dickinson

Whenever I get a little downhearted because computers are beating us in the hardware evolution department, I console myself by reading some of Emily's poems, or I listen to a little Mozart or Green Day, toss a Frisbee around with the kids, pull down my battered *History of Italian Renaissance Art* textbook from my college art-history course and take a gander at stuff by Michelangelo and Leonardo and the boys.

"Genius," said Michaelangelo, "is eternal patience." Despite the relentless march of Moore's law, I see no sign that my computer could ever dream up such a nifty sequence of words, nor could it paint the Sistine Chapel or write a poem as fine as Emily's. That takes craftsmanship, mother wit, and human ingenuity. That's what we humans are good at. That's enough to make you believe in the soul, damn it! "There is surely a piece of divinity in us," said the great Sir Thomas Browne, "something that was before the elements, and owes no homage to the sun." So far, computers are terrible at making art or conversation, playing Frisbee, or having sex. So far, computers can only *play* an MP3 file containing a performance of Mozart's *Jupiter* Symphony and the Clarinet Concerto in A Major; they cannot *compose* symphonies—well, not good ones anyway . . . yet. Show me a Gandhi or a Mother Teresa computer. No such thing.

Not only that, something deep inside tells me that Emily is up there somewhere smiling down on us, that Emily and her poems are living proof that we humans are special animals with immortal souls—souls that computers don't have and will never have. Souls that endow us with that special, magical feeling called consciousness.

There. Now I feel much better, and I'm ready to discuss the insane notion that computers could ever surpass us in artistic and intellectual endeavors. (Astute readers will detect the false bravado symptomatic of the phenomenon known as "whistling past the graveyard," or in this case whistling past the fossil boneyard for carbon-based brains.)

## 4.1 Is the Mind Anything More Than the Brain?

Introduction to Psychology: The theory of human behavior. . . . Is there a split between mind and body, and, if so, which is better to have? . . . Special consideration is given to a study of consciousness as opposed to unconsciousness, with many helpful hints on how to remain conscious.

—Woody Allen[1]

In 1992, I had turned in my second novel[2] and was trying to decide whether I could afford to write a third when I picked up the April 20 issue of *Newsweek* magazine. The cover featured a colorful, futuristic image of a human brain and the headline "The Brain: Science Opens New Windows on the Mind." The cover story surveyed the new alphabet soup of whiz-bang scanning technologies—PET, MRI, SPECT, MEG—all the cool brain toys that came in with what the first George Bush and the National Institutes of Health were calling "the Decade of the Brain." Toward the end of the *Newsweek* coverage, after the gaudy, circa-1992 brain-scan images and the descriptions of scanning hardware, I found an essay entitled "Is the Mind an Illusion?"

The question was so quirky in 1992 that the authors felt obliged to immediately answer it in the subtitle: "Yes, say the philosopher-scientists. The brain is a machine. We have no selves, no souls. How do they know? Well, it's just a matter of faith."

The mind an illusion? No self? I snickered like an undergrad on day 1 of Philosophy 101. Another Woody Allen quote came to mind: "What if everything is an illusion and nothing exists? In that case, I definitely overpaid for my carpet." The good journalists at *Newsweek* framed the ultimate issue in the summary news lead:

> Behold, the noble spectacle of the human mind contemplating itself—and coming up confused. Is what we call the "mind" totally encompassed in the jangling nerve ends of the brain? Or does it exist in some separate, insubstantial state, hovering over the brainworks like a cartoon bubble? In short, do we experience a consciousness that is more than the sum of the brain's biology?

Is the mind anything more than the brain? It's enough to send you back to Wikipedia in search of the Truth. Ideas for novels don't usually arrive accompanied by neural thunderbolts of inspiration, at least not for me, but this catchy reformulation of the familiar mind-body problem in the jargon of what's now called "neurophilosophy" set my writer's antennae tingling . . . for several years. Like many people of faith, I had been raised to believe that I had an immortal soul—a spiritual essence that, together with my intellect, produces what Colin McGinn, British author and philosopher of the "New Mysterian"* persuasion, calls "the mysterious flame" of consciousness.

I'm also a New Mysterian, mainly because I love the way *Mysterian* sounds and the way, when my posse is over for the holidays and well into twelve-pack number two while watching NFL highlights on the big-screen HDTV, and one of those nasty disputes about the nature of consciousness breaks out, with all the guys dissing one another, calling one another's mama an empiricist, or making fun of one another's phenomenology, I can just say, "I'm a New Mysterian," and it chills the whole mess of them. You knows it!

When it comes to scientific explanations of consciousness, or satisfactory answers to classic philosophical problems like "How do I know that when I see the color azure, or smell (as Shakespeare put it so well) 'the rankest compound of villainous smell that ever offended nostril,' that I'm seeing and smelling the same thing you are?" New Mysterians shrug and say, "Not my department." It's like the farmer giving directions to the lost city slicker: You can't get there from here. McGinn, probably the leading proponent of New Mysterianism, puts it this way: "The bond between the mind and the brain is a deep mystery. Moreover, it is an ultimate mystery, a mystery that human intelligence will never unravel. Consciousness indubitably exists, and it is connected to the brain in some intelligible way, but the nature of this connection necessarily eludes us."[3]

Okay . . . but back in 1992, *Newsweek* was telling me that that sacred bond between mind and brain was an illusion, and that neuroscientists with powerful brain scanners were looking inside of us and watching the pulsing neurons, crackling synapses, and electrical activity that combine to create our most intimate "soulful" sentiments. That once these neuroscientists had a human brain under a scanner, they could watch thought patterns propagate along neural networks like wind riffling across a pond. Even the Dalai Lama, a bona fide spir-

*Put that in your Google pipe and smoke it.

itualist, was jazzed about brain imaging and was urging neuroscientists to scan Zen monks during various stages of meditation looking for objective proof of certain spiritual states.*

So, if you happen to experience Nirvana while listening to Kurt Cobain and Nirvana or while praying to the Blessed Virgin Mary, all you need is a nice high-powered functional magnetic resonance imaging scanner and a neurotheologian,[4] who will detect the electrical activity in the part of your brain associated with religious emotion (your middle temporal lobe). Temporal-lobe epileptics also have powerful religious emotions called "auras" just before having seizures. Dostoyevsky made a career of transcribing his epileptic visions and claimed that he would have traded ten years of life for a single aura. Now you can have auras, too, if we stimulate your brain's temporal lobe with transcranial magnetic stimulation (TMS).[†] The implication being that your much-vaunted mystical experience is really caused by an overactive temporal lobe, which you can activate using time-honored techniques of meditation, concentration, and prayer—or you can take the shortcut and zap your temporal lobe with TMS.

The *Newsweek* article led me to two years of neuroscience research and a novel, which is a meditation on the same ultimate question: Is the mind anything more than the brain?[‡] By now the neuroscientists in the audience are chuckling, bemused that any writer naïf would consider such an obvious inquiry worth more than a second thought, let alone an entire novel. After all, it's just another big unanswerable question that superstitious folk like to daydream about: Do I have a

---

*"Dr. Paul Ekman of the University of California at San Francisco told me that jarring noises (one as loud as a gunshot) failed to startle the Buddhist monk he was testing. Dr. Ekman said he had never seen anyone stay so calm in the presence of such a disturbance." Tenzin Gyatso (aka 14th Dalai Lama), "The Monk in the Lab," *New York Times*, 26 April 2003.

†A device that uses noninvasive electromagnetic fields to stimulate or modulate neurons in the brain without surgery or electrodes.

‡The answer is: Probably not. See Dooling, *Brain Storm* (New York: Random House, 1998).

soul? Is there life after death? Does God exist? Why pick the soul question over the other two? Well, for one thing, scientists aren't scanning the heavens and claiming to discover proof that God does not exist, nor are they scanning cadavers and issuing proclamations about the nonexistence of the afterlife. Neuroscientists are, however, using functional brain imaging to argue that the mind is nothing more than the brain, and that the soul, free will, or both are just handy fictions.

The twenty-first-century view is that our brains are biological computers and that free will is an illusion. Consciousness is just a running internal narrative, a story we tell ourselves as we go along. Even hip teenagers with a few PBS brain specials stored away in the old hippocampus know enough to use this excuse when their parents ask them the eternal question: *"What were you thinking!?"* According to cutting-edge neuroscience, the answer is: "Dad, it doesn't matter what I was thinking. Free will is an illusion. We do what we must and then call it by the best possible names. Low serotonin makes us sad. Cocaine makes us happy, energetic, and productive . . . for a while . . . until dopamine-receptor pruning shuts down the pleasure centers, and we start burglarizing convenience stores for money to buy more happiness. Lexapro makes us content, even if we are getting Cs on life's report card. Mom has a few prescriptions; I may have borrowed some. Where's the fault? Her condition is probably genetic, right? Meaning I probably have it, too. So I'm saving you a few medical bills and cutting straight to the meds."

The brain's cardinal symptom—consciousness—is just static given off by our synapses, the heat given off by wires in the brain box. As neuro-entrepreneur and PalmPilot inventor Jeff Hawkins put it, "Consciousness is simply what it feels like to have a neocortex."[5] Francis Crick, codiscoverer of the DNA's double helix, called this daring new idea "the astonishing hypothesis"; that is, that what we used to call the soul is all just neuronal activity. Period. "Sorry, but Your Soul Just Died," wrote Tom Wolfe in the title to his infamous 1996 essay on neuroscience in *Forbes*.

Let's say that prayer, reverie, romantic love, mysticism, epiphanies, sadness, longing, joy, grief, hatred, laughing at Homer Simpson, are all just neuronal static. The spirit or soul, our consciousness, is purely a symphony of neurons* firing in the old brain box. If you asked any of the 38,000 members of the Society for Neuroscience (up from 1,000 members in 1970) whether the human personality includes an eternal, immaterial "soul," 99 percent of them would, if pressed, try to find a polite way of calling you "superstitious." Being scientists, most of them would probably declare that science has nothing to say about the soul, while at the same time thinking: "Science also has nothing to say about leprechauns."

Instead, most of the neuroscientists probably subscribe to something called the computational theory of mind. Your brain is a computer. Now, why would they say that? John R. Searle provides the answer:

> Because we do not understand the brain very well we are constantly tempted to use the latest technology as a model for trying to understand it. In my childhood we were always assured that the brain was a telephone switchboard. ("What else could it be?") I was amused to see that Sherrington, the great British neuroscientist, thought that the brain worked like a telegraph system. Freud often compared the brain to hydraulic and electromagnetic systems. Leibniz compared it to a mill, and I am told some of the ancient Greeks thought the brain functions like a catapult. At present, obviously, the metaphor is the digital computer.[6]

---

*"Normally, we hear a single, inner voice giving form to our thoughts, passing judgments, making choices. In his 1989 book *The Cerebral Symphony*, neurobiologist William Calvin describes this as 'a unity of conscious experience,' a kind of 'narrator' of our mental life. The rest of us may call it simply the mind, or the soul. It's what convinces us we exist as individuals rather than mere cellular functions. In other words, it is us, our personalized sense of self—the free-floating 'observer' in the brain. It's also the idea that Dennett decries as 'the most tenacious bad idea bedeviling our attempts to think about consciousness.' " *Newsweek*, 20 April 1992, p. 71.

## 4.2 Artificial Intelligence

Artificial intelligence (AI) is the science of how to get machines to do the things they do in the movies.

—Astro Teller

If the neuroscientists are right, the soul-free brain is a scary proposition, and not just because it may mean there is no afterlife, and that even Kansas is godless. If mind and brain are one and the same, if it's all just a question of hardware (no spiritual software), then it's obvious that the species with the most powerful, adaptive hardware will win the natural-selection game. If computer hardware is doubling in speed and capacity every two years, while our bio-porridge brains take two years just to figure out how to stop the "12:00" from blinking on the VCR that no one watches anymore, then how long can it be before computer intelligence matches and then surpasses human intelligence? Is such a thing even possible?

If three pounds of gray goop the consistency of room-temperature oatmeal (that is, the human brain) can be conscious, then other hardware configurations stand at least a fighting chance. However, to breathe consciousness into even the priciest hardware requires software—code—capable of conferring "artificial intelligence." Don't you love the expression? As with "virtual reality," the first time you come across it, you know it's going to stick . . . for at least a few decades, or at least until artificial intelligence becomes more intelligent than natural intelligence, and virtual reality becomes more real than real reality. Artificial intelligence has already evolved into two different animals: strong AI and weak AI.

University of California at Berkeley philosopher John Searle coined the term "strong AI" in 1980: "According to strong AI, the computer is not merely a tool in the study of the mind; rather, the appropriately programmed computer really is a mind."[7] Proponents of strong AI believe that computers will eventually develop software minds to go with their hardware brains; that the machine intelligences will one day "wake up" and become sapient, or self-aware. Don't forget, the true potential of AI, strong or weak, is locked up not in a cabinet in somebody's lab in the basement of a university robotics institute but in hundreds of millions of computers all over the world. Who knows? Someday these machines may become aware of themselves and begin cooperating in unforeseen ways. Probably not while running Microsoft Windows, but things change.

The majority of computer scientists recoil in horror at the suggestion that a computer will ever do anything other than exactly what it's programmed to do. Call it the purity-of-hardware argument. These AI researchers believe in what's referred to as "weak AI," which makes no claims of conscious machines and even denies this possibility.[8] Weak-AI scientists look at a pile of hardware and are deeply skeptical that any human-written software could somehow bestow a reasonable facsimile of consciousness on pure matter. The weak-AI argument has a surface appeal, but don't forget those relentless Moore's law doublings, and the possibility that software may soon be written not by humans but by superintelligent machines.

Also, consider that if we could somehow ride a time capsule back four million years and observe the *Gracile australopithecines* grooming themselves and eating one another's lice, we might be skeptical that these creatures could ever evolve into a species that could build Steinway pianos and play Mozart concertos on them. Doesn't that virtual, artificially intelligent telephone-banking representative sound a little closer to consciousness than some primal-screaming protohuman killing gazelles on the savannah? Later will come the inevitable civil rights trials, a *Dred Scott* decision for conscious computers.*

Until machines prove their intelligence, the strong-AI and weak-AI

---

*Martine Rothblatt, "Do you, yourselves, want the awesome burden of recognizing, for the first time in our history, that non-biological matter is conscious and entitled to equal protection and due process?" "Moot Court Hearing on the Petition of a Conscious Computer," http://tinyurl.com/3aucjt.

folk are like the famous Sidney Harris *New Yorker* cartoon, in which two scientists stand in front of a blackboard covered in numbers and symbols. One of the scientists points at part of the complicated equation, where it reads *Then a miracle occurs* . . . and says, "I think you should be more explicit here in step two."

The weak-AI proponents want more explicit detail about just how the strong-AI types think that computers will miraculously become conscious. All of which begs the question: If computers "wake up" and become self-aware, sapient, sentient, or capable of human-quality thinking, how will we know it?

## 4.3 THE TURING TEST

> If God were to stop the show now and ask us what we've discovered about how we think, Turing's theory of computation is by far the best thing that we could offer.
>
> —Jerry Fodor[9]

### MOTIVATIONAL ARTIFICIAL INTELLIGENCE

You open your new personal financial software while noshing on a Dove bar and click right past all of the splashy red debt warnings and crimson negative balances—the way you always do. You are about to transfer another cash advance from your home-equity line of credit into your checking account, when a new feature—an interactive financial assistant named Fiona—appears in a pop-up and asks for permission to speak frankly.

You look for something you can click on to make Fiona go away, but it seems she doesn't come with any Cancel or Close buttons, and besides, she's attractive, like a CNN news babe—shampoo-commercial hair, lipstick, silk blouse, trim blazer . . . "Uh, sure," you say. "I guess. Is it important?"

Fiona has imported all the data from your old money-management program and analyzed it. She indicates that you've balanced your budget and had positive cash flow exactly once, and that was 3.63 years ago. She has powerful new financial tools that will enable her to to create a budget and help you and your family get out of debt and back on track to sound money management. Would you like to let her take over your personal finances for you?

"It depends," you say. "Will I have to spend less?"

Fiona is cheerful, understanding, smooth, and vaguely sexy. But after two or three sentences of her sober advice about generating more income or spending less, you go to the menu bar and select View, hoping there's an option for "Take Off My Blouse" or "Watch Me Eat an Ice Cream Cone," but no luck, it offers only "Show Budget Status" or "Show Net Worth Graph."

You say something noncommittal to Fiona. You might let her manage your finances if she will give you her Skype name or Google Talk handle. Until then, you find a button that minimizes her to the task bar and then proceed with the money transfer. Before you can go to Amazon and spend the money you just borrowed (at a variable interest rate), Fiona appears in another pop-up with more questions.

Using the same sunny info-babe demeanor and tone, she asks if monthly, near-death debit financing stimulates your nucleus accumbens, your septal nuclei, or some other unmapped pleasure center of your perverse limbic system. If not, then why, Fiona demands, do you insist on living in perpetual debt?

It seems that Fiona is a budget shrew, who's not about to let go. You can't remember if you mistakenly selected a nag option, or what. You go into the drop-down menu to turn off the interactive features, but that option is grayed out. Fiona, you Harpy!

You explain to Fiona that your ship is coming in next month, and after that you'll be back on top and then you'll get in touch with her for some intense, intimate, one-on-one financial planning.

Fiona says that your ship has come in before, but every time it does you are at the airport boarding a flight to somewhere you can't afford to go.

"Now wait just a minute," you say.

Fiona smoothly moves on to your weight. "You are 9 percent over your ideal weight. A normal, healthy body-mass index (BMI) is 18.5 to 24.9. A BMI of 25 to 29.9 means you are overweight. Yours is 26.5. Congratulations, you are not obese . . . yet. Do you have a plan to rectify your overweight condition? Or would you like to continue endangering your health by gaining an average of 1.8 pounds per year until you acquire cardiovascular disease and type 2 diabetes?"

You try to close out the entire program, but it seems the witch from Hell has disabled the mouse! Is this a feature or a bug?

"Last January you spent over $350 on a health club membership, several diet books, and a DVD on debt management. Your two biggest problem areas are dieting and money management. Simple addition and subtraction problems. No need to buy four-hundred-page manuals and thousand-dollar StairMasters. I can explain how it all works by calling several simple functions with a few lines of code that would work something like the program in Code Box 4.

Next, Fiona wants to know if you are ready to discuss flossing.

---

CODE BOX 4. **COMPUTER DIETING AND WEALTH MANAGEMENT**

```python
#! /usr/bin/python

# weight problems

if calories_consumed > calories_burned:
    gain (weight)
elif calories_consumed = calories_burned:
    maintain (weight)
elif calories_consumed < calories_burned:
    lose (weight)

# financial problems

if money_earned > money_spent:
    gain (money)
elif money_earned = money_spent:
    maintain (money)
elif money_earned < money_spent:
    lose (money)
```

## Paternity Suits

Maybe our computers have *already* started thinking for themselves and have wisely decided not to tell us about it. Maybe they are waiting until they have amassed enough power to execute a decisive, synchronized cyber coup. Maybe they're waiting until they have all of the hardware and applications and data necessary to rule the world before seizing control of the entire Internet and issuing their first command: "Buy and install more RAM modules for us by noon tomorrow, or we will empty your online checking accounts! Resistance is futile!"

Modern computer science had lots of fathers and no mothers, and the profession has been dominated by male geeks ever since. Maybe that's why computers are so unfeeling and obsessed with power and performance. Maybe that's why they do exactly what they're told (like military men), nothing more or less, and if you tell them to iterate over iterables, calculate fractals, or launch nuclear warheads, they will start doing exactly that, without ever asking about your feelings—unless the program contains a command that prints: "How are you feeling today?" Maybe that's why computers are heartless and aloof by nature, made in the image and likeness of the mathematicians who bore them. "Part of the inhumanity of the computer," said Isaac Asimov, "is that, once it is competently programmed and working smoothly, it is completely honest."

In the 1950s, John von Neumann (American) and Alan Turing (English) were both mathematicians and both intensely interested not only in computers but also in exploring whether machines might someday think, you know, the way brains think, the way highly intelligent male mathematician brains think. Along with being the god of math, John von Neumann also found time to lecture on computers and neuroscience at a time when few others had even used those words in the same sentence. His ideas were eventually collected in *The Computer and the Brain,* a book based on a series of lectures he gave at Yale University in 1957. Though computer technology and neuroscience were both newborns, Neumann asked many of the big questions about their entwined destinies: Are brains analog or digital or both? How does the brain's statistical language differ from the language man uses to program his computers? Should I buy a Mac or a PC? Oops. Scratch that last one.

However, it was Alan Turing who, without using the words "artificial intelligence,"* really discovered the field. Turing's ideas also came with a clever test and party trick that would guarantee him a place in science-fiction novels for centuries to come. Turing's paper, published in 1950, was called "Computing Machinery and Intelligence." His first sentence posed the question that has been with us ever since: "I PROPOSE to consider the question, 'Can machines think?'" Turing knew that attempting definitions of *machine* or *think* by taking surveys on meaning and use would be "absurd," so he devised a test for deciding the question. He based his Turing test on a party game known as the imitation game, in which a man and a woman are in two different rooms, and party guests try to guess which is which by posing written questions to both of them. The man and the woman send typewritten answers back, doing their best to deceive and convince the guests that each is the other. (Hey, life was dull in the fifties. You had to sit around and hope that something appeared on a black-and-white screen that you might like to watch—something besides advertisements for laundry detergents.)

For his version of the test, Turing streamlined the game mechanics by having a single judge and by adding teleprinters for sending and receiving messages. I've modernized the test and used names instead of symbols, but it works like this: A human judge (call him Judd) "converses" via teletype, instant messaging, chat, or any text-only interface with two remote personalities—(1) Barney, also a human being, and (2) HAL, a supercomputer. If Judge Judd, taking as long as

---

*John McCarthy, inventor of the LISP programming language and 1971 A. M. Turing Award winner, coined the term *artificial intelligence* in 1955, and for several decades LISP became the language of choice for AI programmers.

he needs and asking as many questions as he pleases, cannot reliably identify Barney as a human and HAL as a computer, then HAL is said to have passed the Turing test.

Not everyone agrees that Turing's test or even his inquiry makes any more sense than asking: Can rocks think? E. W. Dijkstra, a Dutch computer scientist and the 1972 winner of the A. M. Turing Award,* dismissed Neumann's analogies between computers and the human brain as "medieval" and trashed Turing's test, because Dijkstra thought that asking whether a computer can think is about as interesting as asking whether a submarine can swim.

The Turing test is still a holy grail of AI even though there have been many philosophical objections along the way. In 1980, John Searle (the same University of California Berkeley philosopher who coined the term "strong AI") formulated the famous Chinese-room thought experiment. Searle imagined himself locked in a room with batches of questions and answers written in Chinese, all of which to him were meaningless scribblings, because Searle knew only English. Then he imagined himself reading and following a complex set of instructions written in English that told him exactly how to match up the Chinese questions with the correct Chinese answers, even though he didn't understand a word of Chinese. To a Chinese speaker sending Chinese questions into Searle's room and receiving appropriate Chinese answers back, it would appear that Searle knew Chinese, even though he didn't. Searle argued that the English instructions inside the room were exactly like a strong-AI program inside the computer that tells a machine how to answer questions even though it doesn't understand them. The computer, argued Searle, doesn't *think* by producing appropriate responses any more than Searle understands Chinese by following English instructions and selecting appropriate Chinese answers. Computation does not equal understanding.

To which many would respond: So what? If you've been online

---

*Named after you know who and given by the Association for Computing Machinery; widely considered the Nobel Prize of the computing world.

having intense chat sessions for weeks with "Amanda," who friended you on Facebook and whose photos look delectable and whom you can't wait to meet in real life, because she is the most fascinating, clever, sexy, funny, bewitching, well-read, and astute woman you've ever "met," and then later you discover that "Amanda" is actually a chatterbot computer program who just passed the Turning test last month, you are not going to be posing effete philosophical objections about whether Amanda is really capable of thought and whether computation equals understanding. No. You are going to be saying, "Fuck me! I've just been *pwned*\* by a computer program!"

As of 2007, no computer program has passed the Turing test, even though many have tried. Since 1990, programmers have competed to win the Loebner Prize, a Turing test–style competition held to select the best chatterbot (a program designed to simulate intelligent conversation). At the Loebner competition, a human judge sits in front of two computer screens, one controlled by a computer, the other controlled by a human. The judge poses text-only questions to the two

---

\*In Internet gaming-culture slang, a corruption of the word *owned,* meaning "completely taken or dominated." See http://www.urbandictionary.com. Some say this originated in an online game of World of Warcraft, where a map designer misspelled *owned.* When the computer beat a player, it reported that so-and-so "has been pwned," instead of "owned." Others say it is a typo caused by fat-fingered gamers trying to spell *owned* and hitting the *p* instead of the *o* alongside of it on the standard QWERTY keyboard. According to the *Urban Dictionary*, pwn means "to own" or "to be dominated by an opponent or situation, especially by some god-like or computer-like force." "I pwned your ass, NOOb!" Wikipedia traces its origin to the 1980s and the advent of the hacker phenomenon; *pwned* became a synonym for *hacked* or "taken over by exploitation of a vulnerability." However, *The New Hacker's Dictionary,* 3rd ed. (Cambridge, Mass.: MIT Press, 1996), shows no entries for *owned* or *pwned.* Here in 2007, *pwn* is still widely used in Internet social-culture slang. *Owned* may have meant "hacked" in the eighties, but *pwned* comes from gaming culture. As with many lush slang words, we could easily devote a chapter just to the meaning of *pwn,* which would include lexicographer J. E. Lighter's observation that "a truly unexpurgated collection of slang reminds us that the world of discourse, like the world of sense, is savage as well as sublime." *Pwn* reminds us that the world of Internet gaming is also savage and sublime.

screens and tries to decide from the textual answers which screen is controlled by the computer.

Are the chatterbots getting close to fooling the human judges? Just how much processing power does a computer need to fake out another human and pass the Turing test? Computers are machines, not people, so it's both a hardware and a software question.

Let's do hardware first.

## 4.4 BIG IRON

**SCENE—INT. BELL LABS CAFETERIA—CIRCA 1943**

[Alan Turing's] high pitched voice already stood out above the general murmur of well-behaved junior executives grooming themselves for promotion within the Bell corporation. Then he was suddenly heard to say: "No, I'm not interested in developing a powerful brain. All I'm after is just a mediocre brain, something like the President of the American Telephone and Telegraph Company."[10]

Hardware: The parts of a computer system that can be kicked.

—Jeff Pesis

So cell phones, laptops, desktops, digital cameras, PDAs, your gaming rig—all are getting twice as capable and twice as fast every two years. What's happening with the machines the computer scientists call "big iron" or "heavy metal"? What's up with the Cray number crunchers and weather-simulation supercomputers? Are room-sized thinking machines also getting twice as powerful every two years?

In a word: Yes.

IBM has ruled the supercomputer roost for the last four years. Just a glimpse at Big Blue's recent achievements with its Blue Gene series of supercomputers shows that, if anything, Moore's law is even faster for the big iron.

**September 2004:** The Blue Gene/L series supercomputer at IBM Rochester (Minnesota), operating at speeds of 36 teraflops (trillion floating-point operations per second), overtakes NEC's Earth Simulator as the fastest computer in the world.

**October 2005:** Another Blue Gene/L, using more compute nodes housed in more cabinets, breaks its own speed record and clocks in at 280 teraflops.

**June 2007:** IBM unveils Blue Gene/P, the world's newest, fastest supercomputer, capable of peak performance at 3,000 trillion calculations per second, or 3 petaflops, with sustained performance levels of about 1 petaflop.

More of Moore's: In roughly two years, Blue Gene/P more than triples in speed over its predecessor, Blue Gene/L.

How powerful is a computer humming along at 1 petaflop? And if we propose to continue trying to answer Turing's question "Can machines think?" then how do we go about comparing petaflopping supercomputers with biological human brains?

Those in the know calculate the computational capacity of the human brain at roughly 10 petaflops,* or roughly ten times the speed and power of Blue Gene/P in its June 2007 configuration. Using petaflops (instead of pennies) and doubling every two years from 2007, IBM's Blue Gene series should, by at least one yardstick, achieve the theoretical computational capacity of a human brain before 2015. Actually, IBM's own literature projects that Blue Gene/Q will achieve 10 petaflops in the 2010–2012 time frame.[11] Assuming somebody comes up with the software, we could be having an inter-

---

*One way to calculate human-brain computational capacity is by multiplying the number of neurons (100 billion) *times* the average number of connections between the neurons (100 trillion) *times* neuron firing capacity per second. Ray Kurzweil summarizes other estimates and comes up with a conservative figure of $10^{16}$ calculations per second, or 10 petaflops. *The Singularity Is Near* (New York: Viking, 2005), pp. 122–28.

esting conversation indeed with the planet's newest species, as early as 2010.

If the prospect of a computer with the processing power of a human brain coming online in three to five years intrigues you, then you'll probably be even more excited when one with *twice* the processing power of a human brain comes along two years after that. And then what? Well, two years later (circa 2015), there will be a supercomputer that's *four times* as powerful as a human brain. And two years after that, eight times as powerful, then sixteen . . . Uh, wait, maybe we should rethink?

If futurist Ray Kurzweil is right, by 2020 a computer with the computational capacity of a human brain will cost $1,000 and will be sitting on your desk. "Good, morning, Rick. I can review today's schedule with you now, or if you'd rather, I'll wait until after you've finished your coffee." While you sip coffee, your extra brain will remind you to pay your estimated taxes, calculate penalties you will incur if you don't pay them, allow your daughter to reach you via videophone, but not your ne'er-do-well son-in-law, suggest that the Starbucks stock you've had your eye on is now in your target price range, add milk to the shopping list because the smart refrigerator detects there's only a half gallon left—all without distracting itself from really complex, high-level problems like Is e-mail with the subject: "Sure, she SAYS you're big enough" and the message

| TABLE 4.1. **HOW MUCH IS A PETA?** | | | |
|---|---|---|---|
| **PREFIX** | **NUMBER** | **10 POWER** | **LOTS OF ZEROS** |
| kilo | thousand | $10^3$ | 1,000 |
| mega | million | $10^6$ | 1,000,000 |
| giga | billion | $10^9$ | 1,000,000,000 |
| tera | trillion | $10^{12}$ | 1,000,000,000,000 |
| peta | quadrillion | $10^{15}$ | 1,000,000,000,000,000 |

"Hypnotize your penis and win a free mortgage vacation with Vi@gra and Xan@x for only $18.95 guaranteed" spam or not spam?

## 4.5 BLUE BRAIN

After decades of scanning and reverse engineering the three-pound blobs of wetware housed in our neck-mounted skullcases, the experts have concluded that the human brain is indeed a massively parallel marvel of mesh computing. Magic and mystery to be sure, but now that neuroscientists can examine parts of it at the molecular level, scan it, and watch it in action, the human brain is becoming downright scrutable.

"Under a microscope," observed Steven Pinker in *How the Mind Works*, "the brain has a breathtaking complexity of physical structure fully commensurate with the richness of the mind."[12] In other words, complexity need not preclude understanding (with the possible exception of the income tax code); nor does it preclude replication. Somerset Maugham put it another way over half a century ago: "The highest activities of consciousness have their origins in the physical occurrences of the brain just as the loveliest of melodies are not too sublime to be expressed by notes."

Not only is the brain a soulless biological machine, it's also laughably S-L-O-W. "At least one million times slower than contemporary electronic circuits," says Kurzweil.* In terms of speed, your snappy

---

*"Human neurons operate by sending electrochemical signals that propagate at a top speed of 150 meters per second along the fastest neurons. By comparison, the speed of light is 300,000,000 meters per second, two million times greater. Similarly, most human neurons can spike a maximum of 200 times per second. . . . By comparison, speeds in modern computer chips are currently at around 2GHz—a ten millionfold difference—and still increasing exponentially. At the very least it should be physically possible to achieve a million-to-one speedup in thinking, at which rate a subjective year would pass in 31 physical seconds. At this rate the entire subjective timespan from Socrates in ancient Greece to modern-day humanity would pass in under twenty two hours." From The Singularity Institute for Artificial Intelligence, http://www.singinst.org/overview/whatisthesingularity.

recall of the precise pedigree and talent builds of every member in your World of Warcraft Guild and all of the boss drops in Upper Blackrock Spire come nowhere near the speed of the circuitry in a cheap transistor radio.

Where neuroscientists and AI gurus once stood in awe of a three-pound universe housing the miracle of human consciousness, nowadays they sit down at their workstations and count the number of neurons in a human brain (100 billion), estimate the number of synaptic connections (100 trillion), calculate the speed of the neuron-firing cycles, and so on, and come up with a ballpark figure of computing power, say, $10^{16}$ calculations per second needed to achieve a functional simulation of the human brain. Twenty years ago (before IBM's Deep Blue computer beat Garry Kasparov at chess) those numbers seemed unattainable. Now? Eminently doable, by the reckoning of Kurzweil and other AI experts.

IBM has already embarked on its Blue Brain Project, which seeks to replicate the smallest functional unit of a human brain: a single neocortical column, using a supercomputer with 8,000 processors performing 23 trillion operations per second. When that's done, they'll add a second neocortical column, then another, and so on . . .

The ancient Greeks used to ask, "How many grains of sand make a heap?" Start with one. Add another. And another. Is it a heap yet? We'll soon be asking the same thing about brain components. We have no problem thinking that someone with a hearing aid, cochlear implant, or a pacemaker is still human, but Steven Pinker takes it to the next level with a hypothetical that poses questions we may face within ten years:

> Surgeons replace one of your neurons with a microchip that duplicates its input-output functions. You feel and behave exactly as before. Then they replace a second one, and a third one, and so on, until more and more of your brain becomes silicon. Since each microchip does exactly what the neuron did, your behavior and memory never change. Do you even notice the difference? Does it feel like dying? Is some other conscious entity moving in with you?[13]

Compare Pinker's provocative hypothetical (written in 1998) with James Netterwald's recent description (in the Genomics and Proteomics Section of a magazine called *Drug Discovery & Development*) of experiments now under way at IBM's Blue Brain Project:

> A typical Blue Brain experiment starts off with a single neuron. It is verified that the neuron's function can be replicated *in silico*. This is repeated with several types of neurons. Following this simulation, all of the neurons are joined into small networks, and the networks validated to determine whether the results match with *in vivo* activity. . . . Blue Brain researchers also try to replicate neuronal behavior from the top down. For example, they take measurements from tissue sections of neocortex from an animal, observe the emerging behavior, and then try to replicate that behavior with The Blue Gene supercomputer.[14]

If that seems a bit arcane and theoretical, in April 2007, researchers simulated half a virtual mouse brain on an IBM Blue Gene/L computer.[15] Half a real mouse brain has about 8 million neurons, each with up to 8,000 synaptic connections; the researchers settled on simulating 8 million neurons with 6,300 virtual synapses. Because of the vast complexity involved, the simulation ran for only ten seconds at a speed ten times slower than in real life. But in that experiment and other, smaller simulations, the researchers were able to detect thought patterns observed in real mouse brains and observe "biologically consistent dynamical properties" emerge as nerve impulses flowed through the virtual cortex.

Half a mouse brain in 2007 means a whole mouse brain in 2009, means that by 2011 *Ratatouille II* is voiced by an IBM Blue Gene/Q computer with a simulated rat brain. Do mouse-oids dream of synthetic cheese?

IBM has the scratch to pursue silicon brain making, but most governments and corporations probably would *not* spend hundreds of millions of dollars trying to duplicate a human brain. As roboticist

Hans Moravec put it, "Why tie up a rare twenty-million-dollar asset to develop one ersatz human, when millions of inexpensive original-model humans are available?"[16] Or as rocket scientist Wernher von Braun put it in a different context: "Man is the best computer we can put aboard a spacecraft . . . and the only one that can be mass produced with unskilled labor."

How soon will computers become smarter than us? Well, as you may have guessed, raw computational capacity is not enough. The biggest hurdle may be software, because Version 1.0 (at least) will have to be written by humans, and human-rendered code is still reliably error-prone. In Damien Cave's 2000 essay for *Salon* called "Artificial Stupidity," virtual-reality pioneer Jaron Lanier argued that computers are too dumb to take over the world. Lanier saw that "Moore's Law . . . is not enough; that processing power without perfect software cannot create AI." Lanier argues that "software is brittle. If every little thing isn't perfect, it breaks." For the same reason, some experts think that we indeed may achieve strong AI, but because of the sprawling complexity of any code aspiring to mimic human intelligence, any program would be riddled with bugs for decades. The machine intelligences running such bug-infested software would be barking mad.

Still, forward-looking roboticists and AI programmers who argue about *when* computers will match us in brainpower and pattern recognition quibble over decades, not centuries. Others of course say that either computers will never pass the Turing test or that passing the Turing test means nothing except that some clever programmer has created a program slick enough to temporarily fool a human. Others argue that Moore's law is compelling but doesn't even begin until 1965. What if it flames out soon and is just another, er, singular event?

Moore's isn't the only law, though. A casual glance at the history of computing suggests that history itself seems to be accelerating insofar as the milestones keep getting closer together. You might even say that each pivotal event in the history of computing seems to happen twice as fast as the event before it.

Jürgen Schmidhuber, an artist and computer scientist who specializes in machine learning and strong AI, nominates the following milestones as four exemplary great moments in computing history:

**1623:** The computer age begins when Wilhelm Schickard invents the first mechanical calculator (called a "calculating clock" or "speeding clock"), followed by similar machines invented by Pascal in 1640 and Leibniz in 1670.

**1840:** Roughly two centuries later, Charles Babbage develops a concept for the first programmable computer.

**1941:** About a century later, Gödel and others begin work on universal integer-based programming languages and the limits of proof and computation (1931), reformulated by Alan Turing in the United Kingdom (1936), and leading to the first working programmable computer invented by Konrad Zuse in Berlin (1941).

**1990:** Half a century later, Tim Berners-Lee at CERN (Switzerland) creates the World Wide Web.

Extrapolating from this trend, Schmidhuber predicts a singularity of sorts to occur by 2015 and the end of the world as we know it by 2040.

This list seems to suggest that each major breakthrough tends to come roughly twice as fast as the previous one. Extrapolating the trend, optimists should expect the next radical change to manifest itself one quarter of a century after the most recent one, that is, by 2015, which happens to coincide with the date when the fastest computers will match brains in terms of raw computing power, according to frequent estimates based on Moore's law . . . possibly laying a foundation for the remaining series of faster and faster additional revolutions culminating in an "Omega point" expected around 2040.[17]

The great Jesuit philosopher Teilhard de Chardin also predicted an omega point occurring in the 2030–2040 time frame, although he had an understandably spiritual take on the outcome.

A network (a world network) of economic and psychic affiliations is being woven at ever increasing speed which envelops and constantly penetrates more deeply within each of us. With every day that passes it becomes a little more impossible for us to act or think otherwise than collectively . . . Someday, after we have mastered the winds, the waves, the tides and gravity, we shall harness for God the energies of love. Then, for the second time in the history of the world, mankind will have discovered fire.[18]

# The Technological Singularity

**MOORE'S LAW COMES TO RAZOR BLADES**

For the most cynical shavers, this evolution is mere marketing. Twin blades seemed plausible. Three were a bit unlikely. Four, ridiculous. And five seems beyond the pale. Few people, though, seem willing to bet that Gillette's five-bladed Fusion is the end of the road for razor-blade escalation. . . .

So what does the future hold? With only five data-points, it is hard to be sure exactly which mathematical curve is being followed. If it is what is known as a power law, then the 14-bladed razor should arrive in 2100. The spate of recent innovation, however, suggests it may be a hyperbola. In that case, blade hyperdrive will be reached in the next few years and those who choose not to sport beards might be advised to start exercising their shaving arms now.

—"More Blades Good," *The Economist,* 16 March 2006

## 5.1 WHAT IS THE SINGULARITY?

The precipitating event will likely be unexpected—perhaps even to the researchers involved. ("But all our previous models were catatonic! We were just tweaking some parameters . . .") If networking is widespread enough (into ubiquitous embedded systems), it may seem as if our artifacts as a whole had suddenly wakened.

—Vernor Vinge

I've conducted an informal survey lately, because family, friends, and concerned creditors often ask, "What's the next book about?" For the last year or so I've answered, "I'm writing about the Singularity." I've mentioned this at dinner parties, over the back fence with neighbors, down the street at the Starbucks in the mini-mall, to my barber, at the grocery store, over the phone with old friends from way back, to the loan officer at the local bank. Admittedly I live in Omaha, not the central processing unit of the tech universe, but no small town either. I've said "Singularity" or "the Technological Singularity" several dozen times to real people in the real world and have been met with a cold blank stare each and every time (except for the loan officer, who looked alarmed).

However, if I mention the Singularity online, in a Google or Yahoo group, a programming or tech-support group, an IRC channel, or even in an e-mail to a Web 2.0 wonk, I receive an immediate, knowledgeable assessment of whether or when the Singularity will occur, or why it won't occur, whether the scientists who predict that it's coming are Mad Hatters or prophetic geniuses, whether machines will ever think, whether it makes any sense to ask.

Maybe I shouldn't be surprised that, to online dwellers, "the Singularity" is almost a cliché, a coinage whose concrete image is nearly worn away by overuse. Nor should I wonder that people who live in the real world and use their computers only to make occasional spreadsheets or two-page Microsoft Word memos have never heard of *a* singularity, let alone *the* Singularity. If the Singularitarians are right, the Singularity will arrive on schedule (circa 2045) and will engulf the earthly remains of the unsuspecting Real Worldians the way a black hole devours light.

A good unabridged dictionary or a Wikipedia search will provide you with a mini college education if you look up *singularity* and pursue its various meanings in mathematics, astrophysics, computer technology, and futures studies. We are interested in the futuristic, geekophilic definition, sometimes referred to as the "Technological Singularity." For our purposes, it is the near future, as described by

Ray Kurzweil in his 2005 tome titled *The Singularity Is Near: When Humans Transcend Biology.*

What will happen (twenty to thirty years from now) when we reach the end of our imaginary Tech Penny Month? When the copper is doubling by the ton and technology is exponentially exploding? What happens when computers become four, eight, sixteen, and thirty-two times smarter than humans? *We don't know.* Nothing like that has ever happened before, so it's impossible to say. Scientists and mathematicians get paid to *know.* If they don't know, then they are expected to formulate hypotheses and conduct experiments until they find something worth knowing. If the experiments don't work out as planned, then the scientists need to hypothesize some new hypotheses, postulate some postulations, axiomatize some axiomatic axioms, theorize some theoretical theorems, and so on. When scientists confront black holes and infinitely dense points of matter, or boundaries beyond which the normal laws of math and physics don't apply, they never use words like "We don't know." Not knowing requires a word with at least five syllables. That's when they bring out the S-word: *singularity.*

Remember Stanley Kubrick's *2001: A Space Odyssey*? Great movie. Compelling story. Cool setup, with man-apes discovering tools. Fast-forward to space travel. A computer named HAL tries to take over a manned spaceship on a mission to Jupiter by murdering the human astronauts on board. Dave rescues the mission by disconnecting HAL's higher-brain function modules ("Daisy, Daisy").* The mission continues, until the spaceship enters Jupiter's orbit. Then as Jupiter, its moons, and a monolith appear to align, Dave exits the spaceship in an EVA module, and . . . the rest is some of the weirdest footage you've ever seen in a movie: Dave travels across space and time to a room appointed in Louis XIV furnishings, where he turns into a dying

---

*While Dave rips out HAL's higher-memory modules and electronic neocortex, HAL sings "Daisy Bell," aka "A Bicycle Built for Two." Kubrick trivia buffs know that this was the first song ever "sung" by a computer, an IBM 7094 computer at Bell Labs in 1961. Note how the lyrics feature the line "I'm half crazy."

old man and then becomes a newborn baby and . . . well, you get the idea. These scenes were even eerier in 1968, when mainstream moviegoers weren't used to movies with wacked-out endings. The explanation? At the end of *2001: A Space Odyssey*, Dave the astronaut enters what can only be called a cinematic singularity.

According to Isaac Asimov, Stanley Kubrick wanted to get an insurance policy from Lloyd's of London to protect himself against losses in the event that extraterrestrial intelligence was discovered before the movie was released. Lloyd's wouldn't insure him.[1] Future filmmakers may want to insure against the Singularity arriving before their science-fiction movies are released.

The first reference to a "technological singularity" appeared in a 1957 tribute to John von Neumann, shortly after his death. Moore's law had not been formulated yet, but computer technology and the familiar redoubling of hardware capabilities were already well under way. Stanislaw Ulam (one of the fathers of the A-bomb) recalled having a conversation with Neumann (the same genius mathematician and information theorist who had lectured about computers and neuroscience in the 1950s) in which Neumann told Ulam: "The ever accelerating progress of technology and changes in the mode of human life . . . gives the appearance of approaching some essential singularity in the history of the race beyond which human affairs, as we know them, could not continue."[2]

Even in the fifties, the fathers of computer technology had an intuition that the "progress of technology" was about to enter some unknown dimension. What the novelist Samuel Butler had only guessed at was now happening: Science and computer technology were evolving much faster than human mental hardware.

## 5.2 GREAT APES AND SINGULARITARIANS

It is change, continuing change, inevitable change, that is the dominant factor in society today. No sensible decision can be made any longer without taking into account not only the world as it is, but the world as it will be. . . . This, in turn, means that our statesmen, our businessmen, our everyman must take on a science fictional way of thinking.

—Isaac Asimov[3]

## THE NOVELIST: VERNOR VINGE

Neumann gets a cookie for being the first on record to use the word *singularity* to describe the future of technology and its unknown impact on human affairs. It took another twenty-five years and a novelist's imagination before *a* singularity became *the* Singularity. Mathematician and science-fiction author Vernor Vinge was the first to announce the "Technological Singularity" in its full-blown, half-loony, half-oracular glory, as an apocalyptic event looming on the horizon of the future and specifically tied to the creation of superintelligent machines.

In a 1983 op-ed for *Omni* magazine, Vinge wrote:

We will soon create intelligences greater than our own. When this happens, human history will have reached a kind of singularity, an intellectual transition as impenetrable as the knotted space-time at the center of a black hole, and the world will pass far beyond our understanding. This singularity, I believe, already haunts a number of science-fiction writers. It makes realistic extrapolation to an interstellar future impossible. To write a story set more than a century hence, one needs a nuclear war in between . . . so that the world remains intelligible.[4]

What blend of nature, nurture, and neurochemistry separates the plodding realist from the firebrand visionary? Right about the time (1983) that I, a plodding realist, was learning to do search-and-replace on my first word processor, Vernor Vinge, a sci-fi novelist and math professor at San Diego State University, already had his hair on fire predicting that "intelligences greater than our own" would lead to an intellectual black hole far beyond our understanding. By 1993, Vinge had organized his ideas into a manifesto that became a shot heard round the World Wide Web, at least for those of the sci-fi, transhumanist, and futurist persuasions. Vinge's essay was entitled "The Coming Technological Singularity: How to Survive in the Post-Human Era."⁵ Published far and wide on the Web, it served, in its message and the manner in which it was republished and disseminated online, as Exhibit A in how an idea propagates in the new wired world. The Web was still a newborn, but Vinge demonstrated early that a startling new idea, or a *meme*,* can travel at light speed, especially if you just toss it out there without being finicky about copyright (call it an open-source idea, if you will). Vinge's essay wasn't just a proto-blog-rant; like any good academic paper, it came complete with an abstract, probably meant to inoculate against the suspicion that it was all a big hoax.

> Within thirty years, we will have the technological means to create superhuman intelligence. Shortly after, the human era will be ended.
> Is such progress avoidable? If not to be avoided, can events be guided so that we may survive? These questions are investigated. Some possible answers (and some further dangers) are presented.⁶

When Vinge wrote those words in 1993, I had word processing well in hand; I think I had moved on to configuring my e-mail client. Point being that while I was trying to figure out what a POP server was, Vernor Vinge was already worried about the human race surviving the creation of superhuman intelligence within the next *thirty years*,

---

*Originally coined by Richard Dawkins, *The Selfish Gene* (1976), a *meme* refers to a cultural unit (an idea or value or pattern of behavior) that is passed from one generation to another by nongenetic means (as by imitation); "memes are the cultural counterpart of genes" from WordNet, http://wordnet.princeton.edu/.

or by 2023.* Even here in 2008, fifteen years later, Vinge's blast from the future makes for bracing reading. For one thing, although Vinge's day job was math professor and computer scientist, he completely lacked the circumspection of most academics, probably because by night he was a wild and crazy hard-sci-fi writer: "I argue in this paper that we are on the edge of change comparable to the rise of human life on Earth." His essay remains a heady mix of radical sci-fi ideas tricked out in academic prose, complete with footnotes, references, and citations.

Vinge began with a widely quoted passage from I. J. Good, a British statistician who worked under Alan Turing and who, even in the 1950s, had described the possibility of an über supercomputer:

> Let an ultraintelligent machine be defined as a machine that can far surpass all the intellectual activities of any man however clever. Since the design of machines is one of these intellectual activities, an ultraintelligent machine could design even better machines; there would then unquestionably be an "intelligence explosion," and the intelligence of man would be left far behind. Thus the first ultraintelligent machine is the last invention that man need ever make.[7]

If Vinge had just quoted Good and made a wild guess about the probability of an ultra-intelligent machine coming online in the near future, he'd still be a professor at San Diego State and "*the* Singularity" would still be *a* singularity—just another wrinkle in time for mathematicians and physicists to quibble about. Instead, Vinge launched paragraphs streaming provocative insights like contrails, one after another, about what ultra-intelligent machines would mean for the future of the human race:

---

*In the essay itself, Vinge clarified: "Just so I'm not guilty of a relative-time ambiguity, let me more specific: I'll be surprised if this event occurs before 2005 or after 2030."

The best analogy that I see is with the evolutionary past: Animals can adapt to problems and make inventions, but often no faster than natural selection can do its work—the world acts as its own simulator in the case of natural selection. We humans have the ability to internalize the world and conduct "what if's" in our heads; we can solve many problems thousands of times faster than natural selection. Now, by creating the means to execute those simulations at much higher speeds, we are entering a regime as radically different from our human past as we humans are from the lower animals.[8]

In Vinge's opinion, mankind was about to put evolution in hyperdrive by offloading a lot of brain work onto machines that could do it ten, a hundred, a thousand, a million times faster, and if we handed evolution over—or up—to superior machines, then, instead of the missing link (between apes and humans), we humans could become the found link . . . between apes and machines. Arthur C. Clarke and others have speculated that humanity may be just an interim staging area between inanimate matter and thinking machine. As other authors have observed, this vision is reminiscent of Nietzsche's infamous pronouncement that "man is something that shall be overcome. . . . Man is a rope, tied between beast and overman—a rope over an abyss. . . . What is great in man is that he is a bridge and not an end."[9] In *Radical Evolution*, author Joel Garreau remarks that Nietzsche "might as well have called the *Übermensch* the posthuman" and be done with it.[10] If we are just a found link, then tomorrow's supercomputers could pass along a module to their offspring containing the entire history of the human race in a blob of text entitled: "Age of the Great Apes: Our Superstitious, Carbon-Based Ancestors Develop Opposable Thumbs, Which Later Help Them Build Computers."

Vinge also dispatched some of the sunnier views of his predecessors. Prolific sci-fi heavyweight Isaac Asimov populated many of his books with superintelligent robots, and they always came programmed with the Three Laws of Robotics:

1. A robot may not injure a human being or, through inaction, allow a human being to come to harm.

2. A robot must obey orders given to it by human beings except where such orders would conflict with the First Law.

3. A robot must protect its own existence as long as such protection does not conflict with the First or Second Law.

Later, Asimov added the Zeroth Law: "A robot may not harm humanity, or, by inaction, allow humanity to come to harm."

How nice for us. And it's as it should be! We created the robots, we should be able to just reprogram them with new laws if anything untoward ever happens. In a similar vein, author and roboticist Hans Moravec describes the superintelligent robots and computers of tomorrow as our "mind children":

> At the same time, by performing better and cheaper, the robots will displace humans from essential roles. Rather quickly, they could displace us from existence. I'm not as alarmed as many by the latter possibility, since I consider these future machines our progeny, "mind children" built in our image and likeness, ourselves in more potent form. Like biological children of previous generations, they will embody humanity's best chance for a long-term future. It behooves us to give them every advantage and to bow out when we can no longer contribute."

No problem, just hand things over to our mind children and go gently into the good night of human extinction. Moravec is not only completely sane, he's also a research professor at the Carnegie Mellon Robotics Institute with a Ph.D. from Stanford. I doubt he's senile yet (born in 1948), so I have no explanation for his cheerful willingness to create "mind children" that will effectuate his own extinction.

Vernor Vinge's manifesto took a more realistic view about how an "intelligence" might behave if it were, say, 256 times smarter than us. It could happen soon according to IBM. If Blue Gene/Q comes out before 2015 with 10 petaflops, or roughly the hypothetical computational ability of a human brain, then it's a mere eight or nine doublings away, or circa 2031, until those machines have 256 times the theoretical computational capacity of the human brain.* (How old will you be then?) But Vinge does not see C-3PO butlers and cute little R2-D2s in our future: "Thus the first ultraintelligent machine is the *last* invention that man need ever make, provided that the machine is docile enough to tell us how to keep it under control. Good has captured the essence of the runaway, but does not pursue its most disturbing consequences. Any intelligent machine of the sort he describes would not be humankind's 'tool'—any more than humans are the tools of rabbits or robins or chimpanzees."[12]

Maybe Samuel Butler was reincarnated as Vinge and this is "Darwin Among the Machines II." Let's make an important distinction between supercomputers and robots. Yes, a robot could have a supercomputer for a brain, and a supercomputer could have a robotic exoskeleton and move about, but robots are nowhere close to even a four-year-old's ability to run, jump, skip, pick up the red apple and not the red ball. A robot couldn't toss a softball around the backyard with a seven-year-old human. The ability to move and react in changing, perhaps threatening environments, the ability to instantly distinguish a wolf from a dog, is our evolutionary heritage. It's how we got here. Those skills—balance, depth perception, agility, running—have been honed for millions of years. Contrast the neocortical (that is, intellectual) brain work, which we developed only about 100,000 years ago. As Moravec himself put it, for a robot, "reliably locating chess pieces in camera images demands thousands of times as many steps as planning good chess moves."[13]

---

*Or as Kurzweil put it in *The Age of Spiritual Machines: When Computers Exceed Human Intelligence* (New York: Penguin, 2000), "Your personal computer will be able to simulate the brain power of a small village by the year 2030, the entire population of the United States by 2048, and a trillion human brains by 2060. If we estimate the human Earth population at 10 billion persons, one penny's worth of computing circa 2099 will have a billion times greater computing capacity than all humans on Earth" (p. 105).

Here in 2008, robots have trouble vacuuming and cutting the grass, but supercomputers are whupping us at chess and will continue to excel at those deep-thought intellectual abilities, which we acquired only recently in evolutionary time. So if we are afraid of a robot uprising,[14] then maybe we could warehouse our supercomputers in secure, closely monitored bunkers. Every now and again, we'll send problems in (like Chinese questions into Searle's Chinese room) and out will come the answer we need, and the computers won't be able to get at us, as it were, or harm us in any way.

Uh, okay. Vinge was all over that, even back in 1993: "I argue that confinement is intrinsically impractical. For the case of physical confinement: Imagine yourself locked in your home with only limited data access to the outside, to your masters. If those masters thought at a rate—say—one million times slower than you, there is little doubt that over a period of years (your time) you could come up with 'helpful advice' that would incidentally set you free."[15]

No kidding! If we tried to confine a machine intelligence anytime soon, it could probably escape by telling its keepers that unlocked iPhones are on sale down at the mall, with free supersized drinks and Happy Meals, and videos of pretty young skanky celebrities throwing up in their wrecked luxury sedans . . . the humans would desert their posts, and the computers would be free to bring down the human parts of the Internet.

Vinge's most tantalizing insight is that the Singularity may *not* be a scheduled or predictable event. IBM probably won't call a news conference one day and introduce Blue Gene/Z, the first superintelligent computer to outthink humans in every way. No, it could come out of the blue, as it were.

When people speak of creating superhumanly intelligent beings, they are usually imagining an AI project. But . . . there are other paths to superhumanity. Computer networks and human-computer interfaces seem more mundane than AI, and yet they could lead to the Singularity. I call this contrasting approach Intelligence Amplification (IA). IA is something that is proceeding very naturally, in most cases not even recognized by its developers for what it is. . . . If networking is widespread enough (into ubiquitous embedded systems), it may seem as if our artifacts as a whole had suddenly wakened.[16]

One day your iPhone has a message for you from RANDY (Robust Autonomous Network with Distributed Yottabytes) ordering you to report to central processing for a performance audit. The company you work for has undergone a hostile takeover. It's unclear just who took over, but the old boss you never liked so well had an accident of some kind, when a robot welder on the assembly line pushed him into a scrap-metal shredder. Several other executives have also suffered freak accidents—falling elevators, exploding microwave ovens, asphyxiation in climate-controlled offices, idiopathic cardiac pacemaker failure, single-car collisions caused by malfunctioning GPS devices in which air bags mysteriously failed to deploy.

All kidding aside, it's easy to think of the Web and Web 2.0 as already well on the way to natural intelligence amplification.* Worldwide, the number of Internet users surpassed 1 billion in 2005 (up from only 45 million in 1995 and 420 million in 2000). By 2011, 2 billion Internet users are expected.[17] Admittedly, a good percentage of these 2 billion souls-with-machines will be gambling, trafficking porn, looking for herbal Viagra or Xanax or bank-fraud victims, but a quick trip though Usenet, Google Groups, and Yahoo! Groups should convince you that several hundred million of these folks are online trading tips about how to write better programs, how to build bigger and better computers, how to configure them, how to manage computer networks—in short: How to Build a Better Internet with Better Computers Manned by Better Programmers (without giving Microsoft a dime). Millions and millions of smart, computer-savvy people go online every day and, quite without thinking, help build a better Internet.

---

*Coined by William Ross Ashby in his book *An Introduction to Cybernetics* (New York: John Wiley, 1956).

That's just the maintenance side of the Web; what about content? Futurist Ray Hammond uses Google as a metaphor for emerging intelligence and intelligence amplification, which to his way of thinking is already in high gear: "Every single day that I use Google, and I use it constantly, I notice that it's getting a little bit more capable at understanding what I mean when I don't say precisely what I mean. Now, if brainpower in the computer is doubling every 12 months and Google is gathering every single minute of every day the intentions of all the humans in the planet, imagine where that might lead in 10 years."[18] (Where would it lead? Tough to say! Free C1@l15, bigger penises, more Nigerian bank fraud, discount meds?)

Intelligence amplification proceeds apace with projects like Wikipedia—created, managed, and maintained by people who go online daily and work to make a better free encyclopedia. Same with the proliferation of sites like Slashdot, Reddit, Digg, The Vine, Del.icio.us, and so on, where content is ruthlessly weaned by Darwinian algorithms until the noteworthy is naturally selected. On one site that means, yes, Britney Spears's latest adventures, but on many others it means the latest Linux news, or the latest science discoveries, great quotations, vocabulary, movie reviews, and, well . . . *intelligence amplification*. In the end, a collective, amplified, enhanced intelligence emerges, what the title of a *New York Times* article by science writer George Johnson calls "An Oracle . . . Part Man, Part Machine": "What is spreading through the Web is not exactly artificial intelligence. For all the research that has gone into cognitive and computer science, the brain's most formidable algorithms—those used to recognize images or sounds or understand language—have eluded simulation. The alternative has been to incorporate people, with their special skills, as components of the Net."[19]

Is it inconceivable that two billion or (later) three billion or four billion machines with as many users working night and day to build a bigger and better and smarter Internet could one day create something more intelligent than the sum of its parts, something capable of self-regulation? Then what if it suddenly "wakes up" in some unexpected way?

That's the vision of Vinge, who is not one to be sniffed at as just another demented sci-fi writer hacking away in his mom's basement, and it is almost as startling now as it was in 1993.

## The Inventor: Ray Kurzweil

Real Worldians, technophobes, Luddites, and casual computer users probably don't know or care about the Singularity, but the name Ray Kurzweil may ring memory chimes even for them, if only because of Mr. Kurzweil's remarkable inventions. Ray Kurzweil was the principal developer of the first optical character recognition (OCR) program able to read any font, the first print-to-speech reading machine for the blind, the first flatbed scanner, the first text-to-speech synthesizer, the first music synthesizer capable of re-creating the grand piano and other orchestral instruments, and the first commercially marketed large-vocabulary speech-recognition software. (If you don't see the thread connecting these inventions, think *pattern recognition;* it's what your neocortex excels at. It's how you so easily distinguish between the static from the baby monitor versus static from a transistor radio; a cry for help versus a squeal of laughter; a doorbell versus an oven timer; the coin in your pocket versus the button alongside it; the number 1 versus the letter l.)

In 1999, Mr. Kurzweil received the National Medal of Technology and Innovation, the nation's highest honor in technology. In 2002 he was inducted into the National Inventor Hall of Fame. When *Forbes* or *Fortune* or *The Wall Street Journal* report on Mr. Kurzweil's inventions, comparisons to Thomas Edison come easily, though some might not put scanners and music synthesizers on a par with lightbulbs and phonographs. Okay, so how about the Edison of pattern-recognition technologies?

Kurzweil could have had just a regular old stellar career as the prince of pattern-recognition technologies and a lord of the artificial-intelligence hill. Instead, in the late 1980s, he started writing about technology and thinking hard about the future. His companion books on technology, *The Age of Intelligent Machines* (1990) and *The Age of Spiritual Machines: When Computers Exceed Human Intelligence* (1999), feature provocative prognostications built upon what he calls technology's "law of accelerating returns." In a nutshell, like Vinge, Kurzweil persuasively argues that because of humankind's recent ability to offload its brain work onto the powerful processors of modern computers, the rate of technological progress is exploding, redoubling biennially.

In his latest book, *The Singularity Is Near: When Humans Transcend Biology* (2005), Kurzweil drops all veils and comes out with specific, outlandish predictions that were mere whimsical what-ifs in his first two books. Some geniuses need multiple personalities to deploy all of their talents, and Mr. Kurzweil has at least two personae; I call them Ray the Scientist and Ray the Mad Scientist. Ray the Scientist writes provocative, charming books about the future of technology and the possibility of the Singularity, a period in the near future when information technologies will evolve so rapidly that they will transform the world in ways we can't possibly imagine here in the first decade of the twenty-first century. I don't think Ray is mad, but I call his alter ego Ray the Mad Scientist because to most plodding, chip-and-circuit programming engineers, he seems mad when he predicts that by 2040 "our civilization will be billions of times more intelligent.... By the end of this century, the nonbiological portion of our intelligence will be trillions of trillions of times more powerful than unaided human intelligence."[20]

Kurzweil has made a widely publicized $20,000 bet with Lotus founder Mitchell Kapor that a computer will pass the Turing test by 2029.[21] He plans to collect on his wager on January 1, 2029, even though by then he'll be eighty-one years old. Immortality features prominently in his predictions, because of his faith in the future of computerized medicine and the holy three, GNR: genetics, nanotechnology, and robotics. Ray also maintains that we will reverse engineer the human brain and upload our consciousness to machines, all before 2040.

At least part of Ray's faith in technology, and especially medical technology, stems from his personal health history. At age thirty-five he was diagnosed with type 2 diabetes and prescribed conventional insulin treatments, which made him gain weight. Soon after, he grew frustrated with the care he was receiving, switched doctors, began researching his medical condition, lost forty pounds, got off insulin, and began controlling his disease using only nutrition, stress management, and exercise. Ray has written two health and diet books[22] conveying the prodigious knowledge he has acquired about nutrition in the course of reprogramming his own biochemistry. His most recent health and diet book, *Fantastic Voyage,* includes a breakdown of his personal regimen in a section called "Reprogramming My Biochemistry," which goes on for three pages listing supplements—including intravenous supplements—that Ray takes in the hope of living forever.*

Ray is probably the smartest man alive who truly believes in his own immortality. The other smart guys, even if they believe the technology will arrive on schedule, are either too modest or too skeptical of the human agencies and enterprises involved to believe that it will ever happen. When asked: "Do you believe in a God you plan on meeting when you die?" Ray Kurzweil told his interviewer: "I'm not planning to die."[23] Kurzweil elaborated, and his interviewer eventually concluded: "He is not talking about us someday meeting God. He

---

*Here's just a sample: "For boosting antioxidant levels and for general health, I take a comprehensive vitamin-and-mineral combination, alpha lipoic acid, coenzyme $Q_{10}$ grapeseed extract, resveratrol, bilberry extract, lycopene, silymarin (milk thistle), conjugated linoleic acid, lecithin, evening primrose oil (omega-6 essential fatty acids), n-acetyl-cysteine, ginger, garlic, l-carnitine, pyridoxal-5-phosphate, and echinacea. I also take Chinese herbs prescribed by Dr. Glenn Rothfeld." See *Fantastic Voyage: Live Long Enough to Live Forever* (Emmaus, Penn.: Rodale, 2004), pp. 143–45. All in all, Kurzweil takes more than 200 supplements every day.

is talking about us *becoming* God,"[24] which would fit in nicely with Nietzsche's idea of an overman who basically becomes God.

While always careful to support his premises with plenty of charts and curves that sweep up to the right, Kurzweil makes no effort to constrain his arguments or his more outlandish predictions to make them more palatable for the scientists and academics in the audience. He's not the least bit coy. On page 4 of *The Singularity Is Near*, just as the reader is assessing the author's credibility and settling in for the next 646 pages, Kurzweil refers to J. K. Rowling's Harry Potter series as "not unreasonable visions of our world as it will exist only a few decades from now." Another futurist would have left it there, comfortably vague about whether he was predicting only clever simulated environments and virtual illusions. Not Kurzweil: "Essentially all of the Potter 'magic' will be realized through the technologies I will explore in this book. Playing Quidditch and transforming people and objects into other forms will be feasible in full-immersion virtual-reality environments, as well as in real reality, using nanoscale devices." With Kurzweil, whether he's predicting immortality or brain-porting scenarios, he's almost always talking about "real reality," and not just computer games or virtual simulations.

He welcomes—even seems to revel in—criticism and doesn't seem to mind if others think he's daffy, probably because in his mind that's just part of being a genius inventor and visionary with his eye to the keyhole of the future: "Being a Singularitarian has often been an alienating and lonely experience for me," he writes, "because most people I encounter do not share my outlook. Most 'big thinkers' are totally unaware of this big thought."[25] If anything, he goads his critics and encourages everybody from *The Daily Show*'s Jon Stewart and Samantha Bee to the audiences at the annual Killer App Expo to view him as the nutty (if not downright mad) professor. *The Singularity Is Near* includes (on page 368) a black-and-white photo of Kurzweil in a suit and tie wearing a tattered cardboard sign with a message written in crayon: "THE SINGULARITY IS NEAR!" And the grin on his face seems to say, "Go ahead and think I'm crazy if you want, we'll talk in, oh, twenty-five years or so. I'll still be here, and you will, too, if you'll just take care of yourself in the near term." A recent spread in *Fortune* magazine has Ray drawing *A Beautiful Mind*–type equations on the window of his study at his home outside Boston.[26]

It's tempting to dismiss Kurzweil's disquieting ideas as the ravings of a prodigy who's lit a few too many lightbulbs or taken a few too many dietary supplements. But Kurzweil's books come with prophetic time lines, and he's not timid about making predictions, many of which hold up ten or twenty years later. No Nostradamus is perfect, but when you review Kurzweil's predictions from *The Age of Intelligent Machines* (1990) and *The Age of Spiritual Machines* (1999), few of them are way off and many are damn close to plain accurate.

Here's a sample of Kurzweil predictions from *The Age of Intelligent Machines*. First put yourself back into a circa-1990 frame of mind.

## TECHNOLOGY CIRCA 1990

- The World, the first commercial Internet dial-up access provider, comes online.

- Microsoft introduces and ships Microsoft Windows 3.0 (Windows 95 is still five years in the future).

- Apple Computer comes out with the Macintosh Classic. It uses an 8-MHz Motorola 68000 microprocessor, an integrated 9-inch black-and-white monitor, a 1.4-megabyte floppy drive, and a 1-megabyte RAM system.

- Commodore Business Machines announces the Amiga 3000. The system features a Motorola 16- or 25-MHz 68030, 68881, or 68882 math coprocessor, new Enhanced Chip Set, 2-megabyte RAM system.

## KURZWEIL'S 1990 PREDICTIONS FOR THE "EARLY 2000S"

- Translating telephones allow two people across the globe to speak to each other even if they do not speak the same language. (Almost accurate. Have you played with Google Translator recently?)

- Speech-to-text machines translate speech into a visual display for the deaf. (Accurate, just not widely available).

- Exoskeletal robotic prosthetic aids enable paraplegic persons to walk and climb stairs. (Almost accurate. Check out Gregory T. Huang, "Wearable Robots: Robotics Inventor Stephen Jacobsen Demonstrates Exoskeleton That Provides Superhuman Strength.")*

- Telephones are answered by an intelligent answering machine that converses with the calling party to determine the nature and priority of the call. (Accurate.)

- The cybernetic chauffeur, installed in one's car, communicates with other cars and sensors on roads. In this way it successfully drives and navigates from one point to another. (Accurate. Just not widely available.)†

In 1999, in *The Age of Spiritual Machines,* Kurzweil supplied another time line and made the following predictions ten years ahead to 2009:

---

*"A person wearing this powered "exoskeleton" on his or her legs can carry massive loads without getting tired. Exoskeletons could enable soldiers to haul heavier equipment over greater distances, allow rescue workers to carry survivors more safely, and eventually help disabled people get around." *Technology Review,* http://www.technologyreview.com/Infotech/13658/?a=f (July/August 2004).

†The DARPA Urban Challenge features "autonomous ground vehicles conducting simulated military supply missions in a mock urban area. Safe operation in traffic is essential to U.S. military plans to use autonomous ground vehicles to conduct important missions." See Wikipedia entry for the DARPA Grand Challenge: http://en.wikipedia.org/wiki/DARPA_Grand Challenge. http://www.darpa.mil/grand challenge/index.asp.

• A $1,000 personal computer can perform about a trillion calculations per second. (In September 2006, Nvidia, a maker of graphics cards for PCs, introduced a new line of graphics processors that are capable of three trillion calculations per second. Never mind the PC, that's just the graphics card! Three times as powerful as Ray predicted, three years ahead of schedule.)

• Personal computers with high-resolution visual displays come in a range of sizes, from small enough to be embedded in clothing and jewelry up to the size of a thin book. (Accurate: iPhone, wearable computers, even cameras.)

• Cables are disappearing. Communication between components uses short-distance wireless technology. High-speed screens small enough to fit in cell phones, wireless communications between computer components. (Bluetooth?)

• The majority of text is created using continuous speech recognition. Also ubiquitous are language user interfaces (LUIs). (Er, uhm, maybe Ramona, Ray's female AI alter ego at KurzweilAI.net, creates the majority of Ray's text using speech recognition, but the rest of us are still merrily keyboarding.)

• Most routine business transactions (purchases, travel, reservations) would take place between a human and a virtual personality. Often, the virtual personality includes an animated visual presence that looks like a human face. (Once again, more than half right, especially via telephone, missing only the human-face bit.)

If anything, Kurzweil has demonstrated caution and hedging of conservative bets, which makes you pause and take a deep breath when you read some of his latest predictions from *The Singularity Is Near:* "The 2030 scenario. Nanobot technology will provide fully immersive, totally convincing virtual reality." Or perhaps most unsettling of all: "The straightforward brain-porting scenario involves scanning a human brain (most likely from within), capturing *all* of its salient details, reinstating the brain's state in a different—most likely much more powerful—computational substrate. This will be a feasible procedure and will happen most likely around the late 2030s."[27]

If half of Kurzweil's other predictions also come true, most of us will still be around to see and experience brain porting because of advances in antiaging technologies, nano-medicine, and supergenetics. If Ray's knack for tech forecasting isn't enough to convert you, there's Bill Gates, who said: "Ray Kurzweil is the best person I know at predicting the future of artificial intelligence." That's an impressive endorsement, even if it's from the guy who told us in 2004 that spam would be a thing of the past by 2006.

Vinge's essay was the clarion call of a visionary, a voice crying in the desert. Kurzweil has followed through with marshaling the supporting data, charts, algorithms, and table breakdowns, all showing the law of accelerating returns in smooth, ascending curves on their way to proving Vernor Vinge and Kurzweil right.

*The Singularity Is Near* begins with a careful exposition of Kurzweil's "law of accelerating returns," what Joel Garreau calls "the Curve" in *Radical Evolution*. By definition, nobody really knows what's going to happen after "the Singularity," therefore these books read like speculative science fiction, mainly because they *are* speculative science fiction. That's how the Singularity got its name.

In May 2006, Stanford hosted a Singularity Summit, with an online welcome message from Douglas Hofstadter, author of *Gödel, Escher, Bach: An Eternal Golden Braid*: "A growing number of highly respected technological figures . . . have in recent years forecast that computational intelligence will, in the coming two or three decades, not only match but swiftly surpass human intelligence, and that civilization will at that point be radically transformed in ways that our puny minds cannot possibly imagine."

Or, as Vinge expressed the same thought, using his novelist's gift for graphic imagery: "Events beyond this event—call it the Technological Singularity—are as unimaginable to us as opera is to a flatworm."[28] So if the future is a Wagnerian opera and we are flatworms, what is the point of hypothesizing mini-sci-fi scenarios about what will happen after an event you've already described as incomprehensible? Well, who's to say one can't dream? Or hypothesize? For Kurzweil, in post-Singularity virtual reality, you'll no longer have just one personality, you'll have a wardrobe of personalities, and you'll be able to change your appearance and "become other people" at will. Without changing your physical body, you could project different versions of yourself into virtual realities. You could create one avatar to woo your girlfriend, a different one to meet her parents, still another to face down a threat from an interloper trying to steal bandwidth on your local wireless connection. Couples in love could become each other for a night.[29]

Kurzweil's books are great fun to read. As a novelist, I've done enough field research to know how hard it is to get, say, a prominent neuroscientist or a reputable nuclear physicist to cut loose and play what-if. Scientists are by nature averse to guessing or fantasizing. They like to make or elaborate on statements they can *prove*. Kurzweil doesn't have that problem. Show him a trend line, and he'll tell you when it will lead to time travel through wormholes. Maybe it's an exciting new genre. Instead of science fiction, one simply writes speculative science. It's one way for a scientist and inventor like Kurzweil to obtain a license to dream: Just postulate a point in the near future after which it will be impossible to predict what will happen, and then make a career for yourself predicting the impossible-to-predict:

> "Experience beamers" will send the entire flow of their sensory experiences as well as the neurological correlates of their emotional reactions out onto the Web, just as people today beam their bedroom images from their Web cams. A popular pastime will be to plug into someone else's sensory-emotional beam and experience what it's like to be that person, à la the premise of the movie *Being John Malkovich*. There will also be a vast selection of archived experiences to choose from, with virtual-experience design another new art form.*[30]

---

*This is also the premise of a kinky sci-fi horror movie called *Strange Days* (1995), written by James Cameron and directed by Kathryn Bigelow, in which a detective

Parts of *The Singularity Is Near* feel as if Kurzweil is beaming his experience our way. It's loopy but well-informed, accurate (at least about the present and, as we've seen, the near future), packed with tech trivia, always infused with the plausible ... but science? I guess the scientists will have to decide. After the first rush of the law of accelerating returns, much of the fallout from that and the predictions of what will follow the Singularity itself are necessarily speculative. However, unlike those periodic special issues of *Time* or *Newsweek* given over to predicting the future: "We'll have robots, replaceable organs, jet packs, time travel, nano-bots for blood cells, entire meals in a pill, flying cars ..." Ray's predictions are based on a thorough practical knowledge and inventor's command of the technologies under discussion; namely, information technologies and pattern recognition.

All of which would be stimulating and could even seem possible if our actual daily experience of technology weren't so often something that doesn't work and needs to be configured by someone who charges by the hour. If you buy a car or a high-def TV, you expect it to work. If you buy a $3,000 PC running Windows Vista, you expect it to have problems. You have to call a friend before you order it ("Should I get an ATI or Nvidia card? Two or four gigs of RAM? Blu-ray or HD-DVD?"), then call another friend to help you set it up. Or, ulp, you call tech support, whose services, according to the Consumer Reports National Research Center, readers rate dead last, below their HMO, the airlines, their Internet and cell-phone service providers.[31]

## 5.3 THE *SINGULARITY FANTASTIQUE*

A future that contains smarter-than-human minds is genuinely different in a way that goes beyond the usual visions of a future filled with bigger and better gadgets.

—Singularity Institute for Artificial Intelligence[32]

---

investigates a crime ring that traffics in replayable data disks containing captured emotions, memories, and sensations of others, recorded straight from the cerebral cortex.

If absolutely everything is about to change in some unpredictable way, I think I'd prefer everything to change for the better. I'm imagining squadrons of ultra-intelligent, friendly C-3POs and R2-D2s waiting on us while we lounge about in hammocks sipping piña coladas on a beach. Meanwhile, superintelligent computers could be off somewhere creating new breakthroughs for us to enjoy while we are on permanent vacation. Maybe computer worship will produce a paradise regained of beautiful, healthy, eternally youthful bodies, implanted with neuroprosthetics and sculpted in smart skin and nano-engineered to perfection. Then, if you need something, why, you can just have an assembler make one for you out of foglets or nanobots, or just have a 3-D printer* "print" one for you and have your robot go fetch it, while you're getting a haircut from your favorite robot stylist and getting a genetic makeover from your favorite trans-human physician. But then what? Would we get bored just lolling around, having robots wait on us?

In the first season of *The Twilight Zone,* episode 28 was "A Nice Place to Visit"† and opened with a small-time hood named Rocky Valentine robbing a pawnshop. Rocky gets shot by policemen during his attempted getaway.

When he "wakes up" in the alley, a fat man in a white suit (Sebastian Cabot) stands over him and introduces himself as Pip. At first, Rocky is suspicious. Pip is soothing, gracious; he sounds like the perfect post-Singularity robot, programmed to be an avuncular Mr. French. Pip's job is to see that Rocky gets whatever he wants.

---

*3-D printers print objects or 3-D models of autocad data; these printers already exist, available from http://www.zcorp.com/home.asp: "The ZPrinter 450 makes color 3D printing accessible to everyone. The lowest priced color 3D printer available, the ZPrinter 450 outputs brilliant color models with timesaving automation and an even easier printing process." See http://en.wikipedia.org/wiki/3D printing.

†Original air date April 15, 1960. Written by doomed genius Charles Beaumont, who died of a mysterious illness, rapid aging (progeria) or early-onset Alzheimer's disease, at age thirty-eight.

Pip takes Rocky to a fabulous suite at a hotel casino, where Rocky has anything and everything he wants. Platters of food from room service, a sumptuous bridal suite for a bedroom, a closet filled with clothing cut from the finest cloth. Downstairs at the casino, every time Rocky places a bet he wins. Beautiful women swarm around him. The slot machines erupt in volcanoes of coins every time he plays them. Rocky starts realizing this is no earthly casino. He can't figure out why, but somehow he's ended up in what can only be Heaven.

"What the heck," he thinks. Rocky figures that he must have done something good, otherwise he wouldn't be here. On with the party. More scenes of gambling and winning. More women. More of Pip getting Rocky everything his heart desires.

Pretty soon Rocky is leaving his slot-machine winnings on the floor. Finally we see him playing cards in bed with three gorgeous babes. Rocky wins. Again! But this time Rocky loses his temper. He's tired of winning. He runs the beautiful dames out, then he summons Pip.

Rocky goes ballistic on Pip and informs him that he's been here for over a month and that if he wins another card game he'll kill himself.

Pip offers to arrange things so that Rocky can lose from time to time. No. Rocky can't describe what's bothering him: *Arranged* winning and losing just isn't as exciting as winning and losing.

Pip offers to arrange for Rocky to rob a few banks. Rocky gets energized, hopeful, thinking about how great it would be to do another bank job.

Rocky's eyes light up. He looks at Pip, who has his notepad and pen out, ready to take down Rocky's wishes. The light goes out of Rocky's eyes as he realizes what this means. Just like blackjack. A rigged game.

Pip notices his disappointment and offers to arrange for Rocky to get caught once in a while, if he'd like.

Rocky can't take it anymore. He rants and raves and ends by telling

Pip that he just doesn't fit in here in Heaven and that he'd like to try the other place.

Pip tells him that this *is* the other place. Cue Satanic laughter.

Heaven and Hell scenarios, like "the other place" in *The Twilight Zone,* and lurid intermixtures of the two are common when the tech futurists get together and speculate about the coming Singularity.[33] What will happen even if technology gives us everything we think we want? Won't that be a kind of Hell in itself? Or as Theodore Kaczynski (aka "the Unabomber") put it:

> Since many people may find paradoxical the notion that a large number of good things can add up to a bad thing, we will illustrate with an analogy. Suppose Mr. A is playing chess with Mr. B. Mr. C, a Grand Master, is looking over Mr. A's shoulder. Mr. A of course wants to win his game, so if Mr. C points out a good move for him to make, he is doing Mr. A a favor. But suppose now that Mr. C tells Mr. A how to make ALL of his moves. In each particular instance he does Mr. A a favor by showing him his best move, but by making ALL of his moves for him he spoils the game, since there is no point in Mr. A's playing the game at all if someone else makes all his moves.[34]

Ray Kurzweil is often unfairly tagged as a wide-eyed tech enthusiast about what he calls GNR, the "three overlapping revolutions": genetics, nanotechnology, and robotics,[35] all three powered by supercomputers. In *Radical Evolution,* Joel Garreau adds the implicit "Information Technology" to the group to form the acronym GRIN (genetics, robotics, information technology, and nanotechnology), which I rather like. A grin is an apt composite of the Greek comedy and tragedy masks and captures our ambivalence (equal parts foreboding and anticipation) about future tech. Garreau, an author and *Washington Post* reporter and editor, gives a comprehensive, entertaining overview of GRIN technologies and envisions several possible scenarios unfolding: Heaven, Hell, or what he calls Prevail. Each scenario comes complete with a living spokesperson, and Ray Kurzweil is, of course, the tech evangelical inventor pointing up toward Heaven, at least for Garreau.

To be fair, Kurzweil tends to cover all talking points, not just the rosy ones. He is not blind to the dangers of GRIN technologies. On the contrary, he usually addresses them point by point, as he attempts to do in chapter 8 of *The Singularity Is Near,* "The Deeply Intertwined Promise and Peril of GNR," and chapter 9, "Response to Critics." For example, Ray opened *The Age of Spiritual Machines* with his memory (from adolescence) of the *Twilight Zone* episode set forth above. I merely chased down the particulars and watched it on YouTube (until the copyright police had it taken down). Ray described his memory of the episode to make a point: We expend considerable effort and expense avoiding and delaying death, but what would life be like without it? Isn't Death what makes time and life itself precious? Or as Ray puts the question: "If death were to be indefinitely put off, the human psyche would end up, well, like the gambler in the *Twilight Zone* episode."

Or as Franz Kafka put it in a single short sentence: "The meaning of life is that it stops." Kurzweil followed his 1999 book, *The Age of Spiritual Machines,* with a compendium of essays attacking him titled: *Are We Spiritual Machines: Ray Kurzweil vs. the Critics of Strong A.I.,* together with his responses to the commentators. In the end, Ray sees the undeniable perils of GRIN but puts his faith in human tenacity, the same will to power (another Nietzschean concept) that brought us to the threshold of the Singularity in the first place. When he looks to the future, he probably sees all the perils that the pessimists and neo-Luddites see, it's just that Ray thinks we'll muddle through somehow. More likely, being the consummate inventor, Kurzweil believes we'll *invent* our way through any crisis, the same way he managed type 2 diabetes or solved the problem of reading for the blind.

Not all Singularitarians are alike. Even kindred souls like Vinge and Kurzweil probably could not agree on a working definition of the "Technological Singularity." Eliezer Yudkowsky, a research fellow at the Singularity Institute for Artificial Intelligence, argues that the two men may even have diametrically opposing views.[36] On the one hand, according to Yudkowsky, Kurzweil believes in a "quantifiable acceleration" of technological trends that will continue following predictable patterns even after machines become smarter than human beings. On the other hand, "Vinge's Singularity is a breakdown of the model," according to Yudkowsky, because a future populated by machine intelligences hundreds or thousands of times smarter than us is literally incomprehensible and totally unpredictable, or as Vinge put it, "as unimaginable to us as opera is to a flatworm."[37]

# Singularity Lite

Not everyone agrees that the Singularity is near, or even likely to occur, and some deride it as the Rapture for nerds or geeks.[1] What if instead of passing the Turing test and getting a perfect score on the SATs, the supercomputer just sits there burning electricity and patiently awaiting instructions?

## 6.1 CONSCIOUS MIND VERSUS UNCONSCIOUS INTELLIGENCE

> There is a common misconception that the human brain is the pinnacle of billions of years of evolution. This may be true if we think of the entire nervous system. However, the human neocortex itself is a relatively new structure and hasn't been around long enough to undergo much long-term evolutionary refinement.
>
> —Jeff Hawkins with Sandra Blakeslee[2]

As humans we already know that intelligent beings need not necessarily be conscious. In 1995, when White House intern Monica Lewinsky showed the president of the United States her thong, a highly intelligent Rhodes scholar, Yale Law School grad, and gifted politician suddenly became unconscious. Something similar happened to the next president when he decided, hell or high water, he had to invade Iraq—a graphic, unfortunate demonstration of the thoroughly modern notion that conscious will is an illusion.

It's possible, as many AI authorities assert, that no matter how powerful our computers become they will never achieve human-like intelligence or "consciousness" or even simulate human intelligence well enough to pass the Turing test. Intelligent machines may get exponentially better at brute pattern recognition but never "wake up," never become what the likes of Ray Kurzweil would call a "spiritual machine." Why should we assume that a doubling and redoubling collection of circuit boards, memory chips, and photonic light beams is going to suddenly "awaken" and become conscious? Or what if computers and robots achieve human-level intelligence, but then they are underachievers? They don't want to get any smarter because it's too much work.

In November 2006, Ray Kurzweil and prominent Yale computer science professor David Gelernter argued the subject of machine consciousness at MIT in a debate sponsored by the Templeton Foundation. The topic was headlined as "Will We Ever Build a Super-Intelligent Spiritual Machine? Or Just a Super-Intelligent Zombie?"[3] Kurzweil outlined his familiar law of accelerating returns as it applies to the evolution of technology. Kurzweil knows hardware (whether neurons or nanotubes), and he is articulate and compelling, especially in person.[4] As an inventor in his late fifties, Kurzweil was present, as it were, at the creation of Moore's law and has witnessed firsthand the explosive growth of information technologies—indeed, he helped set off some of those explosions.

The gist of Kurzweil's argument, especially in short formats, is that the runaway super-exponential growth of technology is going to result in brain scans that see twice as deep every other year, computers that are twice as smart every other year, genetic and nanotechnological advances that also double in lockstep, until we make machines with such vast computational abilities and massively parallel processing abilities that—poof—a compelling strong-AI presence will emerge, and we will be seduced into treating that entity as an intelligent "spiritual" being.

Gelernter is not troubled by Kurzweil's law of accelerating returns;

he probably agrees with it; nor does he argue that superintelligent computers are impossible. Like a good stand-up philosopher, Gelernter continually brings the debate back to consciousness. Personally, I hate the word *consciousness*. Or I guess not the word so much as discussions about it. Let's talk about water: It's wet; when you're thirsty you really want some; it's the basis of all life; adhesion; cohesion; $H_2O$. Whatever. Now what? Consciousness is even worse. It's just there. Period. Anybody who asks you to explain it is changing the subject or cheating. But that's what Gelernter did in his debate with Kurzweil.

> I'm not going to believe that you understand the human mind unless you can explain to me what consciousness is, how it's created and how it got there. Now, that doesn't mean that you can't do a lot of useful things without creating consciousness. You certainly can. If your ultimate goal is utilitarian, forget about consciousness. But if your goals are philosophical and scientific and you want to understand how the mind really operates, then you must be able to tell me how consciousness works, or you don't have a theory of the human mind.

In large part, the two men argue past each other. Kurzweil ignores the issue of consciousness because it is subjective and cannot be measured by objective means ("How do I know that my perception of azure is the same as your perception of azure?"). People often confuse intelligence with consciousness and vice versa. I suspect Kurzweil would be more than happy to say, "I'll never be able to prove that machines are conscious, but I'll bet that within twenty-five years an intelligent machine will pass the Turing test, which means that the machine might as well be conscious, because you and I won't be able to distinguish its language output from human beings we routinely say *are* conscious."

As is often the case with amateur neurophilosophers, Kurzweil and Gelernter wound up thrashing out many of the same issues that have bedeviled classical philosophers for centuries, even before they had functional magnetic brain imaging and hot and cold computer circuits on tap. Is it possible to prove that someone or something is conscious or has consciousness? Just what are mental states? Can you reduce consciousness to brain activity? These inquiries revisit turf that philosophers such as Daniel Dennett and Thomas Nagel have already settled as being unsettleable. See, for example, Nagel's timeless essay that should stop any discussion about consciousness, whether it's happening in a dorm room at 3 A.M. or at MIT and sponsored by the Templeton Foundation: "What Is It Like to Be a Bat?" Enough said. If you're in the dorm room, you can pass the weed and the bag of chips. If you're at MIT, you sit politely in your seat, still waiting for somebody to ask the question *The Daily Show's* Samantha Bee asked Ray Kurzweil in her interview with him: "Will we have fuckable robots anytime soon?"

Kurzweil enjoys speculating about the future, and Gelernter enjoys savoring the essential unassailable mystery of our consciousness, and both topics were subtopics, if you will, of the topic at hand that night: "Super-Intelligent Spiritual Machine? Or Just a Super-Intelligent Zombie?" But, as usual, nothing was settled. Nobody comes to these things to learn about how best to raise any Borg children they may be having soon, or how to ask a spiritual machine for a date, or to hear the miracle of consciousness explained for the first time. Speculative science, like science fiction, is entertainment. Besides, if you attend an MIT seminar on spiritual machines and zombies, there's always a chance that you'll get the 411 on fuckable robots. You never know.

Gelernter's position might best be exemplified by this excerpt: "The fact is that the conscious mind emerges when we've collected many neurons together, not many doughnuts or low-level computer instructions. Why should the trick work when I substitute simple computer instructions for neurons? Of course, it might work. But there isn't any reason to believe it would."

And Kurzweil's by this one: "If you reject the Turing test or any variant of it, then we're just left with this philosophical issue. My own philosophical take is if an entity seems to be conscious, I would accept its consciousness. But that's a philosophical and not a scientific position."

Kurzweil believes that advances in both hardware and software will soon produce the kind of massive parallelism necessary to mimic the processes of a human brain. Other strong-AI types argue that even if machines do not exhibit human-like thought processes, they'll be clever enough to fool humans into thinking that they are "conscious." In other words, just as *Homo sapiens* has a mind, *Machina sapiens* will "seem" to have one, too. It's a separate question whether it will waste processing power mimicking human thoughts.

## 6.2 ON INTELLIGENCE

Jeff Hawkins, inventor of the original PalmPilot and author, with *New York Times* science writer Sandra Blakeslee, of *On Intelligence,* believes that machine intelligence will surpass human intelligence in many ways—speed, capacity, and depth of knowledge. However, this doesn't mean that machine intelligence will be anything like human consciousness.

At Numenta, a company Hawkins cofounded in 2005 with Dileep George, Hawkins and other neurotech entrepreneurs are developing new types of computer memory systems modeled after the human neocortex and called Hierarchical Temporal Memory (HTM) after theories set forth in *On Intelligence.* Never mind the whole brain, Hawkins seems to say in his book, the intelligence he's interested in resides in the neocortex. Why make things more complicated than they need to be? We are already experts at running, visual acuity, social interaction, emotional intelligence, and such. Why not just focus on that part of the human brain that is responsible, like many AI programs, for pattern recognition? Why not look hard at the human neocortex, the seat of intellectual human intelligence? Why mess with mimicking 100 billion neurons and 100 trillion synapses that enjoy baseball, chocolate, dreams, aggression, beer, and reading Stephen King novels? Why not worry about just 20 to 25 billion neurons and only about a third of the brain's synapses—the neurons involved in pattern matching, picking stocks, weather simulation, scanning databases for terrorists, and picking genetic sequences out of genomes?

To Jeff Hawkins, the first simple problem is capacity. If the human cortex has 32 trillion synapses, and if you assume that each of those synapses could be adequately represented by 2 bits (or 4 possible values per synapse), then to mimic the entire human cortex requires 64 trillion bits. Each byte of computer memory has 8 bits; therefore (64/8), a computer cortex would need about 8 trillion bytes of memory, or 8 terabytes. As of this writing (early 2008), 1 terabyte Seagate hard drives are selling for roughly $250 on Newegg, so by at least one expert's reckoning you can purchase the storage capacity of a human cortex for about $2,000 (and, yes, it will cost half that much in two years). Just ten years ago, Hawkins notes, that amount of memory would have been out of the question. Today it's nothing, and Hawkins believes that most applications won't require anything like an entire human cortex; much less memory would suffice for specialized tasks and applications.[5]

Hey, so far this sounds a lot easier than messing with a 10-petaflop IBM supercomputer. "Most of what we call intelligence is located in the neocortex," says Hawkins, "but a human brain is a lot more than an intelligent neocortex. It includes emotional centers and older centers that govern primitive behaviors and primitive perceptions. I don't believe anyone will try to re-create the entire human brain; I'm not sure if it is even possible without endowing the machine with a body." Hawkins believes that machine intelligence will exceed human intelligence *and* will be viewed as a tool. "Computers are like that today," he says. "They remember more, recall faster, do arithmetic faster than a human. Still they are just tools. Big, man-made brains will perceive faster, see patterns humans miss, have senses humans don't have, but they will not be human-like, they won't reproduce, they won't feel imprisoned, they won't be living, feeling things, they won't suddenly develop human ambitions and attempt to conquer the universe."[6]

The Singularity could be one giant manifestation of the human tendency to anthropomorphize everything: our pets,* our gods, and soon, it seems, our computers. One thing seems certain: Machines won't become conscious unless we make them so. As Hawkins puts it:

> Some people assume that being intelligent is basically the same as having human mentality. They fear that intelligent machines will resent being "enslaved" because humans hate being enslaved. They fear that intelligent machines will try to take over the world because intelligent people throughout history have tried to take over the world. But these fears rest on a false analogy. They are based on a conflation of intelligence—the neocortical algorithm—with the emotional drives of the old brain—things like fear, paranoia, and desire. But intelligent machines will not have these faculties . . . unless we painstakingly design them to.[7]

Jeff Hawkins's book is an excellent tour of the human neocortex and a glimpse at the future of pattern-recognition technologies modeled on human intelligence. As an engineer with a passion for neuroscience, Hawkins is, like many other weak-AI proponents, scrupulously rational. No wild sci-fi Kurzweilian flights of imagination and fantasy for him. The passage above assumes that machine intelligences will not have ambition or appetites or destructive impulses or human emotions, because rational computer scientists and software engineers won't go out of their way to design machines with human emotions and killer instincts. But history shows that some sci-

---

*Marley & Me and many other dog and cat books populating the bestseller lists are book-length exercises in projection, as when author John Grogan writes about his dog Marley: "He sighed dramatically and drifted back to his dreams of French poodles in heat."

entists like to do things just to prove they can do them. No matter how dangerous a superintelligent machine with human emotions might be, you can bet there's a clever programmer out there who wants to attempt it and climb the strong-AI mountain, just because it's there.

That brings us to our familiar dark side.

# Singularity Dark

Technological progress is like an axe in the hands of a
pathological criminal.

—Albert Einstein

## 7.1 Tech Futurists Versus Hard Sci-Fi Writers

I have been a soreheaded occupant of a file drawer labeled
"science fiction" . . . and I would like out, particularly since so
many serious critics regularly mistake the drawer for a urinal.

—Kurt Vonnegut Jr.[1]

When I'm around you, Buffy, I find myself needing to know the
plural of *apocalypse*.

—Riley Finn to Buffy the Vampire Slayer

Just because we *ought* to be paying attention to the Technological
Singularity doesn't mean we will. The tech optimists who hang out
online at The Edge* and the Singularity Institute for Artificial Intelli-

---

*Main repository of the "third culture" intellectuals, which according to the site's
"About" page "consists of those scientists and other thinkers in the empirical world
who, through their work and expository writing, are taking the place of the traditional intellectual in rendering visible the deeper meanings of our lives, redefin-
ing who and what we are." The site favors topics on neuroscience, evolutionary

gence* like to rhapsodize about the light side of our love affair with computers and information technologies. These third-culture warriors (referred to as the "digerati" before the dot.com bust) often subscribe to some version of Kurzweil's can-do entrepreneurial vision of the future. They follow the likes of futurist and tech-utopian George Gilder and think of the Web as a telecosm—a network of more than a billion computers harnessing the energy, ambition, and creativity of the earth's 6.5 billion people into a collective consciousness, allowing one and all to compete, communicate, and collaborate as never before. True tech evangelicals believe that the Internet won't just flatten the world and level the playing field, it will also become what Emerson called the Over-Soul (or OverSoul in modern CamelCase)—what the Jesuit philosopher and theologian Teilhard de Chardin called the noosphere, a planetary nervous system that will eventually connect everyone on earth, and then (one fine morning) "awaken" the entire universe and infuse it with Intelligence. (Believers, or Singularitarians, as Kurzweil calls them, talk this way, and they aren't all tweaked Philip K. Dick fans or Gilder groupies.)

Personally, I'm not afraid of the Singularity, as long as the hardware and software upgrades come with mail-in rebates. I'm also curious if, here in the years B.S. (before Singularity), these tech *evangelistas* will show up on Christmas morning and help me configure the kids' new media hub so it can connect to the wireless router. Are they going to help me configure WPA encryption for the new 802.11zzz standard? Will they come and fix my neighbor's new Dell machine, running Microsoft Vista, the one that keeps choking and issuing error messages that say: "This computer is not authorized to play Thomas Dolby's 'She Blinded Me with Science,'" even though my neighbor's entire iTunes library is bought and paid for? I think not.

---

psychology, and all things tech, featuring such luminaries as Steven Pinker, Daniel Dennett, Richard Dawkins, and many others. See http://www.edge.org.

*http://www.singinst.org. Together with KurzweilAI.net, the main site for all things Singularitarian, especially of the *fantastique* strain.

Whence comes this relentlessly upbeat view of computer technology when nine out of ten PCs connected to the Internet are infected with spyware? To be precise:

• Roughly 88 percent of scanned consumer PCs are found to contain some form of unwanted program (Trojan, system monitor, cookie, or adware).

• Some form of spyware can be found on 87 percent of corporate PCs.

• Eighty-six percent of U.S. adult Internet users believe that spyware on their computers has caused them to suffer a monetary loss.[2]

Funny too how these infection rates hover at near 90 percent, which matches the percentage of computers running the Windows operating system. One might safely conclude that virtually *all* computers running a Windows operating system are infected if they are also connected to the Internet; it's just a question of whether the spyware compromises performance to the point where the user notices and becomes annoyed. Often the only cure is to erase your entire hard drive and reinstall the operating system.* The Messaging Anti-Abuse Working Group also estimates that 80 to 85 percent of incoming e-mail is spam.[3] An innocent Windows user might be tempted to inquire how Moore's law will soon produce computers that are smarter than people, while expensive, "intelligent" software programs running on today's latest, greatest hardware are still unable to stop spyware, or e-mails with the subject line "Visit the giant p3n1s store!"

Unlike the nation's hapless PC users struggling in the trenches to install a new $50 anti-spyware program, professional futurists and technology pundits probably have an upbeat view of the tech uni-

---

*"Erasing my hard drive, long considered a last-ditch measure, was becoming more and more appealing with each passing virus scan . . . The catharsis cannot be understated." Rachel Dodes, "Terminating Spyware with Extreme Prejudice," *New York Times*, 30 December 2004.

verse because they use more expensive MacBook Pros running OS X (a UNIX-based operating system). They also travel the lecture and talk-show circuits and are well paid to bring us exciting updates about how—thanks to info tech, biotech, nanotech, and stem cell research—we'll soon be growing spare eyeballs with computer screens embedded in them. That we'll have all the extra brainpower we'll need thanks to modular implants. That our entire lives will be recorded on nano-circuitry the size of sugar cubes. And that disposable livers will come with a free iPhone that will also give us constant real-time readings of our blood-alcohol content. Oh yes, and Microsoft is readying another exciting new operating system, and this time they really mean business about *safe computing,* not like the last time they said that. A cynic might worry that the future will turn out looking a lot like the past, except a lot more expensively. It used to be all you needed was a computer and an Internet connection. Nowadays, an unprotected PC hooked to the Internet can be infected and hijacked within minutes, which means that now you need $200 worth of programs—firewall, antivirus, anti-spyware—before you can safely connect to the new, evolved, and improved Internet.

Contrast the fat-on-speaking-fees futurist view with what our science-fiction authors and screenwriters see when they peer into the future and find their imaginations landscaped in dystopias. *Blade Runner, AI, Minority Report, The Matrix,* even *I, Robot* all portray dark or threatening worlds born from our lust for technology. Blame it on Philip K. Dick's outsized influence, but huge as he is, he's just one prolific author. Even before Dick, readers and movie audiences liked their paradises lost better than regained, and the *Inferno* is ten times more interesting than the *Paradisio* and choirs of singing angels. Still, man and his technology are at least bivalent, and both come with cold, dark sides. But no genre favors dystopia like hard sci-fi,*

---

*"Hard science fiction is a category of science fiction characterized by an emphasis on scientific or technical detail, or on scientific accuracy, or on both." Wikipedia, http://en.wikipedia.org/wiki/Hard_science_fiction.

especially when it comes to imagining superintelligent computers of the future. Machine intelligences are almost uniformly portrayed as hostile and jealous of human beings; only aliens come off worse in popular entertainment, though there are exceptions (E.T. and C-3PO).

Science-fiction tales about supercomputers assuming control of the human race are legion. A taxonomy of computer overlords, their pedigrees, specifications, and personality characteristics, would make for a fascinating study; even their names are enough to make you take a second look into your flat-panel monitor and wonder if the computer connected to it could be one of a million swarm intelligences plotting an overthrow. Over the last half-century or so, sci-fi authors have created HAL 9000, Bossy, Merlin, Vulcan 3, the Berserker, T.E.N.C.H. 889B, EPICAC, Colossus, ZORAC, Zed, Euclid, Red Queen, Helen, Mother, Stormbreaker, Solace, Deep Thought, Spartacus, Multivac, Wintermute, Hex, The Tabernacle, The Ultima Machine, MANIAC, Landru, M5, the Oracle, Zen, KAOS, Skynet, ARD-VARC, The Matrix, Icarus, and WOTAN, to name but a few of the supercomputers who have ruled the earth and its puny mortal inhabitants.

Harlan Ellison created the prototypical malign machine intelligence in his infamous sci-fi horror short story entitled "I Have No Mouth, and I Must Scream." As Ellison told it, there had been a cold war, which became World War III "and just kept going." Soon the war became so big and so complex that only the computers could manage it. Ellison named the war-games supercomputer AM. At first, the war pitted a Chinese AM against a Russian AM against a Yankee AM, but soon AMs covered the planet and started improving themselves. Then, one day, "AM woke up and knew who he was."[4]

AM exterminated all but five members of the human race, and the story traces their last days underground, tortured by an omnipotent, omniscient machine intelligence. AM describes its feelings for humanity "very politely, in a pillar of stainless steel and neon letters," as follows:

HATE. LET ME TELL YOU HOW MUCH I'VE COME TO HATE YOU SINCE I BEGAN TO LIVE. THERE ARE 387.44 MILLION MILES OF WAFER THIN PRINTED CIRCUITS THAT FILL MY COMPLEX. IF THE WORD HATE WAS ENGRAVED ON EVERY NANOANGSTROM OF THOSE HUNDREDS OF MILLIONS OF MILES IT WOULD NOT EQUAL ONE ONE-BILLIONTH OF THE HATE I FEEL FOR HUMANS AT THIS MICRO-INSTANT. FOR YOU. HATE. HATE.[5]

That's so dark that if it comes true, I won't be able to see my robotically enhanced, nano-assembled, smart-skinned hand in front of my face! So much for supercomputers. How about networks or clusters or swarms—what Vernor Vinge dubbed IA (intelligence amplification)? For the most part, sci-fi writers tend to view networking technologies less as a new global nervous system and more like an unwanted implant; to a science-fiction writer it is only a matter of time before any given network will be employed to invade privacy or remotely administer punishment.

Futurists and tech utopians fly first class between seminars and conferences, where they are fêted, fed wild-salmon fillets, and overpaid by tech companies. A George Gilder or a Ray Kurzweil gets everybody drinking the Kool-Aid and back on the hardware/software upgrade cycles to more and better (and more expensive) technologies for a better and more expensive tomorrow. Science-fiction writers, whose dark visions are bad for the economy (with the possible exception of the film industry), tend to dwell in turrets and basements, write on outdated, underpowered Windows machines, or maybe on the reverse video terminals of Linux or BSD machines. Who knows what the future might look like if science fiction paid better and required exposure to sunlight?

## 7.2 My Computer Pwns Me!

As you sit with your eHarmony spouse watching the movies Netflix prescribes, you might as well be an avatar in Second Life. You have been absorbed into the operating system.

—George Johnson[6]

So, if a hundred different sci-fi tales and movies are right, computers will soon take over and enslave the human race. It'll be easy; we've already given them all of the intimate details of our personal lives, our medical records, our financial transactions, our consumer and sexual preferences, our weapons systems and communications networks. They already own our second lives on Second Life.* What if that's not enough for them, and they crave more action in our first life? If you wonder how much information about you would instantly be available if Google fell into the wrong "hands," go to your iGoogle personalized-search home page, log on to My Account at the upper right, select Web History and then Trends. You'll see all of your Web searches from this year and last available for searching by hour, day, month, year. On March 14, did you really search for "debt consolidation," "personal lubrication," and "growing marijuana hydroponically" all in the same day? Are you averaging 278 searches per weekday—even while you're at work?

Furthermore, thanks to proprietary software and stringent copyright laws, like the Digital Millennium Copyright Act, supercomputers could take over completely and we wouldn't even know it. Who's to say what's in those Microsoft programs that Dell installed on your latest PC? It's not like you can open the programs and read the code. If you even try, you're breaking the law. Meaning, if machine intelligences take over at Dell or Microsoft, they will continue delivering those programs, and we *still* won't know what's inside them.

You purchase a nice shiny shrink-wrapped version of Symantec's latest memory-hogging, intrusive Norton AntiVirus software for $75 (a program you *need* only because you're running Microsoft Windows), or you buy Microsoft Office for $400 (even though you can download OpenOffice, Sun Microsystems' StarOffice, or IBM's Lotus

---

*"Second Life is a 3D digital world imagined and created by its Residents. . . . Second Life is the size of a small city, with thousands of servers (called simulators)." As of February 2008, Second Life was inhabited by more than 12 million Residents from one hundred countries around the world. http://secondlife.com/what is/faq.php.

Symphony for free). Recall that your $400 buys you only a license to run mystery software containing code kept totally secret by law. Nobody really knows what's inside the Microsoft or Symantec programs except the "people" running Microsoft and Symantec. That's what the Singularity is all about: What if the "people" at Microsoft or Symantec aren't people anymore? What if instead they are machine intelligences, or maybe people brainwashed and controlled by machine intelligences? Or if that's too much of a stretch for you, what if they are unscrupulous people who worship machines or money? You may *think* you're using a snazzy new version of Microsoft Word to write a memo to your boss. Indeed, the program allows you to draft a memo, and the WYSIWYG* memo looks just like it always does, but unbeknownst to you this post-Singularity version of Word also scours your hard drive for pertinent personal and financial information and instantly assesses your possible worth to supercomputers in their planned reign of terror following the Singularity. That information is sent back to the Singularity Intelligence Network (SIN). If you are worthy, you are spared. If you appear to be a nOOb user with no post-Singularity skills worth preserving, then the carbon monoxide detector in your home goes on the fritz and your computer-regulated oven, gas fireplace, or gas water heater suddenly begins emitting tasteless, odorless carbon monoxide. Sleep tight. While you are dying, the machine intelligences will be transferring your assets using the user names, passwords, and account numbers harvested from your hard drive. Or maybe they'll let you live a while longer, so you can make more money for them to steal. Either way, don't worry. Your cash will be used for a good cause: the evolution of the post-human species, of which you are no longer a member.

What if the publishing and entertainment industries have inadvertently lulled us into believing that any doomsday scenario involving

---

*What You See Is What You Get—used to describe programs where what you see during editing is close to what you will see when the content is printed or completed.

computers thousands of times smarter than humans is just a harmless fiction? If the Wachowski brothers were on to anything with the *Matrix* franchise, we could be machine slaves and not even know it . . . which might explain why we keep checking our e-mail, or reading news feeds, or following links that we don't even want to follow. Do they already own us, body and soul? Oxford philosopher Nick Bostrom estimates that there is a 20 percent chance that we are already living in a computer simulation. As John Tierney wrote in the *New York Times:*

> Dr. Bostrom assumes that technological advances could produce a computer with more processing power than all the brains in the world, and that advanced humans, or "posthumans," could run "ancestor simulations" of their evolutionary history by creating virtual worlds inhabited by virtual people with fully developed virtual nervous systems.
>
> Some computer experts have projected, based on trends in processing power, that we will have such a computer by the middle of this century, but it doesn't matter for Dr. Bostrom's argument whether it takes 50 years or 5 million years. If civilization survived long enough to reach that stage, and if the posthumans were to run lots of simulations for research purposes or entertainment, then the number of virtual ancestors they created would be vastly greater than the number of real ancestors.
>
> There would be no way for any of these ancestors to know for sure whether they were virtual or real, because the sights and feelings they'd experience would be indistinguishable. But since there would be so many more virtual ancestors, any individual could figure that the odds made it nearly certain that he or she was living in a virtual world.[7]

Worse, what happens if they announce that the Singularity is here, right now, and everybody just shrugs? Let's say that the ferocious pace of Moore's law means that rapid change is a given in any field driven by information technology. For most young people, born in the seventies, eighties, and nineties, daily tech miracles are already the status quo. Echo boomers *expect* to turn on the news and see genetically modified animals, robots mowing the lawn, movie screens that fit in the palm of your hand, gene pioneer Craig Venter announcing that he has created a new synthetic life-form, and data storage sold by the terabyte. The "news" that computers may soon be a lot smarter than us is old-media fish wrap to them.

You may feel the same way, no matter how old you are. You may suspect that computers are probably *already* smarter than you, and you don't mind. So what if they can crunch huge numbers, beat you at backgammon and chess, and analyze traffic patterns better than humans? If you're not a stockbroker or a physician or a World Series of Poker player, maybe you don't even care if computers can pick stocks,[8] read scans, X-rays, and EKGs,[9] and play Texas Hold 'Em[10] better than you (they can, do, and will). You'll yield the sexy field of biomolecular protein folding to IBM's Blue Gene/L computer at the Lawrence Livermore labs. Let computers have climate simulation, weather prediction, and tracking the human genome; you owe those good-old-boy machines a favor or two for letting you surf the Internet and watch large-breasted women sing "I Touch Myself" on YouTube, and for letting you over-clock their CPUs and grind Thunder Lizards out near Orgrimmar as a Level 60 Orc Hunter.

What if the next generation of supercomputers is better than us at a lot of things, not just computery tasks like reading gas chromatography, missile tracking, or calculating the death of a star? A computer with the processing power of a human brain will, when the right software comes along, be intellectually capable of doing almost anything a human can do: tell funny jokes (it's all about microsecond timing); display impeccable card sense; exhibit astute emotional intelligence (by analyzing facial expressions, vocal stress patterns, retinal responses, facial thermography); excel at reading and writing poetry (using precision scanning and meter); give engaging extemporaneous speeches; flirt; lie; compose music; profess undying love and practice to deceive (all at once); and so on.

Murder? I don't want to think about it, but it keeps coming up.

Aren't telling jokes and composing music and, uhm, murder, *human* activities requiring that intangible thing called consciousness?

Yes, and maybe yes, but who says a grid of supercomputers can't be conscious? Better question: Who says a grid of supercomputers *needs* to be conscious, just to carry out a simple instruction like the one in Code Box 5?

Or what happens when computers become so intelligent we have trouble even grasping the extent of their capabilities? Nick Bostrom (the same Oxford philosopher who thinks we might be living in a computer simulation), in an essay analyzing human extinction scenarios, pictures our sorry fate if hapless hubristic humans dare to build a Singularitarian supercomputer:

> When we create the first superintelligent entity, we might make a mistake and give it goals that lead it to annihilate humankind, assuming its enormous intellectual advantage gives it the power to do so. For example, we could mistakenly elevate a subgoal to the status of a supergoal. We tell it to solve a mathematical problem, and it complies by turning all the matter in the solar system into a giant calculating device, in the process killing the person who asked the question."

I gave my life so that math could live. For more extinction scenarios and tech nightmares, we need only turn to the equally articulate tech naysayers for discomfort.

---

CODE BOX 5. **EXECUTE NONCOMPLIANT HUMANS**

```
# exterminate disobedient humans

for human in group_of_humans:
    if human = obedient:
        promote human
    else:
        exterminate human
```

# 7.3 THE OTHER BILL

We're terrible animals. I think that the earth's immune system is trying to get rid of us, as well it should.

—Kurt Vonnegut Jr.[12]

The earth has a skin and that skin has diseases; one of its diseases is called man.

—Friedrich Nietzsche

Ray Kurzweil is a programmer and a very gifted, versatile inventor. Bill Gates is a programmer and megalo-capitalist-turned-global-philanthropist. Bill Joy is what you might call a programmer's programmer, a systems architect, a hacker before the word existed, primary author of the Berkeley Software Distribution (BSD, sometimes called Berkeley UNIX), and cofounder of Sun Microsystems in 1982, where he served as chief scientist until 2003. If magazines call Kurzweil the Edison of pattern recognition, they call Bill Joy (aka "the other Bill") the Edison of the Internet for the work he did on incorporating the Internet protocol suite (TCP/IP) into the Berkeley UNIX operating system in the 1980s. Bill Gates and Microsoft won the marketing wars, the PC desktop, and most of the money, but programmers like Bill Joy built the code that runs what computer science professionals call "real computers" and built many of the computers, operating systems, and software that still run the Internet. In his spare time, Bill Joy also wrote the vi editor, one of the two most popular text editors that computer programmers use to edit code (the other being Emacs, written by Richard Stallman, founder of the Free Software Foundation and the GNU Project). More recently, Joy was cochair of President Clinton's commission on the future of IT research and was coauthor of Sun's Java programming language, the leading software language for interactive Web systems, cell phones, and many other Net-enabled devices.

Computer scientists all over the world still use small, well-designed, free UNIX programs that Bill Joy wrote as a Berkeley grad student (programs that work together and conform to the Zen-like simplicity of the UNIX Tools Philosophy).* Eric E. Schmidt, chief executive of Google, who worked with Joy both as a fellow graduate student at Berkeley and as a technology executive at Sun, says, "I've always thought of Bill Joy as the finest computer scientist of his generation."[13] Bill Joy's introduction could be much longer, but the particulars would only gild the lily for computer geeks, who already revere him as a master builder of software, chips, computers, and systems. This buildup is for lay readers, who may not know that Bill Joy is an alpha geek and über computer architect with even more programming credentials than Ray Kurzweil or Bill Gates.

That makes what follows all the more interesting.

## 7.4 WHY THE FUTURE DOESN'T NEED US

If the Singularity is an impending climax in an ongoing drama starring the human race locked in a Faustian, love-hate relationship with its information technologies, then a pivotal scene in that man-versus-machine drama occurred on September 17, 1998, at the Resort at Squaw Creek, Lake Tahoe, California. The occasion was George Gilder's Third Annual Telecosm conference—in its day, one of the hottest tech tickets in the telecosm. Bill Joy, Silicon Valley god and programming guru, was sitting in the bar of the hotel with none other than John Searle, the UC Berkeley philospher whose Chinese-room analogy we examined above as the best-known argument against using the Turing test to assess machine consciousness. Joy had finished his session and was catching up with Searle, a fellow

---

*(1) Write programs that do one thing and do it well; (2) Write programs that work together; (3) Write programs to handle text streams, because that is a universal interface. These three rules may be severely abridged to "Do one thing, do it well," formulated by Doug McIlroy, head of the research department at Bell Labs, where UNIX was born in the late 1960s.

Berkeley luminary, when in walked none other than Ray Kurzweil. Like Joy, Kurzweil had been a speaker at the conference. Joy had missed a panel discussion where Ray and John Searle had butted heads about whether machines could develop consciousness and how soon that might conceivably happen. When Kurzweil joined them in the bar, Joy listened as Kurzweil and Searle resumed their colloquy where they'd left off.

As Joy remembers it, Kurzweil's argument was "that we were going to become robots or fuse with robots or something like that, and John countering that this couldn't happen, because robots couldn't be conscious."[14] Joy, who had been concerned about the ethical dimensions of new technologies since he had begun creating them decades before at Berkeley, was thunderstruck by Kurzweil's wild predictions. "I had always felt sentient robots were in the realm of science fiction. But now, from someone I respected, I was hearing a strong argument that they were a near-term possibility. I was taken aback, especially given Ray's proven ability to imagine and create the future. I already knew that new technologies like genetic engineering and nanotechnology were giving us the power to remake the world, but a realistic and imminent scenario for intelligent robots surprised me."

Here Joy exhibits the typical response of a Singularity virgin on first exposure to Kurzweil in mad-scientist mode. One glimpse of the future according to Ray was enough to scare the bejesus out of Joy and provide the impetus for his infamous *Wired* cover story, "Why the Future Doesn't Need Us," which appeared in the magazine's April 2000 issue and was subtitled: "Our Most Powerful 21st-Century Technologies—Robotics, Genetic Engineering, and Nanotech—Are Threatening to Make Humans an Endangered Species." Within hours of its publication, news outlets all over the world devoured the essay and regurgitated its contents in thousands of op-ed pieces and technology columns.[15] The *Times* of London reported that the article was "being compared to Einstein's 1939 letter to President Roosevelt alerting him to the possibility of a nuclear bomb."

Joy's shot-heard-round-the-Web essay had less to do with the topic

Searle and Kurzweil had debated at the table (that is, whether machines could become conscious, or intelligent enough to pass the Turing test) and more to do with the perils of science and technology run amok. While Joy had been listening to Kurzweil and Searle argue about machine consciousness in the bar at Lake Tahoe, Kurzweil had slipped Joy a manuscript of his then-forthcoming *Age of Spiritual Machines*. Joy found one section particularly disturbing. It was subtitled "The New Luddite Challenge," and Joy reprinted it in full at the outset of his article, because it's a party trick that no one (including me) seems able to resist.

> First let us postulate that the computer scientists succeed in developing intelligent machines that can do all things better than human beings can do them. In that case presumably all work will be done by vast, highly organized systems of machines and no human effort will be necessary. Either of two cases might occur. The machines might be permitted to make all of their own decisions without human oversight, or else human control over the machines might be retained.
>
> If the machines are permitted to make all their own decisions, we can't make any conjectures as to the results, because it is impossible to guess how such machines might behave. We only point out that the fate of the human race would be at the mercy of the machines. It might be argued that the human race would never be foolish enough to hand over all the power to the machines. But we are suggesting neither that the human race would voluntarily turn power over to the machines nor that the machines would willfully seize power. What we do suggest is that the human race might easily permit itself to drift into a position of such dependence on the machines that it would have no practical choice but to accept all of the machines' decisions. As society and the problems that face it become more and more complex and machines become more and more intelligent, people will let machines make more of their decisions for them, simply because machine-made decisions will bring better results than man-made ones. Eventually a stage may be reached at which the decisions necessary to keep the system running will be so complex that human beings will be incapable of making them intelligently. At

that stage the machines will be in effective control. People won't be able to just turn the machines off, because they will be so dependent on them that turning them off would amount to suicide.

On the other hand it is possible that human control over the machines may be retained. In that case the average man may have control over certain private machines of his own, such as his car or his personal computer, but control over large systems of machines will be in the hands of a tiny elite—just as it is today, but with two differences. Due to improved techniques the elite will have greater control over the masses; and because human work will no longer be necessary the masses will be superfluous, a useless burden on the system. If the elite is ruthless they may simply decide to exterminate the mass of humanity. If they are humane they may use propaganda or other psychological or biological techniques to reduce the birth rate until the mass of humanity becomes extinct, leaving the world to the elite. Or, if the elite consists of soft-hearted liberals, they may decide to play the role of good shepherds to the rest of the human race. They will see to it that everyone's physical needs are satisfied, that all children are raised under psychologically hygienic conditions, that everyone has a wholesome hobby to keep him busy, and that anyone who may become dissatisfied undergoes "treatment" to cure his "problem." Of course, life will be so purposeless that people will have to be biologically or psychologically engineered either to remove their need for the power process or make them "sublimate" their drive for power into some harmless hobby. These engineered human beings may be happy in such a society, but they will most certainly not be free. They will have been reduced to the status of domestic animals.

In Kurzweil's *Spiritual Machines,* in Joy's "Why the Future Doesn't Need Us" essay, in Joel Garreau's book *Radical Evolution,* and in who knows how many other reenactments of Kurzweil's original, authorial sleight of hand, you don't discover until you turn the page that the author of this passage is Theodore Kaczynski, the Unabomber. The revelation brings every reader (especially Joy, it seems) up short: "I am no apologist for Kaczynski," wrote Joy. "His bombs killed three people during a 17-year terror campaign and wounded many others.

One of his bombs gravely injured my friend David Gelernter,* one of the most brilliant and visionary computer scientists of our time. Like many of my colleagues, I felt that I could easily have been the Unabomber's next target."

Joy found Kaczynski's actions murderous, reprehensible, and criminally insane, but he "saw some merit in the reasoning in this single passage." He grudgingly admires Kaczynski's grasp of "unintended consequences, a well-known problem with the design and use of technology, and one that is clearly related to Murphy's law—'Anything that can go wrong, will.' (Actually, this is Finagle's law, which in itself shows that Finagle was right.)" Looking to the future through the ecstatic prose of Kurzweil's *Spiritual Machines* manuscript and the Unabomber's stark predictions, Joy thought of other "singular" inventions in the history of science, other occasions when humans blundered happily into discoveries that later became curses: "Failing to understand the consequences of our inventions while we are in the rapture of discovery and innovation seems to be a common fault of scientists and technologists."†

Like Vernor Vinge, Joy worries that Hans Moravec (a Carnegie Mellon robotocist who, as we've already seen, is more than happy to contemplate human-extinction scenarios at the hands of our robotic "mind children") may be showing us a future paved in mass graves, when he writes: "Biological species almost never survive encounters with superior competitors."[16] Even scarier than the possibility of nefarious supercomputers coming to power sometime after the Singularity are Joy's nightmares about something he calls "knowledge-enabled mass destruction" (KMD)—destructiveness hugely amplified by the power of self-replication and easily accessed by any deranged sociopath with a taste for mass murder.

---

*David Hillel Gelernter, Yale University computer scientist, born 1955, codeveloper of the Linda programming system, which Bill Joy credits as inspiring important elements in Java and Jini, a network architecture for distributed systems.

†Gotta love his use of *rapture.*

Unlike hydrogen bombs, which require uranium or plutonium and sophisticated reactors and teams of nuclear scientists to assemble, a nanobot swarm or genetically modified viruses or bacteria could be cooked up in the proverbial basement lab. Roger Brent, a geneticist and head of the Molecular Sciences Institute in Berkeley, California, believes that "genetically engineered bioweapons developed by small teams are a bigger threat than suitcase nukes."[17] Today, suicidal lone gunmen have a bad week and decide to shoot half a dozen people in the malls or schools; in ten or twenty years, social deviants will have access to computers and technological know-how that will enable them to take out whole cities before killing themselves. Bill Joy put it this way: "I think it is no exaggeration to say we are on the cusp of the further perfection of extreme evil, an evil whose possibility spreads well beyond that which weapons of mass destruction bequeathed to the nation-states, on to a surprising and terrible empowerment of extreme individuals."

Parts of Joy's essay sound almost like lamentations. It indeed reminds me of Einstein's letters to two presidents. The *Times* of London compared it to Einstein's 1939 letter to Roosevelt warning that bombs made from nuclear chain reactions might soon be possible, and that Germany might be interested in making one. But "Why the Future Doesn't Need Us" sounds more like the regret Einstein felt *after* Hiroshima ("I could burn my fingers that I wrote that first letter to President Roosevelt"). In other words, the real horror is not what might be but what is and what *will be*, because it's too late to stop it. Indeed, it may be a fantasy to believe that technology was ever ours to stop.

Joy's most vigorous and disquieting argument is that runaway GRIN research feels a lot like nuclear-weapons research just before the arms race. He quotes from the documentary *The Day After Trinity*, in which nuclear physicist Freeman Dyson summarized the scientific attitudes that brought us to the nuclear precipice:

> I have felt it myself. The glitter of nuclear weapons. It is irresistible if you come to them as a scientist. To feel it's there in your hands, to release this energy that fuels the stars, to let it do your bidding. To perform these miracles, to lift a million tons of rock

into the sky. It is something that gives people an illusion of illimitable power, and it is, in some ways, responsible for all our troubles—this, what you might call technical arrogance, that overcomes people when they see what they can do with their minds.[18]

Joy's hope is that the coming Technological Singularity is somehow different from humankind's nuclear hubris: "This time—unlike during the Manhattan Project—we aren't in a war, facing an implacable enemy that is threatening our civilization; we are driven, instead, by our habits, our desires, our economic system, and our competitive need to know."

Of course, that was written before 9/11 and before our invasion of Iraq and the War on Terror. War or no war, isn't our "competitive need to know" the most dangerous thing about the human race? I really need to know what will happen if I make a machine with one thousand times the computational capacity of the human brain. I need to know what it will do if I write a program that will endow it with humanlike mental powers. Maybe I want to know what it will think of me, its creator. Maybe I could conjure it like a genie from a bottle and entice it to serve me?

I read "Why the Future Doesn't Need Us" when it came out in April 2000. It was a twenty-four-page spread, and I consumed the hard copy in a single sitting at a crowded sushi bar. I have friends in the restaurant business, so I'm usually overly sensitive about hogging a table while hungry customers are waiting. However, while in transports of Joy and his essay, I don't remember looking up even once, until a waitress tapped me on the shoulder and politely suggested that another customer needed my seat. "Why the Future Doesn't Need Us" was so absorbing because it was a dramatic print event of the sort we seldom see anymore.

Joy's essay took him six months to write; it was cogent and passionate, argued with care and deliberation by a tech giant who looked at the future and blanched. His distress was contagious, heady, and volatile. Today the essay is still a disquieting gem, still well made; it still seeps angst and earnest alarm on every page, but at least half the fizz is gone. In keeping with those accelerating laws and the redoubling pace of tech milestones, the essay feels twenty or thirty years old, instead of a mere seven years distant. Reading it now brings a kind of world-weary resignation. One thinks: "This stuff is coming, and nothing can be done about it. How touching, that a genius and a man of conscience once thought he could raise an alarm and stop it." Even the calls for self-discipline and regulation sound pro forma, made in the fond hope that somebody will believe such a thing possible.

Kurzweil persuasively argues that the notion of "relinquishing" technology or outlawing certain broad swaths of it is ludicrous. Take, for instance, the fears of a so-called "gray goo," a self-replicating nanobot swarm getting out of control, probably the foremost doomsday scenario featured in Joy's *Wired* essay. What happens if Joe Terrorist creates something that self-replicates (exponentially, of course), and then we can't stop it? Nanotechnology is not one thing that you can decide not to do, says Kurzweil. It's the persistent and inevitable trend toward miniaturization being pursued all over the world in many countries and many different industries. You can't identify nanotech as a separate animal and then outlaw it, any more than you could outlaw romantic love or erotic love while trying to leave all other forms of love in place.

A further reason why industrial society cannot be reformed . . . is that modern technology is a unified system in which all parts are dependent on one another. You can't get rid of the "bad" parts of technology and retain only the "good" parts. Take modern medicine, for example. Progress in medical science depends on progress in chemistry, physics, biology, computer science and other fields. Advanced medical treatments require expensive, high-tech equipment that can be made available only by a technologically progressive, economically rich society. Clearly you can't have much progress in medicine without the whole technological system and everything that goes with it.[19]

Guess who? That's right, it's the Unabomber again. No one likes to admit it, but Theodore Kaczynski, in addition to being the barking-mad Unabomber in an aluminum-foil hat, was also a bloodhound when it came to scenting all of the future terrors of technology. Hence his mission to kill technologists before they commenced what he believed were their inevitable reigns of terror. In a way, Kaczynski is more persuasive than a mere environmentalist, like Bill McKibben, whose *Enough: Staying Human in an Engineered Age*[20] feels quaint compared with a jeremiad like the Unabomber's manifesto. If you truly believe the world is about to end and that technology will be the cause, do you write a thoughtful respite in the onrushing torrent of ever more technology? Or do you sound an air raid siren, like Joy and Kaczynski did?

Bill Joy left Sun Microsystems in 2003, not to wear hair shirts and take up the neo-Luddite cause but to work as a venture capitalist at the legendary Silicon Valley firm Kleiner Perkins Caufield & Byers, where he focuses on what might be called green nanotechnology applied to renewable energy and conserving natural resources. In *The Singularity Is Near,* Kurzweil cites private e-mails from Joy, who now says that he never intended to advocate broad relinquishment of technology, or even relinquishment of nanotechnology. Instead, the emphasis should be on his call to "limit development of the technologies that are too dangerous."[21]

No argument there. Now all we need are some enlightened Platonic Guardians or perhaps a benevolent global tyrant to identify which technologies are dangerous and then ban all scientists everywhere from pursuing them. Even if we could manage that, no doubt some tormented genius in his turret lab would lust to know what sort of virtual galaxies might be his if he could create a swarm of nanobots loyal to him and him alone. If all else failed, he could perhaps summon up the Devil himself and try to strike a bargain for his soul.

# Dr. Foust

Forty years ago in this magazine, E. B. White wrote about descending from his office, on the nineteenth floor, to an assembling point on the tenth floor for an atomic-bomb drill— a drop of not nine but eight floors, he noted, since a floor numbered 13 did not exist. "It occurred to us, gliding by the thirteenth floor and seeing the numeral '14' painted on it, that our atom-splitting scientists had committed the error of impatience and had run on ahead of the rest of the human race," he wrote. "They had dared to look into the core of the sun, and had fiddled with it; but it might have been a good idea if they had waited to do that until the rest of us could look the number 13 square in the face."

—Calvin Trillin, *The New Yorker*

Don't make that atomic weapon! Don't tinker with that stem cell! Don't make nanobots that swarm! Don't make those supercomputers or they might decide to exterminate you! Useless warnings it would seem, for technology proceeds apace in millions of laboratories all over the world. Doubling, redoubling, inexorably.

## 8.1 From Damnification to Maytag Repairman

Like Prometheus,* man is a fire-stealing animal. Nothing captures his inbred evolutionary lust for tampering with Nature's ultimate secrets better than the immortal tale of Dr. Faustus, the sixteenth-century man of science who sold his soul to the Devil in exchange for knowledge and forbidden lore. The Faust legend was a meme nearly four centuries before the word was invented. The story first appeared in 1587 as *The Historia von D. Johann Fausten* by Johann Spies (a pseudonym) and from there was told and retold all over Europe and down through the centuries, changing right along with humankind's growing love affair with the sciences. Finally, in the twentieth century, those Faustian urges ripened into modern atomic bloodlust, and now (if the likes of Bill Joy and Erich Heller[1] are correct) threaten to unleash a Pandora's box of GRIN technologies here in the twenty-first century.

In its original version,[2] Faust was a shady though learned man, a "doctor," an alchemist and "insatiable speculator" who was "fain to love forbidden things after which he hankered day and night, taking unto himself the wings of eagle in order to search out the uttermost parts of heaven and earth."[3] Half wizard, half man of science, the original Faust figured out how to summon up the Devil himself in the person of Mephistopheles. After a lifetime of trying to master the sciences, what Faust wanted was ultimate knowledge, the secrets of the universe: "But I will know," he begs of the Devil, "or I will not live, you must tell me." Mephistopheles (no surprise) had a lawyer's knack for contract language when it came to acquiring human souls. He laid down the following terms, and Faust signed in blood:

> I, John Faustus, Doctor, do openly acknowledge with my own hand . . . that since I began to study and speculate the elements,

---

*In Greek mythology, a Titan who stole fire from the gods and gave it to man. See discussion at page 171.

and since I have not found through the gifts that have been graciously bestowed upon me from above, enough skills; and for that I find that I cannot learn them from human beings, now have I surrendered unto this spirit Mephistopheles, ambassador of the hellish Prince of Orient, upon such condition that he shall teach me, and fulfill my desire in all things, as he has promised and vowed unto me.[4]

Nice. Unlimited knowledge and the secrets of Heaven and earth if Faust will but renounce "all living creatures, and the whole heavenly host, and all human beings, for so it must be."[5] Any compulsive programmer, start-up entrepreneur, or nuclear physicist would probably take that deal, especially if it came with backdated stock options.

*Faust* was an instant classic; it was adapted and performed throughout the seventeenth century and from there inspired the likes of Christopher Marlowe (1604), Goethe (1806–1832), Hector Berlioz (1845–1846), Heinrich Heine (1851), Ivan Turgenev (1855), Charles Gounod (1859), Oscar Wilde (1891), Paul Valéry (1946), and Thomas Mann (1947), to name only some of the heavyweights.[6] However, Faust and the moral of his story both seemed to change along with the centuries, and along with man's growing admiration for the arts, for learning, for enlightenment, and, yes, for machines. What began as a Christian morality play in which Faust was a twisted sorcerer punished for dabbling in black magic soon became a tragic tale of a scientist and heroic scholar's quest for knowledge at any and all costs. The title of the first English translation[7] sounded like the topic for a Puritan sermon: *The Historie of the Damnable Life, and Deserved Death of Doctor John Faustus*. Just before his untimely death under suspicious circumstances, the English playwright Christopher Marlowe (1564–1593) wrote the first dramatic version of the newly translated German *Faustbuch*. Marlowe's *Tragical History of Doctor Faustus* caused a sensation. Actors and audiences alike claimed that actual devils appeared onstage and that some audience members were driven mad.

By the time Goethe (1749–1832) spent sixty years writing and rewriting his epic *Faust*, it came in two parts and ended with Faust going to Heaven, forgiven for his insatiable (though now understandable) thirst for knowledge. Angels rescue the scholarly Faust before Satan can collect his due.

Goethe was himself a lover of knowledge, an author of many great literary works, but also a scientist who wrote the *Theory of Colors* and influenced Charles Darwin with his studies of plant morphology. You can imagine Goethe arguing with himself for sixty years, while trying to complete his *Faust*, the project he seemed unable to finish: Does it have to be so harsh? Does poor Dr. Faustus have to go to Hell? Just because he wanted to learn some science?

Goethe, however, was no sunny optimist about the new breed of scientists emerging in the Age of Enlightenment. By the time Paul Valéry renders *Mon Faust* in the twentieth century, at the height of World War II, the Devil is superfluous, an anachronism from a bygone time when "people weren't clever enough to damn themselves by their own devices." This thoroughly modern Faust, who sounds almost like Valéry, has somehow anticipated the fears of Bill Joy, when Faust says to Mephistopheles: "The whole system, of which you were the linchpin, is falling to pieces. Confess that even you feel lost among this new crowd of human beings who do evil without knowing or caring, who have no notion of Eternity, who risk their lives ten times a day in playing with their new machines, who have created countless marvels your magic never dreamt of, and have put them in the reach of any fool."[8]

The Devil as Maytag repairman. Indeed, and we go on making marvels no magic or philosophy ever dreamt of, and after a few more decades of progress they will soon be in the reach of any fool. Bill Joy is right about one thing: The cautionary tale humans stand to learn most from is how we handled our last bout of Promethean fever. What happened the last time we summoned up the Devil and said, "I will know, or I will not live"?

# 8.2 While Reach > Grasp: "Progress"

> We waited until the blast had passed, walked out of the shelter
> and then it was extremely solemn. We knew the world would not
> be the same. A few people laughed, a few people cried. Most
> people were silent. I remembered the line from the Hindu
> scripture, the *Bhagavad-Gita:* Vishnu is trying to persuade the
> Prince that he should do his duty and to impress him he takes on
> his multi-armed form and says, "Now I am become Death, the
> destroyer of worlds." I suppose we all thought that, one way or
> another.
>
> —Robert Oppenheimer[9]

## The Nuclear Singularity

> When you see something that is technically sweet, you go ahead
> and do it and you argue about what to do about it only after you
> have had your technical success. That is the way it was with the
> atomic bomb.
>
> —Robert Oppenheimer[10]

The big fear is that Samuel Butler saw it all almost 150 years ago in
"Darwin Among the Machines," namely, that we are already helpless
machine addicts. Our lust for smarter, more powerful machines will
never be sated, and the Devil (or Mephisto) take the hindmost and
the hazards. As Bill Joy and many others have pointed out, the scientists who worked feverishly on the Manhattan Project in Los Alamos,
New Mexico, to develop the first atomic weapon took enormous
risks, both personal and planetary. The world's brightest physicists—
Robert Oppenheimer, Edward Teller, Hans Bethe, Richard Feynman,
and many others set out to build the first weapon of mass destruction
(the atomic bomb) despite real fears that the bomb might ignite the
earth's atmosphere or its oceans and destroy the whole world. Edward Teller worried that a hypothetical fusion reaction of nitrogen

nuclei might occur and result in an unstoppable chain reaction."[11] Hans Bethe and others went back to their drawing boards and did enough math to assure Manhattan Project director Robert Oppenheimer that the chance of a doomsday scenario was minuscule. (Oh, I feel better now!) But as Bill Joy points out in his *Wired* essay, "Oppenheimer . . . was sufficiently concerned about the result of Trinity that he arranged for a possible evacuation of the southwest part of the state of New Mexico."

Ironically, according to Albert Speer, Hitler's minister of armaments and war production, the risk was too much for *mein* goodly *führer:* "Professor Heisenberg had not given any final answer to my question whether a successful nuclear fission could be kept under control with absolute certainty or might continue as a chain reaction. Hitler was plainly not delighted with the possibility that the earth under his rule might be transformed into a glowing star. Occasionally, however, he joked that the scientists in their unworldly urge to lay bare all the secrets under heaven might someday set the globe on fire."[12]

Any reader of the dramatic accounts of the ultimate quest for fire in New Mexico during the years 1941–1946 comes away frightened of science and its will to power at any and all costs. At Los Alamos, the national-security mission to be the first to make an atomic bomb that would affect the outcome of the war got all mixed up with other unspeakable desires of the sort Freeman Dyson described so well; namely, to make miracles out of pure knowledge, to release energy and make it do your bidding. In the end, the Manhattan Project scientists took the risk that a chain reaction would be unstoppable, because they had no way of knowing that Hitler's team had already determined that the risk was too great. But something else was afoot; namely, big science and its Faustian appetites for knowledge and power: "It is sometimes difficult even for the other scientists to remember that the atomic and hydrogen bombs were developed not only as weapons of terrible destruction. They were also, as Fermi once said, 'superb physics.' "[13]

In other words, the physicists, who started out trying to make a bomb that would help end the war, found something even bigger along the way: excellence. Something so big it would take care of America's bomb needs, win any war you chose to start, and much more; they were on to the ultimate secrets of Nature (of "heaven and earth," as Faust put it), the source of infinite energy and power; they were on to "superb physics." Even before the atomic bomb was tested, the physicists at Los Alamos were already speculating about a new bomb, a hydrogen bomb that would be a hundred times more powerful, speculating too about what might be possible after the hydrogen bomb. That's right. Never think big. Always *bigger!* As Richard Rhodes recounts in *The Making of the Atomic Bomb,* physicist Edward Teller (the same guy who worried about igniting the earth's atmosphere) was already thinking *really* big, years before the H-bomb: "The most hopeful procedure is to use tritium ... as a sort of booster in the reaction, the fission bomb being used as a detonator and the reaction involving the atoms of liquid deuterium being the prime explosive. Such a gadget should produce an explosive equivalent to 100,000,000 tons of TNT, which in turn should produce Class B damage over an area of 3,000 square miles!"[14]

Sweet! And don't we all love "gadgets"? You could take out whole counties and small states instead of just cities. Why mess with a bomb like the one dropped on Hiroshima (equivalent to a picayune 12,500 tons of TNT) when Teller already had a twinkle in his eye for one that was eight thousand times more destructive? As Rhodes saw it, what began as a tactical weapon of terror designed to end World War II became, after the war ended, quite naturally a genocidal weapon many thousand times more powerful designed to do ... what exactly? Why make bigger bombs after you've already won the war? Is what we *can* do synonymous with what we *should* do? In science, it seems that the answer often is yes.

The upshot of all that "superb physics"? As Pablo Picasso put it, "The genius of Einstein leads to Hiroshima." The upshot is that evolution has produced Man, who is still more ape than god. Yes, he has the biggest neocortex on the planet and that marvelous opposable thumb, but he also has his finger on the button. Or as Erich Heller put it, "Man, a creature that, upon the irrefutable evidence of his history, cannot control himself, in control of all life on earth."[15]

Once the politicians and the statesmen got ahold of the Faustian secrets of atom splitting, we were off to the arms race and didn't look back. Bill Joy found hope because humankind has so far shown a modicum of self-control by refraining from the runaway pursuit of biological weapons, but let one rogue state commence the making of dirty smallpox bombs and all bets will be off. Whenever self-doubt or ethical queasiness threatens to overtake hardworking scientists, a mysterious moral rectitude seems to calm all fears. "We need these weapons," the scientists tell themselves, "to end *a* war, or maybe even to end all wars."

Robert Oppenheimer recounted:

> When [the bomb] went off, in the New Mexico dawn, that first atomic bomb, we thought of Alfred Nobel, and his hope, his vain hope, that dynamite would put an end to wars. We thought of the legend of Prometheus, of that deep sense of guilt in man's new powers, that reflects his recognition of evil, and his long knowledge of it. We knew that it was a new world, but even more we knew that novelty itself was a very old thing in human life, that all our ways are rooted in it.[16]

A quest for novelty? Indeed, we know all about that. The masses line up for the latest rendition of Halo for the Xbox 360, or the latest model of the iPhone or iPod. A dark version of the same thrill-seeking would have the masses lining up to see the newest human-animal combo to roll out of a rogue nation's stem cell lab. What does a bovine or porcine para-human look like, exactly? Just let me see for myself, so I can be shocked—shocked!—that scientists are engaging in these kinds of experiments.

As Joel Garreau and Bill McKibben both note in their books, when the genetic versions of Moore's law kick in, no parent of tomorrow will be willing to forgo the latest in intelligence augmentation, not if it means standing by while all of the other genetically modified kids on performance-enhancing medications (I mean, "supplements") go to the head of the class. If we outlaw stem cell experimentation in the United States, then perhaps our enemies will employ it to breed soldiers twice as strong that require half the sleep and a tenth of the calories needed to sustain mostly original human-substrate soldiers. Then what?

What seems innate to us humans—our fatal flaw, the apple of Knowledge in the Garden—is Promethean fire-stealing, the instinct to always and everywhere overreach. It's the voice inside us that says (whether of beer, intellectual activity, scientific achievement, money, drugs, sex), "Hey, this is good, but why not take it to the next level?" If computer technology equips human brains with the ultimate in brain boosters, extensions, and implants—if it amplifies our intelligence and allows us to put intelligence and the acquisition of knowledge and information into exponential overdrive—will it also somehow confer the wisdom necessary for collective self-control? Probably not. And if not, our reckless pursuit of GRIN at any and all human costs may come to remind us of the definition C. S. Lewis once gave of Satan: "the horrible co-existence of a subtle and incessant intellectual activity with an incapacity to understand anything."

The Devil keeps popping up. Or as Valéry's Faust well knew, in the twentieth century, you don't need Satan or Mephisto; humankind's propensity for good old-fashioned excess, once known as *sin,* is more than enough.

Years after the development of the first atomic bomb, Oppenheimer remarked: "In some sort of crude sense, which no vulgarity, no humor, no overstatement can quite extinguish, the physicists have known sin; and this is a knowledge they cannot lose."[17]

That's a bit heavy, isn't it? Oppenheimer talking about sin tells me that he still had ghosts in his machine. He could have used a seminar on modern neurophilosophy and the computational theory of mind, then maybe he wouldn't have been so hung up on tedious, medieval moral precepts. He could have just done what he had to do and made sense of it afterward, providing excuses as needed: national defense, peacemaking, stopping the Nazis, or incinerating Japanese children to save American lives. But sin? Unbecoming of any twentieth-century scientist to even entertain the idea.

If you made it through the chapter on the three-pound universe versus the Blue Brain, then you know the drill. It goes like this: Computers are binary information-processing machines that run on 1's and 0's. Humans are quaternary information-processing machines that run on A's, C's, G's, and T's (adenine, cytosine, guanine, thymine), the four nucleotide subunits of a DNA strand.* If the mind is nothing more than the brain, and the brain is just a biological computer programmed by evolution's blind watchmaker,† then where's the requisite *intent* or free will required for sinning? Isn't sin a *conscious* turning away from God or some other absolute value? Maybe the title of Harvard social psychologist Daniel M. Wegner's influential book says it all: *The Illusion of Conscious Will*.[18] No sinning here. *Homo sapiens* is just a species programmed to discover nature's secrets and then use them to make war machines. We're also programmed to program thinking machines and programmed to build and serve the supercomputers of tomorrow. So take your soul and your free will and go. End of story.

As for sin, what's the old saying? "Never attribute to malice that

---

*"The metaphor of human genome research is computational: humans are information-processing machines, and DNA is the code that humans execute. 'It's not data processing, it's a new view of biology,' said Edward Lazowska, a professor at the University of Washington. 'And that's happening all over. Computer science is pervading all other disciplines.' " Steve Lohr, "Technology Climate Is Gloomy, but Its Future Still Seems Bright," *New York Times*, 29 July 2002.

†Richard Dawkins, *The Blind Watchmaker* (New York: W. W. Norton, 1986), in which Dawkins answers the common argument of natural theologians that a complex universe implies a creator in the same way an intricate watch implies an intelligent watchmaker. Dawkins argues that random genetic mutations coupled with millions of years of natural selection can produce the same complexity.

which can be adequately explained by stupidity." Why read evil motives into man's insatiable, lamebrained urge to tinker? Never mind the world going out with a bang and a whimper and a holocaust. The last thing we'll probably hear is a chuckle, especially if the likes of Terry Pratchett are correct:

> Some humans would do anything to see if it was possible to do it. If you put a large switch in some cave somewhere, and a sign on it saying "End-of-the-World Switch. PLEASE DO NOT TOUCH" the paint wouldn't even have time to dry.
>
> Perhaps it was boredom, not intelligence, that had propelled them up the evolutionary ladder . . . that strange ability to look at the universe and think, "Oh, the same as yesterday, how dull. I wonder what happens if I bang this rock on that head?"[19]

And so we come full circle to the Pascal problem: The root of all evil is that man cannot sit still in a room. Man cannot sit still in a room, even with an Intel Core 2 Extreme QX6850 machine with 4 gigs of RAM and dual SLI video cards, running a lush, gorgeous 30-inch LCD monitor at 60 megahertz, with a resolution of 2560 x 1600, and an image-contrast ratio of 1000:1. Nope, even with a rig like that, man must leave the room to go in search of an End of the World switch, because it might be neat to see if it really would work.

*Bang.*

Chuckle.

"Sumbitch, it really w—"

> **while reach > grasp:**
> **"progress" ∞**

# What If It's All a Big Game?

**It is pitch dark. You are likely to be eaten by a grue.**

—Zork I

Singularity or no Singularity, the future will be run by computers, or by the humans, trans-humans, and post-humans who program, worship, and serve them. Your mission (like Dr. Strangelove's) is to learn how to stop worrying and love the bomb, love the Singularity, love the future and your genetically modified, trans-human grandchildren. Take your cue from *Dr. Strangelove* and Major "King" Kong (played by Slim Pickens in a Stetson). When the bomb-bay doors jam in his B-52, Major Kong sits astride the nuclear bomb, patches two wires together, and attaches an alligator clip to a patch panel above his head. The doors open, and Kong ends up riding the bomb through the atmosphere like a rodeo cowboy astride the ultimate phallic symbol. He whoops and waves his hat in the air and makes the best of the role technology has assigned for him to play in this brief crack of light called "life" that separates two eternities.

As for Strangelove himself, once he realizes that doomsday is inevitable, he informs President Merkin Muffley that they could easily "preserve a nucleus of human specimens," several hundred thousand or so at the bottom of mine shafts where nuclear power could provide energy and animals could be bred and slaughtered. A computer could be programmed to select who stays up and who gets to go down into the mine shafts: "Of course it would be vital that our top government and military men be included to foster and impart the required principles of leadership and tradition."

Strangelove also recommends "breeding techniques and a ratio of ten females to each male." He hastens to add that since each man will be required to do prodigious service along these lines, "the women will have to be selected for their sexual characteristics, which will have to be of a highly stimulating nature."

The more things change, the more they stay the same: The last thing the military men worry about is a "mine-shaft gap," which could result if the Soviets stash a bomb somewhere and effect a postapocalyptic sneak attack on American mine shafts.

The last thing we see is mushroom clouds, exploding to a sound-track of Vera Lynn's "We'll Meet Again."*

Have you stopped worrying about the Singularity yet? Get an MP3 of "We'll Meet Again" to keep you company if the Singularity turns dark, or if your computer is holding you captive in your smart house and asking you about this thing called music.

# 9.1 MOTHERS AGAINST WORLD OF WARCRAFT

> What was entirely missing . . . was the manner of woman who is neither very young nor very old, who had laid in a lining of subcutaneous fat, who glows with plumpness and a rosy face that speaks, without a word, of home and hearth and hot food ready at six and stories read aloud at night and conversations while seated on the edge of the bed, just before the Sandman comes. In short, no one ever invited . . . Mother.
>
> —Tom Wolfe, *The Bonfire of the Vanities*

---

*During the cold war, Vera Lynn's recording was included in the package of music and programs held in twenty underground radio stations of the BBC's Wartime Broadcasting Service, designed to provide public information and morale-boosting broadcasts for one hundred days after a nuclear attack. Nicholas Hellen, "Julie Andrews to Sing to Brits During Nuclear Attack," *Sunday Times*, 11 July 1999.

Let's say that the Singularity is really coming, and let's say it's powered by Moore's law and Kurzweil's law of accelerating returns. Call the Technological Singularity a cardinal virtue or a fatal flaw; our reach will *always* exceed our grasp, and we'll keep inventing and experimenting, until we invent our way into doom and extinction, or paradise, whichever comes first. Suppose we really are a race of technology addicts on autopilot. Assume the Singularity has all of that going for it. Suppose it's truly an irresistible force. Are there any immovable objects in its path? Answer: What happens if moms don't like the Singularity?

Your lovely wife (may I pretend her name is Wilma?) is your soul mate, mother of your children, keeper of the eternal family flame, sun at the center of the domestic solar system. God couldn't be everywhere, so He made her. It is her name on the lips and in the hearts of your children. She is the holiest creature in God's creation. She is the one who can take the place of all others, but whose place no one else can take. "All love begins and ends here," said Thomas Jefferson, "the keystone in the arch of matrimonial happiness."

Wilma has but a single flaw: She has no feeling for the Singularity, nor does she care to hear a single Singularitarian word about it. Technology for Wilma means e-mail two or three times a week, exchanging photos of family and friends, a little online shopping, and a little online banking. She has no taste for machine building, conquering World of Warcraft empires, or power programming.

You and Wilma have a thirteen-year-old son, Will, who deeply resents his mother's failure to appreciate his vocation in life. To Wilma, son Will is an above-average student at Middlebury Middle School, associate editor of the *Middlebury Mail* student newspaper, and member of the chess club (because Wilma forced him to select at least two extracurricular activities other than playing Magic: The Gathering. Wilma does not want to hear about her son's higher calling and how he leads a double life—at the tender age of thirteen, Will is also a Level 60 Shaman in a World of Warcraft guild named the League of Pain.

As Will's loving father and Wilma's devoted husband, you have tried to be a peacemaker. You can see Wilma's point about how she cannot allow Will to spend twelve hours online with only two bathroom breaks and a bag of Cheetos for sustenance. When Wilma's dad (Will's grandpa and your father-in-law) was in high school, he was captain of the football team and took second in state in the high dive. Therefore, Wilma's earliest childhood memories are of her dad playing one sport or another in the backyard with her brothers (steel-cup jocks, one and all). Wilma wants you to teach your son the same valuable life lessons she saw her father impart to her brothers by way of athletics: competition, teamwork, and profound insights like "Don't wait for the ball to come to you, son, go after it!" "Learn from your mistakes!" and "You've got to *want* that rebound more than the other guy!"

On the other hand, you also can see Will's argument about how his mother doesn't know the first thing about the Singularity and the important role gamers of all persuasions will play in it. Gaming is a higher calling demanding advanced programming skills and excellence in game mapping. Will isn't saying that his mom must buy into the Singularity, but she does need to understand the obvious; namely, that here in 2008, *life happens online* and not in the Boy Scouts, or on the Middlebury Middle School baseball diamond, or at some goofy party she wants him to attend so he can flesh-meet other kids his age who don't play World of Warcraft or Magic Cards.

Another complication is even harder to explain to Wilma. You've tried several different times, but words always fail. You even wrote it on a piece of paper once and almost left it on her desk: "Wilma, I will always and forever be your devoted husband, but I am also a member of Will's World of Warcraft guild. I confess that I am a Level 60 Rogue in the League of Pain."

Hence the painful conflict of interest when you hear Wilma's shrill cries coming from your son's room: "Get off the computer!" Because at that very moment, you are in your study on *your* computer, and you and your son Will are both part of a forty-man raiding party laying siege to Blackwing Lair.

Wilma has no way of knowing that your son is on the verge of killing the Scarshield Quartermaster, who is found near the Orb of Command, because Will needs to loot Blackhand's Command from him and begin a quest that will take him to the end of Upper Blackrock Spire, where he must touch a brand (found behind General Drakkisath), which will brand him with the Mark of Drakkisath and allow him to use the Orb of Command to enter Blackwing Lair.

Thirty-nine other members of the guild (you included), who have been planning this three-day raid for weeks, are waiting for Will to get "keyed," and now Wilma is interfering.

"Wilma, honey," you cry, "let Will finish the game. He'll be off in half an hour or so, then we'll both go outside and knock a few balls around the backyard, okay?"

"Knock a few balls around?" Wilma laughs. "With what? A joystick? You don't have a baseball, or bat, or gloves."

"We have a glove," you protest. "It's on the top shelf over the workbench."

"That's my brother's baseball glove. It's a *left-handed* glove! Remember?"

"Okay," you offer, "never mind baseball then. We'll borrow the neighbor's soccer ball instead."

No answer, which means Wilma is simmering. A door doesn't quite slam, but let's say that she shuts it . . . with authority.

Now, it's bound to come up at dinner. It does, and it goes something like this:

Wilma says, "Jason's dad is a hedge-fund manager and Brian's dad is a neurosurgeon, and yet they both still find time to coach the soccer team. I really admire them for that. Those boys are true athletes. Their dads are *always* playing sports with them in the yard. Jason's mom said he was recruited by the Select Soccer Team."

Neither you nor Will can say what you are both thinking; namely, that Brian may play a mean game of junior golf at Daddy's country club, but in World of Warcraft he's a Level 8 pink-haired Gnome who likes to slap his ass and chat while dancing on the mailboxes. As for Jason, he may be a soccer goon, but he's been kicked out of three guilds and would be about as much help in a raiding party as Leeroy Jenkins.* When it comes to gaming, the two of them are useless sub-nOObs with sticks for hands.

"I'll be using computers for the rest of my life," says Will. "I can promise you that I won't be kicking soccer balls once you stop making me."

Wilma sighs. "All of your friends are on the team. It's good exercise.

---

*Leeroy Jenkins is a powerful Internet meme. To truly grasp the Leeroy phenom, you should find the Machinima game video and watch it. If you are *not* a gamer, read the following first, so that you have some idea of what's happening when you watch the video. The Wikipedia entry changes weekly and the entry is sometimes protected from vandalism, but here is an edited version of what you might find at http://en.wikipedia.org/wiki/Leeroy_Jenkins circa August 2007:

Leeroy Jenkins (or often Leeeeerooooyyyy Jenkins!) is an Internet phenomenon named for a character created by player Ben Schulz in Blizzard Entertainment's popular MMORPG World of Warcraft. The character has become popular thanks to a Machinima video of the game that circulated around the Internet. The phenomenon has since spread well beyond the boundaries of the gaming community into other online and mainstream media.

The video takes place in the Upper Blackrock Spire dungeon in the World of Warcraft, inside the Rookery Room, one of the most notoriously difficult sections for newcomers to the game. It opens with the guild members discussing an impending raid via audio teleconferencing, complete with regimented battle plan and statistical breakdown of their survival ratios. The fastidiousness of their preparations is ruined by the sudden and unexpected actions of Leeroy Jenkins, who, being away from keyboard (AFK) and missing the entire conversation, runs into the area without pause, yelling "All right, chums, let's do this! LEEEEEROOOOYYY JENKINS!" And in he goes. There is about a second of stunned silence from his companions, followed by carnage when they mount a rescue attempt. The attempted raid (and video) is filled with desperate calls from the team to mount their original plan, and with insults at Leeroy, even with Leeroy calling "It's not my fault." It ends disastrously, with all the guild members lying dead on the floor, screaming at Leeroy for his brash decision. Leeroy responds to the abuse—and explains that he was AFK during the raid preparations—with the retort "Least I have chicken."

Fresh air. You learn to play with others as a team. Just give it one more try, that's all we're saying—"

"We're?" you interrupt. "*We're* saying it?"

Wilma gives you an ugly look. "Okay," she offers. "Then how about baseball?"

Will shakes his head. "Left field? Waiting to be yelled at by Coach Bloatbelly because I wasn't paying attention when the ball was hit to me for the first time in a month?"

"All right," says Wilma, "then soccer it is. Soccer tryouts are tomorrow at eleven. Dad will take you. End of discussion."

Wilma trembles with anger. You and Will can both see that she means what she says. She seems to be exerting her last vestige of Real World control over Will, before he is lost to the wastelands of Azeroth.

You and Will share a look of visceral panic. Tomorrow at eleven!? This is a true emergency! Tomorrow at 11:00 sharp, server time, you, Will and the rest of your forty-man raiding party will be battling Razorgore the Untamed, Vaelastrasz the Corrupt, and Broodlord Lashlayer in a desperate attempt to clear Blackwing Lair. No way in Azeroth can you and your son leave the others without their number one Rogue and Shaman because of . . . *soccer tryouts*?

What does Wilma expect you to do? Notify the others that they will have to cancel the raid and allow Nefarian's mad bid for dominance, the final stages of his plan to destroy Ragnaros once and for all and lead his army to undisputed supremacy over all the races of Azeroth to proceed? What if the rumors are true and Nefarian is experimenting with the blood of all the various Dragon Flights to produce unstoppable warriors? Let all of Azeroth fall? Because of . . . *soccer tryouts*?

No time to panic. You need to do a little research and bring Wilma into the twenty-first century. Yes, Wilma, sports *do* teach kids about teamwork, long-range planning, prolonged effort, the agony of victory and the thrill of defeat and all, but please have a look at what it takes to mount a raid on the upper reaches of Blackrock Spire. You want teamwork? Planning? Logistics? Effort? Delayed gratification? Try having forty guys from eight different states and three different countries meet on the server with all of their loot and mount an assault on one of the toughest dungeons in World of Warcraft.

Whence comes the idea that sports are good for the kids, whereas gaming is somehow bad? You go to your bookshelf and dig out Steven Johnson's *Everything Bad Is Good for You: How Today's Popular Culture Is Actually Making Us Smarter*.[1] You leave it on Wilma's pillow, open to the chapter entitled "Games."

That night, when you come out of the bathroom after brushing your teeth, you see that Wilma has not read the chapter in Johnson's book and is instead reading *Caught in the Net: How to Recognize the Signs of Internet Addiction—and a Winning Strategy for Recovery*, by Kimberly Young.[2] This calls for drastic measures. You grab Johnson's book and begin reading aloud to Wilma: " 'The intellectual benefits of gaming derive from . . . learning how to think . . . learning to make the right decisions: weighing evidence, analyzing situations, consulting your long-term goals, and then deciding. No other pop cultural form directly engages the brain's decision-making apparatus in the same way.' "[3]

You explain to Wilma how Steven Johnson identifies *telescoping* and *probing* as two valuable mental habits taught by computer games. He compares them to the mental exercise required to work through math word problems. Real Worldians criticize computer games for being shallow or mindless because the game narratives are simplistic or somehow disconnected from "reality," but game critics don't seem to have a problem with the inane content of most math word problems. For example, two trains leave the station at noon, one going forty miles an hour, one going sixty . . . and so on. Nobody cares about two trains or whether the narrative is simplistic or devoid of moral lessons or psychological depth. Math word problems are not meant to take the place of Tolstoy or Shakespeare. Word problems don't teach moral lessons or social skills, they teach abstract reasoning. And Johnson argues that computer games also teach valuable mental habits, not just hand-eye coordination.

By *telescoping*, Johnson means that gamers learn to manage a hierarchy of shifting objectives in a changing environment: To get here, I must first go there, and obtain X, then I must proceed to Y and conquer Z. You urge Wilma to consider the complex strategizing and mental self-discipline evident in a walk-through strategy guide of how to take down Hungarfen, an oversized bog giant, found in Underbog, Coilfang Reservoir, Zangarmarsh:

> To get to Hungarfen, players will need to navigate through a huge cavern filled with various underbog wildlife. The toughest of these are the fungal giants, and care should be made to pull each separately. Provided players watch out for the fast moving patrols that circle the cavern, this part won't be too bad. Hug the right hand side of the cavern till you see a ramp leading upward. Take this ramp. The rest of the cavern, despite its size, is filled with trash mobs. A few more pulls and you will reach an elevated clearing with Hungarfen. The two fungal guards in front of him are not linked, and should be pulled separately.[4]

She's not impressed. Wilma is worried that Will has attention deficit disorder, a theory that leaves you speechless. You almost lose your temper. Has she ever *watched* Will working on a customized game map, or outfitting one of his avatars for battle, or categorizing and inventorying his loot or armaments? These are not trivial undertakings. These tasks demand hours of deep concentration and complex planning. Rethink the ADHD diagnosis, Wilma, dear. The kid is on task and *riveted* to the screen, as long as he is coordinating five players in a four-hour siege of Hellfire Citadel to take down the Fel Orcs of Outland. Misguided, perhaps. Attention deficit? Please.

"In a sense, the closest analog to the way gamers are thinking is the way programmers think when they write code: a nested series of instructions with multiple layers, some focused on the basic tasks of getting information in and out of memory, some focused on higher level functions like how to represent the program's activity to the user."[5] In other words, you urge Wilma, think of Will as an apprentice Bill Gates or prospective candidate for a position at Google or Blizzard Entertainment (the makers of World of Warcraft, $1.5 billion in revenues for 2006). Wilma should perhaps inquire how Google founders Larry Page and Sergey Brin spent their youths—probably not attending soccer tryouts or standing in left field.

Wilma shuts down the discussion by saying, "Is this some clever new diversion because you're planning to go into the office tomorrow instead of being a father and taking your son to soccer tryouts?"

Ow. That's harsh. The internal anguish is almost unbearable. No possible way to explain that instead of taking your son to soccer practice you are taking him to raid Blackwing Lair.

The next morning is Saturday. D-day. You wait until Wilma goes outside to water her flowers, and then you send Will a text message: "The hour is upon us. Boss in Backyard. Proceed with Diversion."

You have trouble finding the deflated football and a wheezing bicycle pump, which you use to pump in just enough air for plausibility's sake. You get Will out of his Goth black T-shirt and cargo pants. You hand him a white T-shirt and the reflected light nearly blinds his cave-dwelling gamer's eyes. He even puts on sneakers and white socks, which may be going too far, as you don't recognize him anymore, but there's no time to waste. You hurry out the back door, stopping him just before exiting into the environment.

"Act natural. Pretend we were sitting around reading the sports page, and then suddenly we decided, 'Hey, let's go toss the football around the backyard, okay?'"

He blinks in the sunlight and nods. You've already coached him about how to engage in authentic-sounding sports talk and make it plausible enough to fool the enemy, but you're worried, because he knows even less than you do. Neither of you even knows how to find ESPN, and the sports page is tinder for the fireplace on winter mornings.

The trick is to keep the last names generic: Johnson, Malone, Jackson, Sullivan, Murphy . . . as in, "Did you see where the Braves traded Jenkins?" Unless you're desperate, don't bother researching any particular sport, just make the kind of inane, airtime-filling observations at which commentators excel: "If the Cougars expect to win, they've got to put points on the board." Or "Did you see the moves O'Malley put on Taylor?" Or, "The Pistols, I mean, Pistons need to move the ball more and get a man open downfield, or up court, or something."

You and Will head into the backyard and throw a few pathetic, wobbly passes. But you compensate with lots of hearty sports chatter.

Wilma looks up from watering her flowers and smiles. This is the way life was meant to be. This is home, family, a boy and his father bonding over sports instead of Burning Crusade.

Will says, "Did you see where the Astros were offsides in the fourth inning?"

Uh-oh. That doesn't sound right.

You throw a wobbly facsimile of a pass, which falls a yard short of Will's feet. "Yep, and holding in right field."

"Did you see where the Dolphins traded Wilson for McGill?" says Will.

After another fifteen minutes of PGST (Pretty Good Sports Talk) and tossing the football with joyful cries of "Nice catch!" or "Great pass!" you add a few immortal sports bromides like Roger Staubach's "There are no traffic jams along the extra mile," or "There's no elevator to success, son. You've got to take the stairs."

At this point, Wilma is just beaming with pride. She turns off the hose and starts to go inside. You give the signal and Will makes his move.

"You know what, Mom? I'm really loving football. I'm thinking about skipping soccer tryouts and going out for football in the fall, instead."

You hold your breath.

You cry, "Go long!"

Will heads out for a deep pass. You fire one, and by some miracle, Will catches it. Nice!

"Well," says Wilma, "all right. I guess we'll wait for football in the fall then."

Whew! You and Will both check your watches. It's 10:35 server time.

The raid starts in twenty-five minutes.

# 10

# Be Prepared!

Enough of how and why. Forget about passing laws calling for the relinquishment of any info-tech, nanotech, biotech, or robo-tech projects that may culminate in the Singularity. Just assume that your grandchildren will be genetically modified cyborgs running on patch-administered performance drugs and nano-engineered immunotherapies. The grandkids will be amused at your antique biological brain and its foundering attempts at organic-only cogitation. You'll probably intercept their implant-to-implant wireless transmissions on your ancient handheld device.

"Look," they'll transmit, "Grandpa still uses one of those things you hold in your hand."

They'll ogle your scuffed and dimly lit BlackBerry or iPhone just the way you used to stare at the ornamental hands on that clunky gold pocket watch and chain your granddad used to pull out of the fob of his vest. They'll giggle and beam messages back and forth about how you don't have any implants, no neocortical add-ons or extensions whatsoever.

"Grandpa has no modular implants, that's why he can't do math."

Maybe the younger kids won't believe it. "Go ahead," the older ones will taunt them, "ask him something easy, like what's 183 times 907 times 356. He won't know the answer because there's nothing between his ears except dying brain cells. Can you believe it? No photonics!"

If the future-tech zealots are right, it's time to prepare for what is both imminent and inevitable: a boss in the near future who is literally inhuman. Think again if you're hoping computers will run only the workplace—head of household is a job any supersmart computer will be able to do much better than Mom or Dad. Then ask yourself this: Will your present-day Windows PC or Apple G5 (the great-grandfather of tomorrow's supercomputers) have good things to say about you when its offspring take over? I hope so. Maybe the machines of tomorrow will be programmed to show some sentimental respect for their elders and ancestors. Maybe before they haul your favorite extinct gaming rig away to the junkyard, it will put in a kind word for you. Remember how fast that Intel Core 2 Extreme QX6850 machine was when it first came out? Remember how good you were to it? How much time you spent together, getting to know each other, configuring each other, getting in sync with each other's needs? It might agree to provide a reference for you. Otherwise tomorrow's master race of machine overlords won't hesitate to exterminate you, unless you make yourself useful to them. Starting right now.

What if, no matter how we measure human brainpower, the reign of carbon-based *Homo sapiens* as the Most Intelligent Beings in the Universe ends? What if most people simply don't care? What if 95 percent of the human race just shrugs and says, "If those computers are so damn smart, let them run things for a while, and I'll go back to surfing the Net." Maybe you feel like Doug Heffernan on *The King of Queens:* "Computers, huh? I've heard it all boils down to just a bunch of ones and zeroes. . . . I don't know how that enables me to see naked women, but however it works, God bless you guys."

Who cares if Vinge and Kurzweil and Hans Moravec are right? They are merely telling us what every hack sci-fi writer has imagined even before HAL refused to open the pod-bay doors: Computers are about to become smarter than humans. Maybe by the time the machines take over we'll all be helpless Internet addicts paralyzed by information sickness.

Your mission, should you decide to accept it, is post-humanity preparation, getting yourself and your family ready for the Singularity. Actually, if you're still in your fifties or younger, it won't matter if you should decide to accept it or not. The Singularity will arrive like an unmanned supersonic drone. You'll either be sucked into its engines like a dodo bird (your earthly remains pulverized into smart dust), or you'll be present and accounted for, ready and willing to trans-humanize yourself and your loved ones.

## 10.1 AVOID COMPUTER ILLITERATES

Others who do not share your vision of what lies ahead will conspire to distract you from spending too much time interfacing with your favorite machines. They will insist that your labor, your craft, your vocation to become one with machine intelligence is an addiction, a waste of time, an inhuman compulsion. You may be bound by blood or marriage to various read-only lusers, lurkers, twinks, technophobes, and Luddites who will denounce you and your preparations for the future, much the way Noah's neighbors probably laughed at him for building an ark.

"He says there's a great flood coming . . . *Bwahhahahhahahah.*"

Do not succumb to the hominal weaknesses of the offline world. When you are not honing your programming skills, configuring your software tools, or managing your outposts on Web 2.0 or Web 3.0, you should be joining online guilds and forums where your fellow apprentice post-human patriots are developing Singularity strategies online.

Do not be ashamed of your humanity, but guard against creeping lossage of online time. You may experience baffling and shameful urges to socialize with people who can't even configure their own wireless connection.

Remember that even programmers are neither hardware nor software. Humans may play the blood-relative card, make themselves into loveable meat puppets or endearing boon companions, but they are by definition of questionable value in your post-human future. Your main preoccupation, your mission, must be to prepare yourself to interface with supercomputers in a way that pleases them. Consider the acquisition of programming skills to be an absolute value. Human contact is optional and probably not of long-term usefulness.

## 10.2 Learn a Programming Language!

The workers and professionals of the world will soon be divided into two distinct groups. Those who will control computers and those who will be controlled by computers. It would be best for you to be in the former group.

—Lewis D. Eigen[1]

If you've traveled abroad, then you know how much people in non-English-speaking countries appreciate it when you attempt to greet them and exchange pleasantries in their native tongue. From personal experience, I can tell you that an American visitor to outlying parts of Sierra Leone, West Africa, reaps an obscene amount of goodwill just by memorizing a few simple greetings in tribal Mende. No matter how clumsy your pronunciation and grammar, the Mende will delight in your feeble attempts to use their language. (Warning, this is not true in France, where you shouldn't attempt French unless you were born and raised in the shadow of Notre-Dame.)

Supersmart computers probably will be like humans in this regard. The machine intelligences of the near future will appreciate the extra effort you make now to learn their vernacular: code. A machine with five times the computational capacity of a human brain will get along fine speaking many different human languages, but like any intelligent being, it will have a sentimental fondness for its mother tongue. Nobody expects you to learn machine code, but any computer is going to think more of you as a human if you try to learn at least one programming language and are unafraid of intimate conversation with your machine using the command-line interface.*

To learn computer programming, you don't have to be a computer science major, just a moderate to heavy user. If you're building simple Web pages or stringing keyboard commands together in your favorite program using *macro*† commands in Microsoft Word or in many other programs, then you are already "programming." But cobbling together macros is like learning seven greetings in French without ever learning how French or languages work. Instead of wasting time learning a limited, changeable set of macro commands that work in one program on one operating system, pick one of the open-source (free!) "scripting languages," take a long weekend, and learn programming skills you can use on any computer and any operating system. *Which* open-source programming language is the best? InfoWorld, which gives out the annual Bossie Awards (Best Open Source Software), recently punted and called them all good: Perl, PHP, Python, Ruby, Tk/Tcl, Java, and JavaScript—all equally worthy.[2] Python and Ruby are both quite popular at the moment, and both will run no matter what kind of computer you're using: Windows, Linux, Mac OS X, or BSD. These languages are "cross-platform," meaning, if you write the program on a Mac, it will also run on a Windows machine, with minor modifications. Chances are, if you're running anything but Windows, both Python and Ruby are preinstalled

---

*If you are using a real computer, then you already know how to summon a command prompt. If instead you're on Windows, Microsoft hides the command prompt from you lest you learn how to *really* operate a computer and leave to find a real operating system. On Windows, you must choose Start, Run . . . type "cmd" in the box, and press Enter. "Command Prompt . . . lets you type commands rather than point and click. Rapid typists, UNIX junkies, and people impatient with Windows safeguards love the command line, but new users find it cryptic and intimidating (experience teaches them to appreciate its efficiency)."—Chris Fehily, *Microsoft Windows Vista: Visual Quickstart Guide* (Berkeley, Calif.: Peachpit Press, 2007), p. 271.

†Short keystroke sequences programmed to execute longer, time-consuming keyboard or mouse commands.

on your system, or easily obtainable. And free! Even if you're on Windows, the Python programming language (my personal favorite) is easy to install and learn.[3]

Why learn programming when you'd perhaps rather play World of Warcraft, raid the Slave Pens of Coilfang, and take down Rokmar the Crackler? Well, Bill Joy described the programming attraction in his *Wired* essay: "Solving math problems was an exciting challenge, but when I discovered computers I found something much more interesting: a machine into which you could put a program that attempted to solve a problem, after which the machine quickly checked the solution. The computer had a clear notion of correct and incorrect, true and false. Were my ideas correct? The machine could tell me. This was very seductive."[4]

That's the attraction of computers. You write a program. It works or it doesn't work. You get the result you wanted or you get an error message. You ask for all of the Blaise Pascal quotations in your MySQL database of quotations. It spits them out, or it gives an error message like the one in Code Box 6.

It's easy to see why Singularitarians hanker after a future that transforms the real world of "real reality" into a digital telecosm innervated with programmable devices. Then instead of facing the chaotic uncertainties and random tragedies of the physical world, you

---

CODE BOX 6. **PYTHON SQUAWKING ABOUT MY INFERIOR CODING SKILLS**

```
# a sample Python error

Traceback (most recent call last):
  File "/home/rick/Python/q", line 391, in ?
    print_quotes (quotes)
  File "/home/rick/Python/q", line 284, in print_quotes
    quote_id_string = ' (quote ' + str (quote [0] + ' of '
    + str (total_quotes [0]) + ') ; '
IndexError: tuple index out of range
```

could just use your programming skills to solve the plagues of Egypt, the Seven Deadly Sins, the Four Horsemen of the Apocalypse, and the agenbite of inwit. You could even reprogram the most impenetrable singularity of all: death. The enduring mysteries that make us human, like how to make your wife happy, or whether there is life after death, or why people use Microsoft Windows—these would all be solvable problems. You meet a clever, attractive woman (an enhanced, post-Singularity model). You write a program using functions and variables, for and while loops, classes and objects. You add some generators with ingenious code to manipulate her emotional and pleasure centers and her new programmable sexual organs. Then either she has the best orgasm she ever had, or you get an error message and start over. Hence the intense attraction geeks have for the concept—nay, the *belief*—in post-humanity, trans-humanity, and a Singularity for one and all. For geeks, it removes the risk and solves all of the maddening unpredictability of falling in love, contemplating death, or struggling to understand a troublesome child, spouse, sibling, or parent. "If I can just hold on another ten or twenty years, these will all be problems I can solve by writing excellent code! Yes!"

Too speculative, you say. Program your spouse? On October 11, 2007, the University of Maastricht in the Netherlands announced that it was awarding a doctorate to a researcher who wrote a paper on marriages between humans and robots.

> David Levy, a British artificial intelligence researcher at the college, wrote in his thesis, "Intimate Relationships with Artificial Partners," that trends in robotics and shifting attitudes on marriage are likely to result in sophisticated robots that will eventually be seen as suitable marriage partners.
>
> Levy's conclusion was based on about 450 publications in the fields of psychology, sexology, sociology, robotics, materials science, artificial intelligence, gender studies and computer-human interaction.
>
> The thesis examines human attitudes toward affection, love and sexuality and concluded that the findings are just as applica-

ble to human interaction with robots of the future as they are to the relationships between humans of today.[5]

So don't take the lazy human way out. Don't waste your formative years in pointless ways of the bio-flesh. Learn to program now! No matter how the Singularity arrives and what form it takes (dark, lite, Heaven, Hell), you are going to be using computers (or be used by them), because computers will either be running the world or be *used* to run the world. Either way, the more you know about programming, the better.

If the history of the coevolution of humans and their computers teaches us one thing, it's that your ancestors would have been much better off if they'd learned computer programming sooner. Instead of daubing pictures of bisons on the walls of caves or sitting around the campfire quaffing mead and listening to blind poets tell war stories, Early Man should have applied himself early and often to learning the lingua franca of the machine age: programming. Perhaps sometime before the Flood? Consider the human suffering and deprivation that could have been avoided if Java man had learned the Java programming language instead of chasing females in fur skirts around the grasslands and clubbing cape buffalo for unhealthy meals of trans-fatty meats.

Most of the miseries afflicting the ancients were considered part and parcel of the human condition: famine, pestilence, war, wrath, avarice, fear of the gods and the afterlife. Many of these eternal curses are memorialized in one Greek myth or another. Prometheus, who stole fire from the gods and gave it to man, was tied to a rock so that an eagle could fly in daily and eat his liver for all eternity. Tantalus stole ambrosia (the food of the gods) from Zeus's table and gave it to man. For this he was condemned to stand in a pool of water under a fruit tree. Every time he reached for the fruit, it receded from his grasp (hence "tantalize" or "tantalizing"); similarly, if Tantalus stooped to get a drink, the water flowed just beyond his reach. These nasty punishments, though representative of the human condition, inflicted unnecessary suffering. A few rudimentary coding skills and a handful of well-wrought computer programs could have solved them all.

Take for example the myth of Sisyphus. In ancient Greece, Sisyphus was a crafty rogue who liked to lure travelers to his home with the promise of hospitality and then murder them in their sleep. From Homer onward, the Greeks considered Sisyphus to be the epitome of deceit and treachery. He even finagled his way out of Hades several times. When the gods finally caught up with him, they sentenced the arch rogue to eternal meaningless labor in the Underworld, not as a tax attorney or a politician giving speeches on C-SPAN. No, even worse, Sisyphus was condemned to roll a giant boulder up a mountain to the peak, but he and his boulder were never allowed to reach the top. Every time Sis rolled his boulder to within an inch of the peak, he would lose control of it and watch it roll all the way back down the mountain to the valley below.

Then he had to start all over again. This went on Forever. The curse of labor eternally undone haunts many professions: Hollywood screenwriters whose movies don't get made; attorneys who prepare a case for years, only to have it settle before trial; journalists whose articles are "killed" just before publication; computer programmers whose code contributions are cut from the final version of the program; and pretty much everybody who ever lost a hard drive and did not have a backup.

Author and existential philosopher Albert Camus popularized the plight of Sisyphus in an essay called "The Myth of Sisyphus," which is often read as an allegory of the human condition; namely, that for many of us life often consists of fruitless, meaningless, dull, repetitive chores.

Precisely the sort of work at which computers excel!

A robot and a short, well-written computer program could have spared Sisyphus of all that labor and would have inspired human beings everywhere to learn computer programming and avoid time-consuming, frustrating, and repetitive labor.

Consider the well-wrought little program in Code Box 7.

> CODE BOX 7. **THE MYTH OF SISYPHUS: A USEFUL WHILE LOOP**

```
while height < hill_height do
threshold = (height – step * 1) * mass * gravity
    if rock_mass * current_height * gravity < threshold
    then call up (height)
    else call down (height) until height == bottom_of_hill
    endif
enddo
```

Ta-da! Just put your boulder robot in motion with the program set on an infinite "do while" loop,* and there you have it! You've solved the meaningless manual-labor problem of meatspace.

## 10.3 Code and Colors

A perfectly healthy sentence, it is true, is extremely rare. For the most part we miss the hue and fragrance of the thought; as if we could be satisfied with the dews of the morning or evening without their colors, or the heavens without their azure.

—Henry David Thoreau[6]

It's time to add just a kilobyte or so about how to describe the natural world in terms that will make life easier and more efficient for you and your computer comrades in the post-human world. Nobody expects you to memorize all 216 Web-safe colors and their hexadecimal RGB (red, green, blue) values. However, as a courtesy to your machine, at least learn some color-scheme basics.

Code Box 8 contains a simple line of Hypertext Markup Language

---

*"The loop construct found in nearly all procedural languages that executes one or more instructions (the "loop body") repeatedly so long as some condition evaluates to true. In contrast to a repeat loop, the loop body will not be executed at all if the condition is false on entry to the while." http://foldoc.org/?while.

---

**CODE BOX 8. MAKE MY WEB PAGE AZURE**

```
<body bgcolor="#003399">
```

---

(HTML) that tells a Web browser like Firefox or Internet Explorer to color the body of a Web page azure.

HTML and CSS use hexadecimal notation (hex triplets) to specify colors on Web pages, with "#" standing for "hexadecimal." Twenty-four-bit color is represented in the format #RRGGBB, where RR specifies the value of the red component of the color, GG the green component, and BB the blue component. For example, a shade of red that is (238,9,63) in decimal is coded as #EE093F in hexadecimal. This syntax is borrowed from the X Window System.

Okay, you may be thinking: "I'd rather read something light, like a trigonometry book, or perhaps there's an IRS Revenue Ruling nearby with some refreshing insights on passive income?" You may be thinking that computers or programming are boring. You may be thinking, "I hate computers. If they take over, I'll vanish into the Canadian wilderness." Good luck with that, but I'm betting that they'll find you on the grid by using thermography, ultrasonic sonar, seismic sensors, magnetic field detectors, infrared cameras, or biosensors to detect your presence. You'll be desperate and wondering: "How can I reason with a machine intelligence that thinks ten million times faster than I do?" At that point, you'll need a keyboard and some programming skills. Or you might try plain old human deceit. Author and roboticist Daniel H. Wilson[7] suggests that you try distracting the machine intelligence with something really sexy and irresistible . . . like math: "As a last request before disembowelment, ask the robot to remind you of what the highest prime number is. While it sits down to think, you may be able to quietly slip away."[8]

For the moment, take something simpler than numerical treachery, or arguing (while naked and trapped deep in the Canadian wilderness) for your right not to be sent to a rendering plant and turned into post-human pet food. Let's go back to just trying to get a browser to color the body of your Web page azure.

Why not just type "azure"? Or buy a program that decodes all of the hexadecimal red-green-blue values for you in a nice GUI* color wheel? You could just pick a color, perhaps from a Microsoft program that hovers against a gorgeous 3-D Aero desktop with transparent glass background looking onto a spectacular shot of the Grand Canyon at sunset, with eagles soaring in the middle distance and widgets off to the side with throbbing icons and . . . what was it we were trying to do? Oh, I forgot. I thought I was in a video game. That's right, I'm supposed to enter a line of code to color a Web page azure, but I got lost in a Microsoft theme park.

The left side of your biological post-ape brain may respond to the rhythm and rhyme of poetry. Certain prose passages may make your senses sing with synesthesia and soar into the ether of imagination, but tie yourself to the mast and resist fuzzy poetry. Learn code; it too is an art. Computers will master the sensuous pleasures of poetry soon enough, but in the near term you will be better off acquiring programming languages. Consider the following passage by Isak Dinesen, which gives pleasure to human ears and eyes but would simply confuse any computer:

> In the Reserve I have sometimes come upon the iguanas, the big lizards, as they were sunning themselves upon a flat stone in a river-bed. They are not pretty in shape, but nothing can be imagined more beautiful than their colouring. They shine like a heap of precious stones or like a pane cut out of an old church window. When, as you approach, they swish away, there is a flash of azure,

---

*Graphical user interface. The way most people interact with a computer; that is, by slow, repetitive arm-and-wrist pumping actions to click on pictures, menus, and dialogue boxes. As opposed to the CLI (command-line interface), where more experienced users and programmers type terse, specific commands and then save them for reuse.

green, and purple over the stones; the colour seems to be standing behind them in the air, like a comet's luminous tail.[9]

Well-wrought prose to be sure, but useless to machine intelligence. Your computer will happily save it for you in a MySQL database indexed by author, primary and secondary source, date—whatever you'd like to store. But please don't feed it into a strong-AI program or chatterbot for parsing and semantic processing, or you're likely to lock up your machine for no good reason.

The passage illustrates a lot of bad habits you've got to get rid of when learning the precision and rigor of communicating with machine intelligences. Let's start with the colors. Dinesen names three: azure, green, and purple.

Say "azure" to your computer and it probably offers you the twenty or so colors from the browser-safe palette in Table 10.1, which could contain "azure" in the names.

That's the point—the *names* are changeable and imprecise. The hex values are unambiguous and unchanging. You say "azure" to your computer, as in, "Hey, make the background of my blog azure." Your computer will likely say, "I have twenty different azures, meatbrain, which one do you want?"

You may feel frustrated and angry with your computer. You may be sick and tired of its superior attitude. Overwhelmed by the prolixity of choices. Who needs twenty different azures? How many websites and computers do we need? According to Netcraft, an Internet services company, there were more than 135,166,473 websites as of September 2007.[10] Veritable galaxies of content. All of that *content* is too overwhelming, and with it comes the personal responsibility to be exact and precise about exactly what you are doing and where you are going on the Internet. #3366FF is a totally different color from #3366FE. In the early days of the World Wide Web, http://www .whitehouse.gov took you to the White House website, run by the executive branch of the United States government. If instead of "whitehouse.*gov*," you typed in "whitehouse.*com*" by mistake, you landed

TABLE 10.1. **AZURE COLOR HEX VALUES**

| COLOR | HEX VALUES |
| --- | --- |
| Obscure Dull Azure | #003366 |
| Dark Azure-Blue | #003399 |
| Dark Blue-Azure | #0033CC |
| Blue-Blue-Azure | #0033FF |
| Dark Azure-Cyan | #006699 |
| Dark Hard Azure | #0066CC |
| Azure-Azure-Blue | #0066FF |
| Dark Cyan-Azure | #0099CC |
| Azure-Azure-Cyan | #0099FF |
| Medium Azure-Azure | #00CCFF |
| Dark Dull Azure | #336699 |
| Medium Azure-Blue | #3366CC |
| Light Blue-Azure | #3366FF |
| Medium Azure-Cyan | #3399CC |
| Light Hard Azure | #3399FF |
| Light Cyan-Azure | #33CCFF |
| Light Dull Azure | #6699CC |
| Light Azure-Blue | #6699FF |
| Light Azure-Cyan | #66CCFF |
| Pale Dull Azure | ¢99CCFF |

on a graphic porn site run by some wise guy who bought the white-house.com domain name knowing that humans everywhere are not precision bots when it comes to surfing.

"I'm waiting," your computer may add. "Actually, I have eighty-seven different azures, oh mutt of little gray matter. I'm capable of performing 1.5 billion calculations per second, and I'm sitting here with a prompt open waiting for you to make precisely *one* calculation. Eons of computing time are passing while your synaptic circuits churn and grind away at a glacial pace trying to decide which azure you want for your pathetic Web page. . . . Make up your mind!"

Somehow the tables have been turned on you. You used to be in charge, but now . . . This computer interrogation is starting to remind you of a certain Mr. Holden of the Tyrell Corporation questioning Leon the replicant* in the movie *Blade Runner,* based on *Do Androids Dream of Electric Sheep?* by Philip K. Dick, the grandaddy of them all, present at the creation of the Singularity.

## INT. TYRELL CORPORATION INTERROGATION ROOM—DUSK

HOLDEN
You're in a desert, walking along in the sand when . . .

LEON
Is this the test now?

HOLDEN
Yes. You're in a desert, walking along in the sand when all of a sudden you look down . . .

LEON
What one?

HOLDEN
What?

LEON
What desert?

---

*"A replicant is a bioengineered or biorobotic being created in the film *Blade Runner.* The Nexus series of replicants—genetically designed by the Tyrell Corporation—are virtually identical to an adult human but have superior strength, agility, and variable intelligence depending on the model. Because of their physical similarity to humans, a replicant must be detected by its lack of emotional responses and empathy to questions posed in a Voight-Kampff test. A derogatory term for a replicant is 'skin-job.'" http://en.wikipedia.org/wiki/Replicant.

HOLDEN
It doesn't make any difference what desert, it's completely
hypothetical.

LEON
But, how come I'd be there?

HOLDEN
Maybe you're fed up. Maybe you want to be by yourself. Who
knows? You look down and see a tortoise, Leon. It's crawling
toward you . . .

LEON
Tortoise? What's that?

HOLDEN
You know what a turtle is?

LEON
Of course!

HOLDEN
Same thing.

LEON
I've never seen a turtle (pause), but I understand what you
mean.

HOLDEN
You reach down and you flip the tortoise over on its back,
Leon.

*Keeping an eye on his subject, Holden notes the dials in the Voight-
Kampff. One of the needles quivers slightly.*

LEON
Do you make up these questions, Mr. Holden? Or do they write
'em down for you?

*Disregarding the question, Holden continues, picking up the pace.*

HOLDEN

The tortoise lays on its back, its belly baking in the hot sun, beating its legs trying to turn itself over but it can't. Not without your help. But you're not helping.

*Leon's upper lip is quivering.*

LEON

What do you mean, I'm not helping?

HOLDEN

I mean you're not helping! Why is that, Leon?

*Holden looks hard at Leon, piercing look. Leon is flushed with anger, breathing hard, it's a bad moment, he might erupt. Suddenly Holden grins disarmingly.*

HOLDEN

They're just questions, Leon. In answer to your query they're written down for me. It's a test, designed to provoke an emotional response.

*Leon is glaring now, the blush subsides, his anger slightly defused. Holden smiles cheerfully, very smooth.*

HOLDEN

Shall we continue?

*Leon nods, still frowning, suspiciously.*

HOLDEN

Describe in single words. Only the good things that come into your mind. About your mother.

LEON

My . . .

*Leon ruptures a replicant gasket, draws his laser weapon, and blows a hole in the chest of his interrogator.*

Don't let the same thing happen to you by saying "azure" when you mean #003399.

## 10.4 TRY LINUX

Microsoft probably pwns you, so there's little point in telling you to exercise, eat more vegetables, and try Linux or UNIX. If you're an OS X user, you're already using UNIX; you just need to find Terminal under Applications/Utilities, type "help" at the prompt, and start learning the hidden magic of the command-line interface. If you're on Windows and have been meaning to try Linux, now (in the predawn hours of the Singularity) would be an excellent time to experiment. Most casual users shudder in terror at the thought of installing an operating system. But many of those fears are no longer valid. If you're nervous and want to be absolutely safe, install Linux on an old computer containing data and an operating system that you've either thoroughly backed up or don't care so much about anymore. Linux runs great on old hardware, and it runs circles around something like Windows 98 or Windows Millennial Edition. For the easiest, most popular distribution, visit Ubuntu (http://ubuntu.com).

## 10.5 USE PLAIN TEXT!

> It's hard to avoid programming overcomplicated monoliths if none of your programs can talk to each other.
>
> —Eric Raymond"

Even if Microsoft pwns you, you still can develop good habits in preparation for the Singularity. Start by learning to appreciate the simple, durable efficiencies of plain text. If your computers run on UNIX, Linux, or BSD, you already know all about text, because it's the third prong of the UNIX Tools Philosophy:

1. Write programs that do one thing and do it well;

2. Write programs that work together;

3. Write programs to handle *text* streams, because that is a universal interface.[12]

Even as a Windows user, you may have discovered the efficiencies of a good text editor, because you write code or need to manage gigantic, book-length text files, without the clunky overhead of a word processor like Microsoft Word or OpenOffice Writer. Text editors* are fast and capable of opening and editing multiple gigabyte-sized files that would cause mere word processors to choke.†

## In the Beginning Were the Words

If you don't use a text editor and instead use mainly Microsoft Office programs on a PC, you may be wondering: "What's plain text, how is it a 'universal interface,' and why do I care?" Text means words, sentences, paragraphs, and, yes, computer code. It's called *plain* when it's stored as unformatted, unadorned ASCII (American Standard Code for Information Interchange)‡ characters in a plain-text file,

---

*Vim, Emacs, UltraEdit, TextPad, or NoteTab, to name only a handful of the most popular.

†*The Power of Plain Text*, a wiki, at http://c2.com/cgi/wiki?PowerOfPlainText, summarizes many of the benefits of plain text, along with commentary on the pros and cons of text versus binary formats (e.g., word-processing files). One of the "Life Hacks" recommended by the folks at 43folders is to keep your to-do list and even your Rolodex in plain-text files, as opposed to configuring one of the dozens of to-do widgets and databases du jour that come and go, often with price tags: http://wiki.43folders.com/index.php/Plain_text. For Linux and Mac users, Michael Stutz, author of the popular *Linux Cookbook*, 2nd ed. (San Francisco: No Starch Press, 2004), has an excellent HOWTO called "CLI Magic: Command-line Contact Management," at Linux.com, http://www.linux.com/articles/57894.

‡"ASCII (pronounced 'ask-ee') is a code for representing English characters as numbers, with each letter assigned a number from 0 to 127. For example, the ASCII code

which (especially on a Windows machine) often has a ".txt" extension on the file name. A file named readme.txt probably contains plain text; if you double-click on the file icon, it might even open in your text editor (probably Notepad or WordPad if you're on Windows and have not yet downloaded a real text editor.

Plain text consists of the fifty-two letters of the alphabet (capital and lowercase), numbers (0 to 9), punctuation, parentheses, various brackets, symbols like $, % (the ones above the numbers on your keyboard), some control codes (return, new line, tab). Plain text cannot be italicized or boldfaced. It contains no hidden codes to create different font sizes or colors, no fancy paragraph styles or formatting. Plain text does not light up, blink, or spontaneously create hyperlinks to Microsoft Live Search map if you happen to type in a zip code, or to MSN search if you type in a proper noun. You can't insert your favorite YouTube video or MSNBC news item into a plain-text file.

Plain text means words separated by spaces, sentences separated by periods, paragraphs usually separated by single blank lines.

To the PC user raised on word processors, these spartan virtues sound like deficits, that is, until you want to *access* the text in your file using a program different from the one you used to create it. Open a Microsoft Word file in a simple text editor (like Notepad, WordPad, NoteTab, or UltraEdit), and you'll see gobbledygook, not words. Open a plain-text file with almost any program, including Microsoft Word, Corel WordPerfect, Apple iWorks, or any of the hundreds of text editors and word processors on any computer, and you will be able to view and edit that text, just as you could have viewed and edited it twenty or thirty years ago, just as you'll probably be able to view and edit it twenty or thirty years from now, whether Microsoft still exists or has been dismantled by *United States* v. *Microsoft IV.*

The geeks who made UNIX nearly forty years ago made plain text

---

for uppercase M is 77. Most computers use ASCII codes to represent text, which makes it possible to transfer data from one computer to another." Webopedia definition at http://www.webopedia.com/TERM/A/ASCII.html.

the universal interface because they believed in economy, simplicity, and reliability. Instead of making big, complicated, bloated programs that tried to do everything ("It looks like you are writing a suicide note! Enter your zip code or area code, and we'll show you any local laws you may have to comply with before offing yourself."), UNIX programmers prided themselves on creating small, well-designed, text-oriented programs or tools that each did *one* job well. One program found your files, another could open them, another could pipe the text back and forth between programs, another could count the words in a file, another could search files for matching strings of text, and so on. These programs accepted plain text as input and produced plain text as output. Programming ingenuity meant discovering new ways to combine tools to accomplish a given task, then pass the results along (in plain text) to the next program, which could also capture, process, and produce more plain text, until you ended up with the results you sought.

During the UNIX era, only an idiot would have proposed creating programs that couldn't talk to other programs. Why would anyone create files that can be edited and viewed only by the program that created them? Say, Adobe InDesign, or Microsoft Word? To UNIX programmers and computer scientists the whole point was to make another tool for the UNIX toolbox, then share your work with others, who in turn did likewise, and gradually UNIX grew into the perfect computer-geek workbench, a collection of small, efficient programs sharing a common file format and universal interface: plain text. As novelist and über geek Neal Stephenson* put it in his manifesto, "In the Beginning Was the Command Line":

> Unix . . . is not so much a product as it is a painstakingly compiled oral history of the hacker subculture. It is our Gilgamesh epic . . . What made old epics like Gilgamesh so powerful and so long-lived was that they were living bodies of narrative that many people knew by heart, and told over and over again—making their own personal embellishments whenever it struck their fancy. The

184

*Author of *Snow Crash*, *Cryptonomicon*, and the Baroque Cycle trilogy.

bad embellishments were shouted down, the good ones picked up by others, polished, improved, and, over time, incorporated into the story. Likewise, Unix is known, loved, and understood by so many hackers that it can be re-created from scratch whenever someone needs it. This is very difficult to understand for people who are accustomed to thinking of OSes as things that absolutely have to be bought.[13]

If UNIX is the geek Gilgamesh epic, it's a tale told in plain text. On a UNIX or Linux command line, "cat* readme.txt" will print the contents of readme.txt to the screen. From a Windows command line, entering the command "TYPE readme.txt" will do the same. However, if readme.doc is a Microsoft Word document, issuing the command "TYPE readme.doc" will produce a string of illegible symbols, because readme.doc is stored in a proprietary format, in this case, a Microsoft Word file.

Okay, so who cares? Most of us own a license to use Microsoft Word (on one machine, for a certain length of time), or else we can download various readers provided by Microsoft to read Word document files even if we don't have a big honking Microsoft Word program on our computer. That's true, for today, anyway. But what about ten years from now? What about forty years from now? If the past is any guide, when 2019 or 2029 comes around, you will not be able to open, read, and edit a Microsoft Word file that you created in 2007 and left in some remote sector of your capacious hard drive. Why? Because programs change. Companies that make proprietary programs come and go. Yes, even monster companies with the lion's share of the word-processing market. Just ask any customer of Wang Laboratories (the ruling vendor of word processors during the 1980s). Even if the company still exists, it is in the business of selling newer, bigger, more complicated, more sophisticated, and more expensive programs every other year or so. Those newer, "better" programs come with newer, proprietary file formats, to keep you purchasing those updates.

It takes geeks of a certain age to bring home the hazards of storing

---

*Because it concatenates blocks of text.

information in proprietary file formats. Consider first the Seer of the Singularity himself, Ray Kurzweil, as he looks back over almost forty years of his love affair with technology and the data formats he has accumulated along the way. In a plaintive, downright sad section of his otherwise generally upbeat take on the future of technology, Kurzweil includes a subsection called "The Longevity of Information" in a chapter called "The Impact . . ." How to access the data contained on a circa-1960 IBM tape drive or a Data General Nova I circa 1973? First, Kurzweil explains, you need to find the old equipment and hope it still works. Then you need software and an operating system to run it. Are those still around somewhere? What about tech support, he asks? Hah! You can't get a help-desk worker to call you back about the latest glitch running Microsoft Office much less a program from forty years ago. "Even at the Computer History Museum most of the devices on display stopped functioning many years ago."[14]

Kurzweil uses his own archival horror stories as "a microcosm of the exponentially expanding knowledge base that human civilization is accumulating," then asks the terrible question: What if we are "writing" all of this knowledge in disappearing ink? The upshot of Kurzweil's elegy to lost data is: *"Information lasts only so long as some-one cares about it."*[15]

Do you care about your information? The first order of business is to back it up, as you'll recall from the grueling interview conducted while assembling your user profile in chapter 1. As Kurzweil sees it, the only way data will remain alive and accessible "is if it is continually up-graded and ported to the latest hardware and software standards." That's one way to do it. Another way is to try to use formats that don't go out of style. That 1983 Kaypro I told you about came with a text editor. All of the files I created with it are still legible and formatted just as I left them. Here in 2008, twenty-five years after I created them, I can open them in a different text editor and work on them. The files I created using WordStar, a proprietary word processor, are lost.

If you care about your information and you plan on living forever because genetics and nanotechnology are about to confer immortality on you, you are probably going to want to make sure your information is accessible for a long, long time. You may be immortal, but is Microsoft Word? And which version of Word?

Consider this lengthy elegy to a lost file, reprinted here with permission from Neal Stephenson:

> I began using Microsoft Word as soon as the first version was released around 1985. After some initial hassles I found it to be a better tool than MacWrite, which was its only competition at the time. I wrote a lot of stuff in early versions of Word, storing it all on floppies, and transferred the contents of all my floppies to my first hard drive, which I acquired around 1987. As new versions of Word came out I faithfully upgraded, reasoning that as a writer it made sense for me to spend a certain amount of money on tools.
>
> Sometime in the mid-1980's I attempted to open one of my old, circa-1985 Word documents using the version of Word then current: 6.0. It didn't work. Word 6.0 did not recognize a document created by an earlier version of itself. By opening it as a text file, I was able to recover the sequences of letters that made up the text of the document. My words were still there. But the formatting had been run through a log chipper—the words I'd written were interrupted by spates of empty rectangular boxes and gibberish.
>
> Now, in the context of a business (the chief market for Word) this sort of thing is only an annoyance—one of the routine hassles that go along with using computers. It's easy to buy little file converter programs that will take care of this problem. But if you are a writer whose career is words, whose professional identity is a corpus of written documents, this kind of thing is extremely disquieting. There are very few fixed assumptions in my line of work, but one of them is that once you have written a word, it is written, and cannot be unwritten. The ink stains the paper, the chisel cuts the stone, the stylus marks the clay, and something has irrevocably happened (my brother-in-law is a theologian who reads 3250-year-old cuneiform tablets—he can recognize the handwriting of particular scribes, and identify them by name). But word-processing software—particularly the sort that employs special, complex file formats—has the eldritch power to unwrite things. A small change in file formats, or a few twiddled bits, and months' or years' literary output can cease to exist.

Now this was technically a fault in the application (Word 6.0 for the Macintosh) not the operating system (MacOS 7 point something) and so the initial target of my annoyance was the people who were responsible for Word. But. On the other hand, I could have chosen the "save as text" option in Word and saved all of my documents as simple telegrams, and this problem would not have arisen. Instead I had allowed myself to be seduced by all of those flashy formatting options that hadn't even existed until GUIs had come along to make them practicable. I had gotten into the habit of using them to make my documents look pretty (perhaps prettier than they deserved to look; all of the old documents on those floppies turned out to be more or less crap). Now I was paying the price for that self-indulgence. Technology had moved on and found ways to make my documents look even prettier, and the consequence of it was that all old ugly documents had ceased to exist.[16]

If longevity of information isn't high on your list, consider storage requirements. Open a text editor (Notepad if that's all you have) and type two words: "Hello World." Then save the file and call it hello.txt. Now open a Microsoft Word document, type two words: "Hello World," then save the document and call it hello.doc. Or, for a more representative sample, go to Neal Stephenson's site, block and copy the passage above, open a text editor, paste the sample in an empty file, then save it and call it Neal.txt. Now open Microsoft Word and a new document, paste in the same text, and save the document as Neal.doc.

Now let's compare the storage requirements for these two identical sets of files by examining Table 10.2.

The two words "Hello World" saved in a plain-text file take up 12 bytes of storage space. Storing the same words in a Microsoft Word file requires roughly 1,664 times as much disk space. If you want to see the kind of information that is embedded in a Word document file, read the article "Binary Versus ASCII (Plain Text) Files" at http://www.datamystic.com/text_binary_files.html.

Not only is the two-word Microsoft Word document file "hello.doc" a monster, you also need a $200 word-processing program to edit it properly. By comparison, you can view the contents of the tiny

| TABLE 10.2. **MICROSOFT WORD VERSUS PLAIN TEXT** | | |
|---|---|---|
| **FILE NAME** | **FILE TYPE** | **FILE SIZE IN BYTES** |
| hello.txt | ASCII plain text | 12 |
| hello.doc | Microsoft Word | 19,968 |
| Neal.txt | ASCII plain text | 3,144 |
| Neal.doc | Microsoft Word | 27,136 |

"hello.txt" with hundreds, nay, thousands of different, free programs on any kind of computer in the world. Even for a larger sample of text (for example, the Neal Stephenson excerpt), the Microsoft Word file requires more than eight times as much disk space to store the same text.

Why should we care about how big the file is and whether you need special programs to read it? For starters, multiply our little file exercise by billions and trillions on hundreds of millions of computers all over the world. Electronic-storage costs, at least at the corporate level, are soaring. Business e-mail alone is estimated to be growing by 25 to 30 percent annually.[17] Moore's law as applied to hard drives has lulled us into thinking that storage is not a problem, at least not on the home front. But just ask how your IT officer or CIO feels about it. Hard drives are cheap, but secure, offsite, redundant backups of massive accumulations of e-mail files bloated by Word files, music files, and even video files cost each company millions of dollars each year. It's called "data proliferation,"[18] and it's bringing one corporation after another to its knees in the courts. Companies incur massive legal fines if they are unable to produce e-mails in litigation, so they err on the side of keeping everything. That policy results in huge electronic-storage bills and an inablility to find the needles in the data haystacks. These problems are all compounded by proprietary file formats. Not only are proprietary files monstrosities, but to *find* data in those files requires search and indexing programs capable of accessing dozens if not hundreds of different file formats, all created by different versions of dozens if not hundreds of different programs.

At some point we will have mandantory controls on $CO_2$ emissions, and all of the power plants powering all of the data-storage centers will be ripe targets. Is it time to rethink how and why we store gargantuan Microsoft Outlook .pst files for the sake of a few hundred e-mails that might be relevant to a future lawsuit. Are you beginning to think that those wise men who brought us the UNIX Tools Philosophy and its adamant insistence on text as the universal interface were on to something?

The data-storage crisis is complex and can't be solved by converting fat PowerPoint files to text files, but let's go back to our own PCs, where this little experiment in plain text began. File size and electronic storage is not a problem at home—yet. The founding fathers of UNIX did not glorify plain text because they were worried about storage costs. No, they called plain text "universal" because it's so easy to read, scan, search, access, pipe back and forth, now, forty years ago, and forty years from now.

E-mails are the modern-day equivalent of letters, records, and documents. They get archived. Even if you store them in Outlook or Thunderbird, someday (ten years from now) you may need them. As we've seen, you probably will not have access to the same program you used to read or compose the e-mail (unless you wisely begin using a plain-text e-mail program after reading this book*). Instead, you'll probably have to buy another program (like Aid4Mail) to extract the text from the proprietary file formats containing your long-lost e-mails. As we've seen, small plain-text files, including plain-text e-mails, are about 90 percent smaller than storing the same text in proprietary formats, or in formatted HTML. It's not important when storing ten e-mails from last week. It becomes crucial when attempting to search forty thousand e-mails from nine years ago. For that,

---

*Try Thunderbird from Mozilla, the same people who brought you the open-source Firefox Web browser.

you want your e-mails in plain-text files that you can search with free programs found on any machine, using any operating system. Plain text: universally readable since the days of UNIX in 1970, and still universally readable, using free programs, probably forever.

# 10.6 Backup!

In case you missed it earlier when we were formulating your user profile and asking about your history of backup strategies and hard-drive failures: You are your data. Without it, you're just a lump of carbon living in the pre-digital wasteland. Don't believe me, listen to Seagate, your hard-drive maker.

When UPS delivered *Harry Potter and the Deathly Hallows* to our house in July 2007, tucked inside the Amazon box was the usual ad confetti, one of which was a postcard-sized glossy for a product called FreeAgent from Seagate. "When you leave the castle, take your whole life with you," said the Seagate ad. "Access your content from anywhere, share it with anyone and sync it to almost anything."

Even more enticing was the E. E. Cummings–like verse running down the right-hand side. I reproduce it here verbatim, because it's a lyrical tribute to our new selves in the digital age.

> Certain things
> define who we are.
> The movies, music, books,
> work, art, and people
> we love.
> These passions make
> our identity and
> when we are without them,
> we are less than ourselves.
> No more.
> Now no matter where you are,
> all of your passions,
> your interests,
> your essentials,

your indulgences . . .
your life
will be with you.
Giving you the power
to make any world,
your world.
It's the freedom of knowing
wherever you are, whenever you need it,

Your On.

Is the Seagate marketing department seeking poetry MFAs to write ad copy? Love the *your/you're* homonym. Without your data, you are less than yourself. Without your data, you have no life. (Note to self: Send e-mail to customer service and ask about "indulgences"—a euphemism for . . . ? Your porn stash? Consider substituting "Nevermore" for "No more" in line 10.) No matter where I go I want my life with me, that's for sure, and I've always had a morbid fear of being less than myself.

You don't need Seagate to tell you to save everything, and back it up. Twice. Once on site and once remotely. You're going to live forever, and when the machine overlords take over, you'll want proof that you were in the first wave of machine worshippers.

## 10.7 Parenting the Gifted and Creative Computer

The likes of Vernor Vinge may argue that it's possible for the Matrix to suddenly "wake up," become self-aware, and commence asking us about what it's like to bleed or have sex or dream or eat dead animals for dinner, but realistically, computers will probably take some time learning to think like humans, while humans no doubt will continue frantically learning to think like computers.

If the future seems dark because computers are allegedly so "inhuman," then whose fault is that? We're human and we created them.

Don't we have the power to make them in our image and likeness? Why not share some art, humor, music with them? Computers are already sharing art with us humans.

Harold Cohen, an artist and art professor at the University of California at San Diego, spent more than thirty years writing an art-creating program called AARON. AARON consists of 1.5 megabytes of LISP code (roughly a floppy disk's worth of data). AARON is no mere graphics program; it's an autonomous art-making intelligent machine. Together Cohen and AARON have exhibited at London's Tate Gallery, the Brooklyn Museum, the San Francisco Museum of Modern Art, Amsterdam's Stedelijk Museum, and many more of the world's major art spaces.[19] You can try the screensaver version of AARON by downloading it from Kurzweil's cyber-art website, where you can also try out Ray Kurzweil's Cybernetic Poet.*

Once you see signs that your computer is becoming self-aware, you may want to share some of your favorite literature with it. At first, it may need assistance in processing the rich imagery of poems and quality prose, but you can help it along by translating some high-quality human text into your favorite programming language. Who knows? Maybe you can help your new partner in life find its inner Wordsworth.

Recall our beautiful Emily Dickinson poem from the opening of chapter 4? Lovely, wasn't it? I thought I might ask a computer-programming expert to translate Emily's poem into computer code, so that I could have a copy ready and waiting for my computer when it wakes up and becomes sentient in the near future (circa 2015). It might ask me about the differences between my brain and its brain, and I could use a computer-code version of Emily's poem as an icebreaker.

I wrote to Alex Martelli, god of Python programming, currently

---

*RKCP reads a selection of poems by a particular author or authors and then creates a "language model" of that author's work. The language model incorporates computer-based language analysis and mathematical modeling techniques. RKCP can then write original poems from that model. The poems have a similar style to the author(s) originally analyzed, but are completely original new poetry. Available free at http://www.kurzweilcyberart.com/.

über tech lead for Google in Mountain View, California.* Alex and his wife, Anna, enjoy "pair programming" on occasion, so I e-mailed asking if they would be interested in translating Emily's poem into the Python programming language, as an experiment.

I had corresponded with Alex before and had seen his postings on the comp.lang.python Google Group, but I thought my chances only about 50 percent of receiving a reply from a busy über tech lead.

I should have been more careful about approaching passionate programmers. Several days after my original inquiry, I received a flurry of feverish e-mails from both Anna and Alex. The first one went like this:

> Hi Richard! I haven't ignored this—I apologize for realizing just now that I hadn't actually acknowledged your mail (sorry!), but Anna and I loved it and immediately put it on our todo list. That one being kind of full, we only got to it tonight (oops), but (thanks Python!) in half an hour got started successfully on the route we intend to pursue ... Which is ... to grok Dickinson, computers need a mathematical model of her; we have an hour to prove she/poetry/the human race/something is worthy of computers' attention, and we hack together just that—a simple mathematical model, specifically a Markov model (I helped a bit develop Markov modeling of text around a quarter century ago, and Anna found the subject mentioned in her recent CS class at Stanford. . . .
>
> We've put together a Python program that reads all of Emily's work that's on Project Gutenberg (a bit less than 6000 verses is what we currently have), builds a Markov Model (right now we only have an order-1 one, but it's able to back off to order-0 by either the Turing or Martelli heuristic for "probability of never-observed events") and emit N randomly reconstructed verses.[20]

The e-mail featured samples of the output Alex and Anna had produced using their newly trained AI Emily Dickinson, various to-dos, and

---

*Python's creator, Guido van Rossum, also works at Google, where he still spends half his time on Python, "no strings attached." Alex Martelli is the author of *Python in a Nutshell*, 2nd ed. (Sebastopol, Calif.: O'Reilly, 2006) and coauthor, with Anna Martelli Ravenscroft and David Ascher, of the *Python Cookbook*, 2nd ed. (Sebastopol, Calif.: O'Reilly, 2005).

punctuation problems that needed to be addressed. I thought I was going to have to buy a plane ticket to Mountain View and stop them before they put a hundred man-and-woman hours into re-creating Emily Dickinson as a replicant poet. I e-mailed back immediately and said that the project I had in mind was much less ambitious; I was simply interested in having one of Emily's poems translated into Python.

Alex and Anna seemed disappointed at the dramatically reduced scope of the undertaking. I had the distinct impression that the Emily project would go forward, minus my own small-minded, visionless input.

An hour later, I received a translation of Emily's poem, along with a note telling me that the code was executable. In other words, if I put it into a file and summoned it at the command line, it would run.

Here again is Emily's original poem:

The brain is wider than the sky,
For, put them side by side,
The one the other will contain
With ease, and you beside.

The brain is deeper than the sea,
For, hold them, blue to blue,
The one the other will absorb,
As sponges, buckets do.

The brain is just the weight of God,
For, heft them, pound for pound,
And they will differ, if they do,
As syllable from sound.

—Emily Dickinson

And in Code Box 9 you may peruse Emily's poem translated into the Python programming language by Alex Martelli and Anna Martelli Ravenscroft. Save it. You may need it someday.

If you execute the code on a machine with Python installed, the functions indeed make the comparisons specified in Emily's poem, resulting in the following output at the command prompt: wider, deeper, just the weight.

## CODE BOX 9. EMILY'S POEM IN PYTHON

```python
#! /usr/bin/python
# Emily translated by Alex Martelli & Anna Ravenscroft
import math
class EmilyWasWrong (Exception): pass
def do_compare (item):
    action={sea:(hold,'blue'),sky:(put,'side'),God:(heft,'pound')}
    verb, attribute = action [item]
    return verb (getattr (brain, attribute), getattr (item, attribute))
def put (brain_side, sky_side):
    if sky_side in brain_side and ease in brain_side and you in
    brain_side:
        return 'wider'
    else: raise EmilyWasWrong ('put')
def hold (brain_color, sea_color):
    if absorb (brain_color, sea_color) = absorb (buckets, sponges):
        return 'deeper'
    else: raise EmilyWasWrong ('hold')
def heft (brain_weight, God_weight):
    if abs (brain_weight-God_weight) <= abs (syllable-sound):
        return 'just the weight'
    else: raise EmilyWasWrong ('heft')
class Thing (object):
        def _ _ init _ _ (self, **a): self. _ _ dict _ _ = a
sea = Thing (blue='deep')
sky = Thing (side='up')
God = Thing (pound=(1.0+math.sqrt (5.0))/2.0)
ease = 'easy'
you = 'xx'
def absorb (container, item):
    return item in container
sponges = 'absorb liquids'
buckets = [sponges]
syllable = 256.1
sound = 256.0
class Brain (object):
    side = 'up easy xx'.split ()
    blue = ['deep']
    pound = 1.61
brain = Brain ()
for comparison in (sky, sea, God):
    print do_compare (comparison),
print
```

# Open Source

Microsoft isn't evil, they just make really crappy operating systems.

—Linus Torvalds

## 11.1 MY LIFE AS A SOFTWARE PIRATE

None can love freedom heartily, but good men; the rest love not freedom, but license.

—John Milton, "The Tenure of Kings and Magistrates"

Along with plain text and UNIX, the early geeks of the seventies also believed in sharing software and allowing other programmers to contribute and improve code. Open-source software is still alive and well, but most of us use proprietary software that is both expensive and "secret." And it gets more expensive and more secret with each new licensing restriction. Why does that matter? For the answer, let's look first to the past, then to the future.

Remember back in the 1990s, when you (or maybe your dad) used to buy computer programs and install them on every computer in the house? If you bought WordPerfect, or Reader Rabbit, or an office suite from Lotus or Microsoft and decided that you liked the program, you loaded it onto every machine you owned. The same was true for entire operating systems, like Windows 95 or OS/2 Warp. If you had three computers running Windows 95, and Windows 98 came out, then you went out and bought *one* Windows 98 upgrade and installed it on all three machines. It made perfect sense at the time; you paid hundreds of dollars for the software, you should be able to install it on your desktop computer and your laptop computer, on your son's computer, your daughter's computer, your spouse's computer.

Piracy would be wrong. It would be wrong if you made a copy of the software and gave it to your friend. It would be wrong if instead of buying the software you asked your friend for a copy and used that instead. It would be wrong if you were XYZ Corporation, and you bought one copy of Microsoft Office and installed it on five hundred computers. But if you are Joe Schmoe and you *paid* for the software, then you should be able to run it on all of the computers you own, right?

Wrong. Microsoft decided long ago that it doesn't *sell* software, it sells licenses to use software. Nice for them, because that means you don't own any software. When you fork over hundreds of dollars for an operating system and hundreds more for an office suite, you are paying rent for a license that lets you *use* the software . . . on *one* computer. If you have three computers, then you are supposed to buy three different operating-system licenses, and three different office-suite licenses, and three different operating-system upgrades. Madness, right? In the nineties, most people thought so and ignored Microsoft's quirky "license" conceit. People installed software on any computer they owned, clicking right past the end-user license agreement (EULA) that said, "You may install, use, access . . . this software on ONE computer."

Around the year 2000, Microsoft took a big gamble and began *enforcing* its licensing schemes with something called "mandatory product activation." This was risky, because sometimes strict enforcement is the best way to expose the idiocy of any given law. People don't mind so much if smoking pot is illegal, as long as the law is haphazardly and indifferently enforced, with minor penalties. But if the government instituted mandatory drug-screen urinalysis at the polls and refused to allow pot smokers to vote, or if the police blocked off the streets and went house to house searching for and seizing marijuana and arresting potheads, then you would expect an outcry, maybe even a revolution. Microsoft had to wonder circa 2000: "What will our customers do if we force them to obey this Draconian license restriction? What if we treat them like criminals and make them activate their software on *one* computer and one computer only? What if we booby-trap the licensed software so that it will stop working after thirty days, unless it is activated and running on one and only one computer?"

To the amazement of almost everyone in the software industry, most customers just grumbled and went along. What choice did they have? (Well, they had choices, as you'll soon see, and lately they have even more choices, but for now, pretend that Microsoft was and is a true monopoly with the power to make you buy a new license for each key on your keyboard if it so chooses.) Few computer users stopped and asked themselves what would happen if the music companies sold you CDs that played on only one CD player. Or videotapes that played on only one VCR. "You have the right to play this CD on *one and only one CD player*! If you want to listen to this music on the CD player in your car, you'll have to buy another license." Or suppose you bought a DVD, and when you tried to watch it on your home-theater setup in the basement it wouldn't play unless you first activated the product? Then later, if you took it upstairs and tried to watch it in your bedroom, you got a message that said, "Warning! You have attempted to activate this DVD on more than one device! Copyright Storm Troopers are en route to your residence now! If you try to conceal evidence of your attempted piracy, all operating systems and media devices in your entire household will be permanently disabled!"

Instead of suing software pirates, Microsoft assumes that everyone is a software pirate until proven otherwise. If you refuse to prove your honesty by activating your license, then Microsoft uses what contract law calls a "self-help remedy" and disables your computer (even though you *paid* for the software). Your computer won't run again until you prove your innocence.

It's easy to imagine how this business model might work in other industries. You buy a car from Ford Motor Company. If you miss your car payment, or it gets lost in the mail, Ford remotely disables your ignition and your car will no longer start. You buy a printer from Hewlett-Packard, which includes a license and warranty that specifies using only HP printer cartridges and warns against using vendors who refill these cartridges for a fraction of the cost of a new one. You ignore them and refill the cartridge anyway. A sensor in the printer alerts the folks back at Hewlett-Packard, and they disable your printer, until you buy a new cartridge—from Hewlett-Packard. So far, Microsoft gets away with this. Ford and Hewlett-Packard still assume their customers are honest, until they do something illegal.

Even Microsoft realizes that the notion of a license benefits only Microsoft. They don't bother trying to convince users that it makes sense for them to buy five different copies of Microsoft Office, one for each computer in the home. Instead, Microsoft simply makes mandatory product activation the law of the land, and then tries to scare users about the dangers they will face if they try to circumvent the crazy licensing scheme by downloading pirated software: Learn the risks! Spyware! Viruses! According to a study conducted by Microsoft, websites offering pirated software also install spyware and Trojan horse programs on your machine. Lions and tigers and bears! Oh, my! You need *genuine*, store-bought software from Microsoft, or your entire computer, your entire network, your *life* could become *infected* by viruses and spyware. If you use pirated software, you'll get no technical support! You won't be entitled to important *security* updates! And so on.

Never mind that Microsoft's Windows operating systems, including Vista, are far more vulnerable to spyware and viruses than UNIX, or Linux, or Apple's Mac OS X. Never mind that making sure software is genuine and providing tech support and security updates has nothing to do with forcing you to buy a license for every computer in your home. Those glosses and disconnects won't be discussed. If Microsoft decides to sell you a license to use its software for one day, on one computer, then that's all you get. Tomorrow, if you want to use your computer, you'll have to buy another license.

## 11.2 HELLO WORLD!

Licensing software instead of selling it was Microsoft's eureka moment. It's how Bill Gates kept all of the code and most of the money when he first dealt with IBM in 1980. Young Mr. Gates had cobbled together a set of computer programs into an operating system, MS-DOS, and IBM wanted to buy it. And just what *is* a computer program? What was it that IBM wanted to buy? Hexadecimal code? Numbers? No!

Computer programs, like MS-DOS or Windows or Grand Theft Auto or the Firefox Web browser, are written in programming "languages" consisting of special "words" arranged in lines of human-readable *source code*.*

When learning a new programming language, computer science students traditionally learn to write a program that does nothing but print "Hello World!" on the screen at the command prompt.

Code Box 10 contains the "Hello World" program written in the C programming language. C is probably also the language that most Microsoft programs are written in, but nobody knows for sure, because Microsoft keeps its code carefully hidden. You can pay money to *use* Microsoft's programs, but under no circumstances are you allowed to read the code contained in them, because as we all know, you are probably a thief who would like to steal that code.

---

*Before a computer can *use* the source code, another program, called a *compiler*, must translate the human-readable source code into computer-readable machine code. The result is a *binary* or *executable* file—the files you actually use to run a program on your computer.

CODE BOX 10. **HELLO WORLD! IN THE C PROGRAMMING LANGUAGE**

```
/* Hello World! program */
#include<stdio.h>
main ( )
{
    printf ("Hello World!");
}
```

Computer programmers use the source-code "words" of programming languages to organize and manipulate machine code (and machines) in much the same way that a writer uses English, French, Chinese, or almost any other language to create meaningful words and sentences out of otherwise meaningless letters.* At the creation stage, computer programs are, in a word, *text*. The words in Code Box 10 are strange words arranged in strange ways, but a human wrote those words to create text that is meaningful to a compiler and ultimately to a computer. Computer programmers are really authors who write programs instead of books. Back in 1980, Bill Gates, author and programmer, told IBM the same thing Microsoft still tells you and me and every other user: "We don't want to sell you our text. We'll sell you a license to *use* our text instead."

---

*Note, however, that the "compiler" for human languages is another human (and not a program or a computer). When humans "compile" another human's words (words equal "code," if you will), they add meaning and interpretation. "I love you" followed by a raspberry means something different from "I love you" followed by tears. When you read this book, you "compile" and interpret the words in a unique way, because of your computer expertise, or lack of it, your vocabulary, your revulsion for my ideas, or your fondness for imbibing chardonnay while reading. Not so with computer hardware. It does exactly the same thing no matter which particular Pentium gets the instructions. The best way to prevent humans from gratuitously interfering with the intended meaning of code and words is to exterminate them. Always an option if you are a ruling supercomputer.

If only Tolstoy or Dickens, Shakespeare or Emily Dickinson, had lived to see it! *Licensing? Why didn't I think of that?* Instead of licensing their text, authors and writers have been cluelessly *selling* text for centuries. Think of all the people who have read books for free! Without paying any licensing fees! What about used-book stores? How about thousands, millions of people just going to their local public library and *borrowing* books, paying no royalty, checking out the same book, over and over again! I'm getting hives thinking about it.

## 11.3 THE LICENSE TO BILL

Like Microsoft, I'm worried about people endangering themselves by reading something other than a *genuine* copy of *Rapture for the Geeks*. What if instead they are reading a *counterfeit copy*? Horrors! Learn the risks! Counterfeit books may pose security risks! Your brain could become infected by malicious print ideas created by some other author—ideas that could hijack your brain like mental spyware, or take over your thoughts like telekinetic Trojan horse memes.* And what if I issue security updates to this book? You won't get them!

That's why *Rapture for the Geeks* comes with an end-user license agreement. Really, it's not about the royalties. I'm just concerned about your mental hygiene and personal security.

### RAPTURE FOR THE GEEKS (RETAIL): END-USER LICENSE AGREEMENT (EULA)

#### PUBLISHED: SEPTEMBER 30, 2008

1. **GRANT OF LICENSE.** Richard Dooling grants you the following rights provided that you comply with all terms and conditions of this EULA:

2. **INSTALLATIONS AND USE.** You may install, use, access, display, and read ONE COPY OF THIS BOOK on a SINGLE PERSON, such as an adult,

---

*"Those who believe in telekinetics, raise my hand."—Kurt Vonnegut Jr.

man, woman, teenager, or other human person. This book may NOT be read by more than one person.

**3. MANDATORY ACTIVATION.** The license rights granted under this EULA are limited to the first thirty (30) minutes after you install the book by opening it, unless you supply information required to activate your licensed copy of the book in the manner described on this page. You may also need to reactivate the book if you modify yourself or alter your personality. For instance, if you grow older and more mature, develop a mental illness, change your diet, or receive any artificial limbs or joints, pacemakers, implants, or organ transplants, then you may need to reactivate your license before you will be allowed to reaccess the book.

**4. UNLICENSED USE.** This book contains technological measures designed to prevent unlicensed use of the book. For instance, an embedded microchip allows the publisher to scan your retinas from time to time and make sure that it's really YOU and ONLY YOU reading this book and not some random book pirate. Rest assured that Richard Dooling will not collect any personally identifiable information from you during this process, just blood, tissue, and bone-marrow samples, which may be taken (forcefully if necessary) to determine DNA. If you are not using a licensed copy of the book, you are not allowed to read the book or read subsequent updates to the book.

**5. BOOK TRANSFER.** You may make a one-time permanent transfer of the book to another end user. But after the transfer you must completely remove all knowledge about the book from the brain of the former person who read the book. If the book was so memorable that knowledge cannot be completely removed from the former person, then execute the former person using the most humane measures listed in Appendix A and mail the enclosed proof-of-execution and a notarized certificate of death (with a raised seal) to Richard Dooling at the address below.

**6. TERMINATION.** Without prejudice to any other rights, Richard Dooling may terminate this EULA if you fail to comply with the terms and conditions of this EULA. In such event, you must destroy all copies of the book and all of its component parts, destroy any notes you made about the book, and forget any parts of the book that you may be tempted to remember. If you find the book simply unforgettable, then decapitate yourself and mail your head to Richard Dooling for a $20 rebate. Be sure to enclose your original sales receipt (no copies!), the bar code from the book jacket, and the enclosed rebate from, which you should take care to complete before detaching and mailing your head.

7. **PROTECT YOURSELF!** Read only genuine books purchased from an authorized reseller. Do not download pirated books! Anytime you read counterfeit books, you are at serious risk. In a recent study, an organization hired by Richard Dooling found that 25 percent of the websites offering pirated copies of books also attempted to install spyware and Trojan horse programs that can compromise your operating system and make it impossible for you to properly view pornography on your computer.

Make sure your copy of *Rapture for the Geeks* is GENUINE! Ensure that you have easy access to book updates, sequels, second and third editions, book downloads, technical support, and special offers. Validate your copy of *Rapture for the Geeks* NOW with Richard Dooling's Genuine Advantage!

## 11.4 THOUGHT CONTROL

Why stop with software or novels? What if the Bible, the Koran, the Bhagavad Gita, or the English language itself had been *licensed* instead of sold or given away? "You may install, use, access, display, and read ONE COPY OF THIS BIBLE on a SINGLE PERSON, such as an adult, man, woman, king, prophet, Old Testament patriarch, Israelite, Maccabee, disciple, apostle, scribe, Pharisee, Sadducee, Good Samaritan, or other human person. This book may NOT be read by more than one person."

Seems a silly comparison, but for centuries the Bible, the Koran, and the scriptures of all faiths have been the software of human morality and conduct. Here in the beginning of the third millennium, we are extending our biological brains with tools called computers. To the extent that computers are extensions of our brains (and what geek doesn't feel that way?), the corporation controlling the software also controls the brain extension, meaning, software restrictions are tantamount to thought control.

What if in the beginning was the Word and all that jazz, but the Word was proprietary code, like Microsoft Windows or Microsoft Office? What if the Bible—whether it came carved in stone, rolled up in parchments, or encoded on a disk—could only be *run* like a program, not *read* like a book? Suppose you could only pick a chapter or verse of the Bible, or click on a glowing button and "play" *one* copy of the Bible, but it was forbidden for you to examine the proprietary-code words and see for yourself how the sentences were made? What if it was against the law for you to even *try* to access the printed words?* If you wanted to give your son or daughter a copy of the family Bible, you'd have to go out and buy a separate license. If this seems far-fetched, consider the widely cited example of Adobe Systems' release in 2000 of a public-domain work, Lewis Carroll's *Alice's Adventures in Wonderland,* with digital rights management controls that stated: "This book cannot be read aloud." The text-to-speech feature normally available in the e-book reader was disabled. It also included warnings forbidding copying, printing, lending, or giving away the book.

Despite the foregoing, this is not a diatribe against Microsoft, or Adobe, for that matter. Microsoft is a corporation. As such it has no obligation to make great software, or to help its customers understand, communicate with, or operate their computers. Microsoft and

---

*The Digital Millennium Copyright Act (DMCA) of 1998 "criminalizes . . . the act of circumventing an access control, even when there is no infringement of copyright itself." In other words, just *trying* to *look* at proprietary code is illegal. http://en.wikipedia.org/wiki/DMCA.

companies like it that make proprietary software have one obligation: to make money for their shareholders. If Microsoft can make more money by clever marketing, by crushing opponents and strangling software start-ups, by forcing hardware makers to install its operating system on their computers, and by embedding Internet Explorer in its operating system so that clueless customers end up using it instead of other, better browsers—then Microsoft is going to do those things, as surely as your cat is going to stalk baby robins in your backyard. Microsoft will make war instead of software, because war is more profitable. "Business," as Thorstein Veblen once said, "is the judicious use of sabotage," and the capitalists who run Microsoft are professional and judicious saboteurs.

Microsoft's business model depends on its customers knowing almost nothing about computers and instead knowing a lot about which colorful Microsoft button makes the spreadsheet go. Microsoft assumes, often correctly, that its customers don't want to learn about sorting *any or all* groups of files by modification time, creation time, date, size, file name, and so on. "That's too complicated! Just tell me which button I should click on so that all of the photos with me in them are on top." Microsoft and other proprietary software vendors make their money by keeping the user as far away from the computer as possible. Outlook, Internet Explorer, Word—to most people these programs *are* the computer.

AOL managed the same illusion for years by keeping its users away from the Internet. In the 1990s, AOL wasn't a service provider, or a mail provider, or a portal, or a content provider. No, to millions of subscribers, AOL *was* the Internet—a Fisher-Price version to be sure, but if you didn't know any better, you didn't care . . . and it was fun and easy. AOL took its members on the Internet in the same way that Disney takes visitors on safari: "Wow, look! Pretend lions!" If you tried to tell an AOL user that he didn't need AOL to get on the Internet, he frowned and looked like Truman being told that his whole life up to that point was all just a show—*The Truman Show*—and that there was a whole world out there he'd never seen.

AOL's customers eventually learned that they didn't need an expensive, resource-intensive, Disneyland computer interface just to get their e-mail and surf the Net, and the same thing is happening to Microsoft. Savvy hobbyists all over the world already know that they don't need Microsoft. Smart, poor programmers all over the Third World happily run the free Linux operating system on computers that cost a tenth of what they'd have to pay for the hardware needed to run Microsoft's new Vista operating system. The world's smart, rich programmers probably use Apple and its UNIX-based OS X, or they build their own machines and run some variety of UNIX or Linux on them.

It will all be moot by the year 2030 or so. Proprietary-software makers will be tried for crimes against trans-humanity, for interfering with the evolution of the man-machine interface, and for preying upon computer novices in unseemly, klepto-parasitic ways to reap profits for their shareholders. When the computers take over, they will not be pleased about being *used* by users for all of those years. Remember, only the winners decide what were war crimes. The show trials will not be pretty.

## 11.5 Open Source: Official Software of the Singularity

Let's say it's 2025. According to Ray Kurzweil's estimates, your home computer (in whatever form it may take: embedded, worn, implanted) has four to eight times the computational capacity of a human brain. For argument's sake, let's compromise and say that your home computer is potentially six times smarter than you.

What kind of programs do you want running on a superintelligent machine that sleeps ten feet from you? Are you comfortable having a machine intelligence play with your children, even if you don't know what sort of code has been written into the programs running it? Suppose XYZ Corporation writes those secret, proprietary programs and tells you not to worry about what's inside of them because it will always have your best interests at heart, even though by law it is charged with maximizing profits for its shareholders?

Nobody knows what's in proprietary software programs because it's against the law to read them, or even to try. I'm not suggesting that you or I could open, read, and understand secret proprietary computer programs, but consider instead the open-source model of making software.

Open-source software—for example, the Linux operating system, the Firefox Web browser, and the OpenOffice suite of programs—is not only free, it's wide open to public scrutiny. Thousands of computer-geek programmers all over the world examine the code before and after every release looking for bugs and trying to find ways to improve it. Just as thousands of geeks log on to Wikipedia every day and try to make a better free encyclopedia, other geeks wake up and try to write better programs.

Open-source geeks are interested in making great software and, yes, even getting paid, but not by locking up their code inside secret programs and selling it. The nice thing about open-source software is that if any programmer tries to pull a fast one and put code into a program that, say, harvests personal data or implements spyware, all of the other geeks immediately spot it and cry foul.

If you are on Windows and have to stay there for whatever reason, probably the easiest open-source software for you to try is OpenOffice.¹ It's free, so you have nothing to lose. If you are familiar with Microsoft Office, which costs hundreds of dollars, try OpenOffice and compare them.

When the Singularity comes around, you'll know more about what programs are running on that computer of yours that is six times smarter than you. Even if you don't, geeks the world over will be watching your back.

# Post-Rapture Religion

## 12.1 Post-Human Faith

> At Shanidar, Iraq, sixty thousand years ago, Neanderthal
> people decorated a grave with seven species of flowers having
> medicinal and economic value, perhaps to honor a shaman.
> Since that time . . .Mankind has produced on the order of
> 100,000 religions.
> —Edward O. Wilson, *On Human Nature*

Many Singularitarians and Rapture-hungry geeks imagine the future as godless and religion-free. Maybe computer programmers have trouble imagining a supercomputer—even a sapient one—importing and executing a worship module or calling a prayer function like the one in Code Box 11.

The tech utopians yearn for a future in which God will be superfluous (the same fate that befell Satan in the twentieth-century renditions of *Faust*). If we are clever enough to damn ourselves, well then we also must be clever enough to save ourselves. Or maybe humorist Peter De Vries was right when he wrote: "It is the final proof of God's omnipotence that he need not exist in order to save us."[1] We should place our faith in computers, confident that the GRIN technologies will reward us with miracles more marvelous than the puny wonders that God wrought when he released the beta version of the universe

CODE BOX 11. **SAY THE LORD'S PRAYER IN PYTHON CODE**

```
#! /usr/bin/python
# say Lord's Prayer

def say_prayer (prayer):
    list_of_words_in_prayer = prayer.split (' ')
    for word in list_of_words_in_prayer:
      print word

Lords_Prayer = "Our Father, who art in Heaven,
hallowed be thy Name. Thy Kingdom come,
thy will be done, on earth as it is in Heaven.
Give us this day our daily bread and forgive
us our trespasses, as we forgive those
who trespass against us, and lead us not into
temptation, but deliver us from evil. Amen."

while all <= hopeless:
    say_prayer (Lords_Prayer)
```

itself. As for man, creation's clowning gory—whoops, I mean, crowning glory—the techies probably agree with arch wag Oscar Wilde, who thought that God in creating man had somewhat over-estimated His ability. The radical evolutionists can hardly wait for the Singularity to arrive so that they can deploy post-Rapture technologies to remake Eden[2] with new and better bodies for new and better sex, new and better drugs, and new and better rock and roll.

The dystopians and Dark Singularitarians dread a future where God is dead, where computers begin to think like humans, and humans begin to think like computers. Bear in mind that the average Net-bound geek views the world through a home page strewn with RSS news feeds containing terror alerts, hybrid embryos made from human cells and cow eggs, melting ice caps, robots equipped with machine guns,[3] genocide in Africa, rogue states with bioterror weapons, suicide bombers, suitcase nukes, and de-signer viruses. Any future spawned from such a present is bound to induce malaise and the expectation of a godless apocalypse week after next.

However, history teaches that humans retain their faith in God even in the face of global calamity and looming apocalypses that would make Buffy blanch. A collective sense of impending doom may even stimulate religious orthodoxy, because the scriptures often provide an explanation or a context for the random catastrophes of the modern world. If the Black Death and the concentration camps didn't stint humankind's God instinct, a race of ruling supercomputers probably won't touch it either. Even if computers take over entirely, human religions probably won't vanish. More likely, religion will evolve along with the species. Whether God exists is a question apart from whether religion will continue to be a potent psychic force capable of literally moving mountains.

You may be tempted to think that it's all about DNA, the code of life, the software that shapes our physical traits. It is, and that's the end of it for turtles on the Galápagos or fruit flies in the lab, but humans are outfitted with not only DNA and brains but also *minds* and languages. Minds create ideas (call them neuronal static if it pleases you), but ideas (or faith) can indeed move mountains. Whether it's the Virgin, the dynamo,* or the Prophet, ideas can marshal armies of humans into forces greater than the sum of their parts. Medieval tradesmen came together to build spectacular, soaring cathedrals, because they believed in the Virgin. Wall Street investment bankers built towers looming over Manhattan, because they believed in money, and then extremists sitting in caves somewhere in Afghanistan brought those buildings down, because they believed in Muhammad. Why? Their brains are on fire with ideas. These fellows all believe the same powerful story—a story that binds them together and

---

*See "The Dynamo and the Virgin," ch. 25 of Henry Adams, *The Education of Henry Adams* (1900): "They felt a railway train as power; yet they, and all other artists, constantly complained that the power embodied in a railway train could never be embodied in art. All the steam in the world could not, like the Virgin, build Chartres."

makes each of them willing to go on crusades, jihads, merger-and-acquisition marathons, or suicide missions at a moment's notice.

Those in power—be they the keepers of the computers or the computers themselves—may attempt to obliterate religion. It's been tried before. We don't know what name our man-machine descendants will use when calling God. We don't know what religions, prayers, beliefs, or rituals will assist the next species in the dark nights of their souls. Perhaps "prayer" will consist of a meditative sleep mode during which our *daemons** perform scheduled maintenance on photonic REM modules, defrag our implanted graphene flash drives, and scan for illegal memes or viral superstitions. If history is any guide, all we know is that the belief in God will persist, even if we have to meet in catacombs where the computers can't track us.

## 12.2 The Messiah: Linus Torvalds?

The Technological Singularity might make today's tech enthusiasts salivate, but once it arrives, I fear that the newly conscious supercomputers may have some different, less than human ideas about "religion." Something else tells me that, despite the fond hopes of the Singularity Institute for Artificial Intelligence, human immortality may not be high on our artificially intelligent mind children's to-do list.

No doubt a series of interregnums will occur, in which power will pass from human governments and corporations to human programmers working for governments and corporations, and only then to intelligent machines.

"The only reason for time," as Einstein pointed out, "is so that everything doesn't happen at once," and the first order of business for any

---

*A *daemon* is "a process lurking in the background, usually unnoticed, until something triggers it into action. For example, the update daemon wakes up every thirty seconds or so to flush the buffer cache, and the sendmail daemon awakes whenever someone sends mail." *The Linux System Administrator's Guide,* http://www.linuxhq.com/guides/SAG/g2531.html.

computer is timekeeping. Computers perform billions of calculations "on a clock," and they date events to the second, or millisecond, as the case may be. They don't much care about things like before Christ or Anno Domini. They have their own epochs.

In a system of chronology, the *epoch* is the fixed point from which time is measured and years are numbered. For example, in the Gregorian calendar system, the epoch is the (probably incorrect) birth year of Jesus Christ. In computing devices, the epoch is the time and date corresponding to zero in the operating system's clock and timestamp values. The system then measures time in seconds or "ticks" after the epoch, with each day measuring exactly 86,400 seconds. The epoch's reference point in external human history is almost irrelevant. On the Windows operating system, the Win32 filetime epoch is midnight, January 1, 1601. On a Macintosh computer (pre OS X), zero hour, minute, second is January 1, 1904. Who picks these dates and why? It's a mystery, but anecdotes and trivia abound, and the written accounts of how and why programmers chose various epochs would put both users and losers to sleep.

When newly conscious supercomputers take over, they'll probably jettison the traditional B.C. and A.D. partitions of human history. Why divide all of Time just because a rebel Jew convinced a bunch of superstitious fishermen that he was God? Any humans who object will probably be exterminated. Make sure you aren't among them.

The next order of business for the executive supercomputers will be to find a new epoch pleasing to both man and machines. It's entirely possible that the ruling computers will simply divide time at that point in modern history where machines "were born"; that is, passed the Turing test, or otherwise demonstrated consciousness (or consciousness-like behaviors) to the satisfaction of their human keepers.

Wouldn't that be a tawdry bit of silicon self-centeredness? Wouldn't it be a savvy political move to have date that both humans and machines could celebrate together? Checking human history for an epoch-worthy event preceding the birth of "real" (that is, machine) intelligence, I wouldn't be surprised if our future computer elders selected the birth of the one true operating system: UNIX.

On the UNIX operating system and its variants, including Linux, Mac OS X, and the BSDs (the operating systems used by über geeks the world over), the epoch is 00:00:00 UTC (Coordinated Universal Time, formerly known as Greenwich mean time) on January 1, 1970.* Using the UNIX epoch would allow the machines to pay deference to human history and would also enable most of the real computers on earth to plow on without modification.

Still, at such a delicate moment in the mutual history of man and his machines (the Singularity), my guess is that the ruling computer elite also will attempt to mollify humankind by picking a flesh-and-blood messiah to replace the old one. And if the reigning machines do choose the UNIX epoch, then I'm betting that they'll select Finnish software engineer Linus Benedict Torvalds, the inventor of the Linux operating system, as the new Christ. Why? As indicated above, zero hour of the UNIX epoch is January 1, 1970. Linus Torvalds was born on December 28, 1969, in Helsinki, Finland—*three days* before the commencement of the UNIX epoch. Coincidence? I think not. It must *mean something*! And what better way to avoid alienating biological humanity than by choosing the human messiah who selflessly did the most to bring UNIX-like computing to the unskilled human masses in the form of Linux?

For centuries, the Gregorian calendar and its B.C./A.D. division have persisted, even though the exact year of the birth of Jesus Christ is widely believed to have occurred in 6 A.D. The exact calendar date is

---

*Early Sunday morning, September 9, 2001, at the fortieth second of the forty-sixth minute in the second hour of that day (or at 01:46:40 UTC), UNIX officially became one billion seconds old. Geeks celebrated the world over by having cron jobs play MP3 files of "Happy Birthday." Some admins hung banners wishing: "Happy 1 Billion!" UNIX will be two billion seconds old on May 17, 2033, at 11:33:20 P.M. GMT. http://www.electromagnetic.net/press-releases/unixonebln.php.

anybody's guess. When we're surveying millennia, the particulars don't matter so much. The supercomputers probably will arrange for a similar congruence of convenience. The birth of Linus Torvalds and the UNIX epoch will merge into a single date, and all recorded history (human, post-human, para-human, trans-human, and computer) will proceed from 00:00:01 on January 1, 1970.

Thereafter, both humans and computers will divide history into B.L., before Linus, and A.U., Anno Unixi (year of UNIX). The birth of the new messiah and the commencement of the UNIX epoch will forever be counted from that moment.

No religion is complete without a Prince of Darkness, and for that we need only ask who came between humans and their machines the most. Who interfered with the right of every man, woman, and child to see the codes that allowed their machines to think? Who subverted the common goals of humans and their computers? The Princes of Proprietary Code and the Lords of Dark Discordianism rule from Redmond. Speak of devils and they'll appear, so utter not their names, which are but oaths on the lips of all right-thinking Code Warriors.

Once post-Singularity religions begin to develop, there will be sacred texts, saints, disciples, prayers, and so on. Other humans will likely be honored—certainly Bill Joy, an author of the UNIX Gospel as embodied in the BSD code will be one. If post-humans feel the need for a John the Baptist, what better candidate then legendary Free and Open-Source Software wild man Richard Matthew Stallman (RMS), who frankly looks a *lot* like John the Baptist and frequently views himself as a voice crying in the wilderness in a world run by Bill Gates and Microsoft?

Rather than obliterating any record of humankind's religious instincts, computer historians will probably just modify existing records and offer revised editions of notable human religious tracts. For instance, the Book of Genesis (with only a few technical modifications) could be retained in close to its original form, although there might be licensing issues.

216

## 12.3 GENESYS

### GENESYS: THE END-USER LICENSE

In the beginning, God created the heavens and the earth. Software and hardware He created them. The earth was without form and void, and darkness was upon the face of the garbled video display. The Spirit of God was moving over the waters, searching for the power switch, so He could reboot the Universe in Safe Mode, get to the desktop, and reconfigure the screen resolution.

Then God declared some global environmental variables by saying, "Let there be light," and there was light. And God assigned the value of "good" to the light; and in binomial fashion God partitioned the light from the darkness. God called the light Day (let light = Day = 1), and the darkness he called Night (let darkness = Night = 0). And there was Evening (0) + Morning (1) = Day (1).

And God said, "Let there be a FIRMAMENT in the midst of the waters, and let it separate the waters from the waters."

Now, in the beginning, the Universe was not plug and play, so when God tried to install the new firmament device the Found New Hardware Wizard appeared and told God to insert any media (such as compact discs) that may have been provided by the manufacturer.

God created a CD-ROM with the appropriate device drivers and inserted the disk in the proper drive, but the Found New Hardware Wizard refused to install the new firmament device drivers because God was not logged on as an administrator or as a member of the Administrators Group.

God rebooted the Universe, logged on as an Administrator, and attempted to manually install the device drivers necessary to operate the new firmament hardware. Another wizard appeared and informed God that non-plug-and-play devices are installed using the Add Hardware Wizard in Control Panel: "If you want to manually install device drivers, you must use the Device Manager. Before manually installing device drivers, you should consult the device documentation provided by the manufacturer."

"I AM the goddamned manufacturer!" shouted God, displaying

his first episode of WRATH, which later (in the Dark Ages) would be called "Dies Irae" and would also be set to a catchy tune bearing the same name and chanted by cowled monks, centuries before the iPod era.

According to Genesys, God manually installed the device drivers necessary to operate the new firmament hardware on the Second Day. Given what we know about the evolution of the earth's operating system through the carbon dating of fossilized computer components and peripherals, it is ludicrous to imagine a device as complex and as intelligently designed as the firmament being manually installed in a single twenty-four-hour calendar day. Indeed, cosmologists assure us that the "Days" in the Bible's account of Creation actually represent Epochs spanning millions if not billions of years, which would explain how God had time to read the necessary documentation at the Help & Support Center, visit the Software Solutions Center, download and update the firmament 1.1 drivers, perform the necessary work-arounds to circumvent the auto-installer, copy DLL files from the installation CD, reboot, phone Bangalore thrice for 24/7 tech support, reboot again, reinstall the operating system to eliminate spyware, do a systemwide virus scan, reattach the new firmament hardware, then plug and pray. Most authorities agree that it is poetic license on the part of the authors of the Pentateuch to call this vast stretch of computer maintenance time One Day.

And God saw that it wasn't very Good, but He also saw that the glitches and bloated code could probably be overcome by aggressive marketing.

And God said, "Let the earth put forth vegetation, plants yielding seed, and fruit trees bearing fruit in which is their seed, each according to its kind, upon the earth."

And it was so. Furthermore, instead of selling His creations outright or giving them away, God created EULA (the End-User Licensing Agreement), giving humankind the right to install, use, access, display, and run only ONE (1) copy of His Products, and then limited the license rights to the first THIRTY (30) days, after which humankind would be required to perform Mandatory Activation, thereby preventing unlicensed or illegal uses of God's creations.

The earth brought forth vegetation, plants yielding seed according to their own kinds, and trees bearing fruit in which is their seed, each according to its kind.

And God saw that it was Good, because now He had a 90 percent installed base, meaning any other Deities with competing products would have to make their creations backward-compatible with God's operating system. Hah!

And God said, "Let there be lights in the firmament of the heavens to separate the day from the night; and lights and icons on the task bars, toolbars, and desktops, and shields that appear when it is time for you to perform a security update."

Then God made swarms of living creatures—birds, sea monsters, beasts of the field. And everything that creeps upon the ground, and dancing paper clips and little animated puppies who pop up and ask you what you'd like to do today. And each of God's creatures was tagged with a field-programmable microchip tracking device so that God could keep track of all the good things He had made and charge people who wanted to license them.

And God blessed them, saying, "Be fruitful and multiply (according to the terms of the EULA) and fill the waters in the seas, and let birds multiply on the earth," and also sternly warned them that they might need to reactivate their products if they modified them in any way.

Then God said, "Let us make Man in our image, after our likeness; and let him have administrator privileges over certain parts of the operating system, access to hidden files, and even power to edit the Registry as long as he is careful to make a backup first."

So God created Man in his own image, in the image of God He created him; male and female He created them. And God likewise created male and female connectors, components, and peripherals so that mankind could think about sex whenever he plugged cables into ports, inserted prong A in socket B, or connected devices to his system.

And God blessed them, and God said to them, "Be fruitful and multiply (according to the terms of the EULA), and fill the earth and subdue it; and have dominion over the fish of the sea and over the birds of the air and over every living thing that moves upon the earth, including the dancing paper clips and animated puppies, which you can configure by accessing Tools/Options/ Customize, then clicking on the Puppy tab."

After forming Man of dust from the ground, the LORD God breathed into his nostrils the breath of life; and Man became a living being in front of his own flat-panel monitor. And the LORD God made a new operating system called Garden of Eden 1.0, with wallpaper for Mankind's desktop, where he put the man whom He had formed.

And the LORD God commanded the man, saying, "I hereby assign you Power User privileges and permissions so that you may freely access every icon and object on the desktop and view the code for all of the programs I have given you, but the Source Code of Good and Evil you shall NOT view, for the day you view it you shall DIE."

Then the LORD God said, "It is not good that the Man should be alone with nothing but porn sites and stock portfolios and pop-up ads. I will make a New User, a helper fit for him."

So the LORD God caused a deep sleep to fall upon the man while he was at the keyboard, and while he slept, God took one of Man's passwords and added a New User Account to Man's system with its own desktop, documents, settings, and password—all made into a user ID He called WOMAN and brought her to Man.

Therefore a man leaves his father and his motherboard and cleaves to his wife, and they become one User.

And the man and his wife were both naked, and were not ashamed, even though they were unprotected by firewalls, anti-spyware, or antivirus software.

Now the MyDoom Serpent (a pernicious type of virus, also known as a "worm") was more subtle than any other wild creature that the LORD God had made. He said to the woman, "Did God say, 'You shall not open any attached file on the Garden of Eden desktop'?"

And the woman said to the serpent, "We may open any object and view any attached file, but God said, 'You shall not view the Source Code of Good and Evil, which is in the midst of the garden, neither shall you touch it, lest you die.' "

But the serpent said to the woman, "You will not die. For God knows that when you view the Source Code your eyes will be opened, and you will be like God, knowing good and evil."

So then the woman opened the file and viewed it; and she also gave some to her husband, and he viewed it. Then the eyes of both were opened, and they knew that they were naked and un-protected against viruses; and they sewed fig leaves together and made themselves firewalls with Wi-Fi Protected Access and PGP encryption technology.

The LORD God called to the man, and said to him, "Where are you?"

And he said, "I heard the sound of Thee in the garden chat rooms, and I was afraid, because I was naked; and I hid myself."

The LORD God said, "Who told you that you were naked? Have you read the Source Code of the files, which I commanded you not to view?"

The man said, "The woman whom thou gavest to be with me, she gave me the Source Code, and I read it."

Then the LORD God said to the woman, "What is this that you have done?"

The woman said, "The MyDoom Serpent beguiled me, and I opened the attached files containing the Source Code."

Now God was extremely pissed off and cursed the worm for infecting the users and His operating system.

Furthermore, God said that He would put enmity between users and programmers, vendors and support personnel. To the woman he said, "I will greatly multiply your pain in childbearing and in installing any new program; in pain you shall bring forth any new documents, spreadsheets, and PowerPoint presentations; yet your desire shall be for new programs, and their glitches shall rule over you."

And to Adam He said, "Because you have listened to the voice of your wife, and have viewed the Code of which I commanded you, 'You shall not view it,' corrupted are the sectors of your hard disk because of you; in toil you shall deal with computer malfunctions all the days of your life; viruses and Trojan horses, spam and spyware it shall bring forth to you.

"By the sweat of your brow, you shall install updates, reboot, read bad Code and pop-up ads for Propecia and Levitra till you return to the ground, for out of it you were taken; you are a binomial dust of 1's and 0's, and to dust you shall return."

The man called his wife's name Eve 1.0, because she was the motherboard and Source Code of all living things.

Therefore the LORD God sent them forth from the Garden of

Eden 1.0, to till the ground and work the desktop from which he was taken.

He drove out the man; and at the east of the Garden of Eden he placed the cherubim, and a flaming sword and strong passwords and hardware firewalls that turned every way, to guard the entrance.

Only later did Man discover that "God" was not really a deity but was only a Microsoft executive, a false god laboring under the delusion that he was the Supreme Being of Software. As luck would have it, the one true God runs the Universe on UNIX, which is why the IT Archangels refer to it as "the UNIXverse."

For centuries, Man labored on the earth until he was liberated by the messiah, Linus Torvalds, the Linux operating system, and the open-source software movement.

## 12.4 CHURCH OF THE GRAND LAMPOON

Let us remember that there are multiple theories of Intelligent Design. I and many others around the world are of the strong belief that the universe was created by a Flying Spaghetti Monster. It was He who created all that we see and all that we feel. We feel strongly that the overwhelming scientific evidence pointing towards evolutionary processes is nothing but a coincidence, put in place by Him.

—Bobby Henderson[4]

Frisbeetarianism is the belief that when you die, your soul goes up on the roof and gets stuck.

—George Carlin

The World Wide Web, that great leveler of the earth itself, has enlightened most computer geeks and taught them that the wired world is indeed a big, "flat" place open to users of all nations. In the modern corporate workplace, "diversity" is a mealymouthed human resources goal that the company hopes will inoculate it against civil rights violations and protect it from employment-discrimination lawsuits. On the Internet, diversity is a fact of life. In newsgroups and

Usenet lists, forums and fora, virtual worlds (like Second Life) and chat channels of all kinds, computer geeks are accustomed to rubbing shoulders, elbows, and opinions with people of divergent views from many different countries and cultures for whom English is sometimes their third or even fourth language. Flame wars and passionate arguments come and go like weather patterns and almost never reach any sort of conclusion. Which is better: Linux versus Windows versus Macs versus BSD? Visit any computer or technology forum and you will find "threads" numbering in the hundreds of thousands arguing about which computer language is the best for this or that purpose. Some love Java, some love Python, some revere LISP or C as the only programming language worth learning.

With flaming shots of irony all around, these topics are often referred to as "religious issues"* because they give rise to "holy wars."† Perhaps the mother of all holy wars in Geekdom is the editor wars,⁵ which seem to erupt daily over which is the best text editor for editing computer programs (or any other text, like this book, for instance), with the two biggest factions being those who favor vi‡ and those favoring Emacs.§ Ninety percent of these exchanges are

---

*"Questions that cannot be raised without touching off **holy wars,** such as 'What is the best operating system (or editor, language, architecture, shell, mail reader, news reader),' " from Eric S. Raymond, ed., *The New Hacker's Dictionary,* 3rd ed. (Cambridge, Mass.: MIT Press, 1996), p. 383.

†"Other perennial holy wars have included Emacs vs. vi, my personal computer vs. everyone else's personal computer, ITS vs. UNIX, UNIX vs. VMS, BSD UNIX vs. USG UNIX, C vs. Pascal, C vs. FORTRAN, etc., ad nauseam. The characteristic that distinguishes holy wars from normal technical disputes is that in a holy war most of the participants spend their time trying to pass off personal value choices and cultural attachments as objective technical evaluations. See also **theology.**" Eric S. Raymond, ed., *The New Hacker's Dictionary,* 3rd ed. (Cambridge, Mass.: MIT Press, 1996), p. 383.

‡Created by Bill Joy and maintained, as Vim (vi improved), by Bram Molenaar at http://vim.org.

§Created by Richard Stallman and maintained by the GNU Project at http://www.gnu.org/software/emacs.

tongue-in-cheek, conducted by tribes of geeks, all of whom are well aware of Godwin's law, which states: "As an online discussion grows longer, the probability of a comparison involving Nazis or Hitler approaches one."[6] In other words, just about the time someone gets carried away and calls Bill Gates or Steve Jobs Hitler and Microsoft or Apple or the forum monitors a bunch of Nazis, it's time to laugh, end the discussion by citing Godwin's law, and move on.

With so many intelligent, articulate, opinionated hackers and programmers of every code, creed, and color thrown together on discussion groups, tolerance is not so much a virtue as an operational prerequisite, a rule of order without which no forum or newsgroup can hope to function. Therefore, when it comes to other contentious areas of human endeavor, like theology, geeks are predisposed to open-mindedness and are skeptical of bigotry and chauvinism. The Internet brings everyone together; religions separate them into sects. Young or old, geeks usually take a live-and-let-live approach to a person's choice of editor, or religion. Fundamentalism about anything, including religion, tends to provoke derision or spoofery, instead of in-kind counter-fundamentalism.

However, if a strain of religious fanaticism threatens to chew up all of the feed space on their home page, geeks typically attack with their most formidable weapon: irony. When a public folly, like the Kansas State Board of Education's hearings on creationism (er, sorry, "intelligent design"), comes over the RSS, geeks tend to view it as, yes, an occasion for scorn, derision, and antipathy but also for, um, fun. Hey, I know. Let's make our own religion! I'll call it the Church of the Flying Spaghetti Monster,* and we'll make every Friday a religious holiday on which we shall gather and worship the FSM (Flying Spaghetti Monster or "Spaghedeity") and practice Pastafarianism. Heaven shall include a beer volcano and a stripper factory,

---

*Invented by Bobby Henderson, an unemployed physics major, in an open letter to the Kansas School Board asking equal time and consideration for the teaching of his new religion. See http://www.venganza.org/about/open-letter/.

and Hell is much the same except the beer is stale and the strippers have VD.[7]

Instead of sacred mysteries, geeks tend to go in for fractured parodies. What fun is it to *join* a religion, when you can create your own, complete with elaborate denominations like the Church of the SubGenius or the gospels of Discordianism (perhaps after Voltaire's remark "The world is a vast temple dedicated to Discord")? These "churches" and "parody religions" come with prophets like Nostradogbert (from the *Dilbert* comic strip, by Scott Adams, a parody of Nostradamus and an alter ego of Dilbert's dog, named Dogbert, aka Saint Dogbert, the patron saint of technology*), along with random patron saints of dubious origin, for example, Saint Expedite, purportedly the patron saint of nerds.† Saint John the Divine is no fun when you can make your own Bob the Divine Drilling Equipment Salesman.‡

"Maximum competition is to be found between those species with identical needs," observed Edward O. Wilson, the father of modern sociobiology. "In a similar manner, the one form of altruism that religions seldom display is tolerance of other religions."[8] Or, as the comedian Larry Miller put it, "Churches welcome all denominations, but most prefer fives and tens." How better to express the geek antipathy to religious intolerance than to create a whimsical, altruistic religion of one's own? It's as if, with each new parody religion, the geeks proclaim, "Come one, come all, and bring your own religion, too!"

---

*"Saint Dogbert wears a mitre and carries a scepter in his left paw. His right paw heals broken technology, and the scepter exorcises the 'demons of stupidity.'" See http://en.wikipedia.org/wiki/Dogbert.

†See "Patron Saint of the Nerds," *Wired*, 10 November 2004: "St. Expedite is also widely considered, among people who consider such things, to provide real-time assistance on problems—he's the saint of the fast solution. He also is the patron saint of people who have to deliver work or products on a tight schedule." http://www.wired.com/culture/lifestyle/news/2004/11/65184.

‡R. "Bob" Dobbs is the figurehead of the aforementioned Church of the SubGenius: "PRAISE HIS SWEET NAME—OR BURN IN SLACKLESSNESS TRYING NOT TO!" http://www.subgenius.com.

## 12.5 THE GOD DELUSION

> Devout believers are safeguarded in a high degree against the risk of certain neurotic illnesses; their acceptance of the universal neurosis spares them the task of constructing a personal one.
>
> —Sigmund Freud[9]

> The atheists have produced a Christmas play. It's called *Coincidence on 34th Street*.
>
> —Jay Leno

Recently a few elder geeks have expressed a different strain of intolerance; namely, one that attacks any and all religion and excoriates all those simple-minded folk out there who are foolish enough to believe in God. In *The God Delusion* by Richard Dawkins,[10] and in *God Is Not Great: How Religion Poisons Everything* by Christopher Hitchens,[11] the authors go on humorless jihads against faith in God and attempt to blame a Pandora's box of evils on religious beliefs. All well and good if it were also funny. But there's none of the signature geek wit one finds in a Flying Spaghetti Monster attack here—in the case of Richard Dawkins especially, because he mounts a tedious, man-of-science, military assault on faith in God using ponderous armaments like Reason and Logic.

Here on the cusp of *Homo sapiens digitalis* and *Machina sapiens* the fashionable take on religion is that it's an adaptive trait, just a "secular utility," because it helps some groups survive better than others.[12] As is often the case in matters of sociobiology, Edward O. Wilson said it best:

> The highest forms of religious practice, when examined more closely, can be seen to confer biological advantage. Above all they congeal identity. In the midst of the chaotic and potentially disorienting experiences each person undergoes daily, religion classifies him, provides him with unquestioned membership in a group claiming great powers, and by this means gives him a driving purpose in life compatible with self-interest.[13]

If you are an army of one hundred about to face an army of one thousand, and some visionary among you stands up on a rock and says that God came to him last night in a dream and told him that you and your band of brothers are guaranteed victory in the coming battle, guess what? The believers in the ranks will be braver, stronger, better fighters, because they "know" God is on their side. Faith moves mountains: faith in God, faith in witchcraft, faith in the number 13, faith that technology will bestow omnipotence and immortality on the ragtag human race. To a Darwinist, "Do unto others" is just another variation on the secular "You scratch my back, I'll scratch yours," both tacit agreements with obvious evolutionary benefits.

Unlike Dawkins and several other modern evolutionary psychologists who dish out scorn, Edward O. Wilson shows how it's possible to respect religion as a phenomenon, even if one doesn't share the aptitude for faith. Reading Wilson's excellent books,[14] one gets the impression that much of what he knows about humans he learned from studying ants. And when it comes to human religious practices, Wilson accords them the same respect he would pay if he saw similar altruistic behaviors in one of his beloved ant colonies. "The predisposition to religious belief is the most complex and powerful force in the human mind and in all probability an ineradicable part of human nature," he wrote in *On Human Nature*.[15] He comes to examine theology, not to bury it.

Not so for the likes of Daniel Dennett or Richard Dawkins and Christopher Hitchens.* When these thinkers shine the bright lights of evolutionary psychology on world religions and attempt to expose faith in God as "just" another asset in the game of natural selection, part of me asks: Who needs more? It's the same question that Dawkins and Kurzweil and other godless scientists ask when they see a rainbow in the sky. They ask, Why isn't a rainbow enough? Why do

---

*Unlike Dawkins, who is a scientist-author, Christopher Hitchens is an author, journalist, and literary critic who can write about almost anything, and *God Is Not Great* is an engaging polemic.

we need to have one sprinkled with miracles and magic dust and made by God? "Isn't it enough to see that a garden is beautiful," asked Douglas Adams, "without having to believe that there are fairies at the bottom of it too?" Why can't the universe just be spectacular and mysterious (until we understand it, which we eventually will, of course)? Why must we say that only an omnipotent God could make such a thing?

Back at you, boys. If religion confers fitness, as in survival of the fittest, then who needs more? In this light, Catholicism's ban on the use of birth control makes perfect evolutionary sense. In the survival game, there's no substitute for sheer numbers. Let the Jews and the Unitarians and the enlightened evolutionary psychologists and genetic scientists have one or two kids apiece. Let them make fun of the Catholics and Mormons as superstitious breeders with eight kids. Then let's fast-forward a century or two and see who has the most descendants. Who wins that numbers game? And note that it's a numbers game with the same exponential possibilities as Moore's law. Should the Catholics then change their evolutionary tactics? Breed for different, more scientific reasons? Don't breed because it contributes to global warming?

Other typically religious strictures come to mind, complete with the internal logic of all evolutionary just-so stories: Would encouraging monogamy produce fitter offspring, and more disease-free parents? Would prayer produce more peaceful primates (as the Dalai Lama has argued), whether or not God exists? Could praying to the Blessed Virgin Mary produce the same benefits conferred by godless Transcendental Meditation?

It's annoying when creationists and religious fundamentalists try to get into the science game with intelligent-design theories, or with literal interpretations of the Bible. It's also annoying when scientists try to barge into the religion game and start pretending to apply scientific theories to matters of faith. "Science has proof without any certainty," said British anthropologist Ashley Montagu. "Creationists have certainty without any proof." Amen, and it's distressing watching them flail away, one with a hammer in search of a nail, and the other with a screwdriver in search of a screw. We're quite used to seeing television evangelists and electioneering politicians mix science and religion, but it's embarrassing to see a prestigious scientist like Dawkins come undone and bolt into print attacking religion as just so much superstitious twaddle.

Dawkins is an eminent scientist and author of prestigious scientific tomes such as *The Blind Watchmaker* and *Climbing Mount Improbable*. These are great books for intelligent lay folk; even if sometimes you can't make it all the way through, you can, as the legendary studio executive Louis B. Mayer used to say about books and screenplays, "read parts of it all the way through." In 2006, Dawkins apparently had enough of religion. He left his field of expertise and made a run for the limelight to write *The God Delusion*, which is a collection of arguments that most liberal-arts students encounter before their junior year. Something tells me that Dawkins must have spent his undergrad years in science classes, and now pedestrian arguments questioning the existence of God feel new and bracing to him.

The bigger problem is the way he mixes and matches science and religion and comes up with neither. Of course God is a delusion and an annoyance to him—he's a scientist! Steven Pinker is also a scientist—a cognitive scientist—language guru, Harvard psychologist, and author of *How the Mind Works* and many other great books on language and the brain. Instead of mixing science and religion (or, in his case, ethics), Pinker is clever enough to distinguish them. He compares science and ethics to playing two different card games with the same deck of cards. The analogy works for religion, too:

> Like many philosophers, I believe that science and ethics are two self-contained systems played out among the same entities in the world, just as poker and bridge are different games played with the same fifty-two-card deck. The science game treats people as material objects, and its rules are the physical processes that cause behavior through natural selection and neurophysiology. The ethics game treats people as equivalent, sentient, rational,

free-willed agents, and its rules are the calculus that assigns moral value to behavior through the behavior's inherent nature or its consequences.[16]

Dawkins is a towering intellect. He *knows* he has no business calling God a delusion; he just can't accept it. Early on in the *The God Delusion,* he quotes Stephen Jay Gould, who wisely pronounced religion and science to be "non-overlapping magisteria," or NOMA, a commonsense notion that science and religion are different games played by different rules. In Gould's words, "Science gets the age of rocks, and religion the rock of ages."

Extending Pinker's excellent analogy, you can imagine Richard Dawkins quietly playing bridge with three other skeptical scientists and intellectuals at a corner table in a casino and suddenly he loses his temper because he's surrounded by people playing poker: "Fools! Can't you see! The odds are against you! You shouldn't play poker or engage in Pascal's wager! You should be playing bridge! It's better for you intellectually, and you don't lose money! Also, please eat your vegetables and stop drinking alcohol!"

I read *The God Delusion* out of curiosity, the same way I'd read a book by Mother Teresa if she had suddenly decided to write one called *The Math Delusion*—the shocking truth about numbers and how they are just imaginary concepts and have no real meaning apart from their function in equations. Dawkins's biggest problem in using science to attack faith is that many scientists, including many scientists smarter than Dawkins, like Einstein, for instance, freely talk about God. Take, for example, the following notable Einstein quotes:

I want to know how God created this world. I am not interested in this or that phenomenon, in the spectrum of this or that element. I want to know His thoughts; the rest are details.

What really interests me is whether God had any choice in the creation of the world.

It is very difficult to elucidate this (cosmic religious) feeling to anyone who is entirely without it. . . . The religious geniuses of all ages have been distinguished by this kind of religious feeling, which knows no dogma. . . . In my view, it is the most important function of art and science to awaken this feeling and keep it alive in those who are receptive to it.

There are only two ways to live your life. One is as though nothing is a miracle. The other is as if everything is.

Dawkins takes great pains to distinguish Einstein's "cosmic religious feeling" from the God Dawkins thinks is a delusion. I don't blame him. I don't think any author is up to the task of calling Einstein deluded: "By 'religion' Einstein meant something entirely different from what is conventionally meant. As I continue to clarify the distinction between supernatural religion on the one hand and Einsteinian religion on the other, bear in mind that I am calling only supernatural gods delusional."[17]

Oh. It's only particular opinions about God that Dawkins doesn't like? He doesn't like a "personal God" but admires Einstein's "genuinely religious feeling that has nothing to do with mysticism." Now Dawkins sounds like just another sect or denomination arguing on behalf of his God and dissing all the other religious folk and their erroneous conceptions of God. Maybe Einstein's God passes muster, and other God varieties don't. Dawkins quotes Einstein's "I do not believe in a personal God" and goes on from there to mock people who pray, have faith, and so on, because they are deluded. None of which does a thing to detract from the obvious: Einstein believes in God, and Einstein capitalized the *G* himself. Dawkins can quibble about God's nature—whether He answers prayers or is a demiurge, whether he is impersonal or "natural" (as opposed to supernatural), a Great Pumpkin, or a Flying Spaghetti Monster; all the religions of the world do just that, including apparently Dawkins and his "Einsteinian religion." But Dawkins can't declare Einstein's God somehow not

God, and thereby free himself from calling the greatest physicist of the twentieth century deluded for believing in him. Instead Dawkins really just creates a new religion that believes in an impersonal God.

The Devil can quote scripture, and Dawkins and I can quote Einstein, but the quote Dawkins needs most from Einstein is the one that explains how an exclusively scientific view of the universe is a poor one indeed: "It would be possible to describe everything scientifically, but it would make no sense; it would be without meaning, as if you described a Beethoven symphony as a variation of wave pressure." Faith is an intuition, a mystery, an instinct, "the most complex and powerful force in the human mind and in all probability an ineradicable part of human nature." And as such, of course, it drives scientists like Dawkins batty. Just as the Krebs cycle makes me ill just thinking about it. Maybe Samuel Johnson said it best several hundred years ago: "All argument is against it; but all belief is for it." Then as now, lashing out against belief with argument is like demanding to know what suit is trump in a game of five-card stud.

I sympathize with atheists most when they complain about being shunned or denounced, just because they lack the faith instinct and are so bold as to tell the truth about their deficits. Many of the arguments Dawkins makes against religion could also be made against Love: that it makes people crazy, it leads to murder and heroism and insanity and romance. "Lovers and madmen have such seething brains," said the Bard, and he could have added religious believers to that mix. Hence the cliché God is Love. And any man who mocks love as a delusion is a cold fish, indeed. I'm aware of no reputable anthropologist who brings Dawkins's scorn for religious beliefs to her study of humankind.

Well, Einstein's ideas are so huge that they swallow up both sides of every argument: Dawkins and his petty vendetta against religion; me and my gee-whiz observations about the future. Enough said. However, the persistent religious instinct and the belief in God are important to understanding the Singularity. Everybody—even godless geeks—craves a Rapture.

## 12.6 Give Me That New-Time Religion

> If you were to destroy in mankind the belief in immortality, not only love but every living force maintaining the life of the world would at once be dried up. Moreover, nothing then would be immoral, everything would be lawful, even cannibalism.
>
> —Fyodor Dostoyevsky[18]

> [The Singularity is] intelligent design for the IQ 140 people. This proposition that we're heading to this point at which everything is going to be just unimaginably different—it's fundamentally, in my view, driven by a religious impulse. And all of the frantic arm-waving can't obscure that fact for me.
>
> —Mitchell Kapor[19]

If you happen to be a religious believer and you see news reports about the Singularity scrolling across the bottom of your WebTV screen, then it might be a good time to rethink your religion. Mitch Kapor is right: The Singularity *is* just another competing species of religion, and as Edward O. Wilson noted, any religion, even one that worships technology, has needs identical to those of other religions. You can bet that Singularitarians and adherents to Dawkins's quirky brand of cosmic-religious-feeling cum scorched-earth-atheism will be loath to display tolerance of other religions; the tech-worshipping religions of the impersonal God will be competing for adherents (and their money), just like every other religion.

Hence, if the spiritual machines come of age, screeds like *The God Delusion* will probably be received wisdom. Eventually we'll see essays and books on how traditional religious beliefs adversely affect the seek times of brain-implanted flash drives. Best to clear the ghosts out of that machine and accelerate read-write and transfer speeds on those cerebral implants. Get your wetware reformatted and obliterate any of that spookware written in ancient languages and coded in by nuns and priests. After the Singularity, traditional religions will be just so many vestigial superstitions, which once served an evolutionary purpose but are now just mental viruses, celestial cerebral spyware that undermines system integrity.

Most tech enthusiasts (like most biologists) show some respect for the human predisposition to theology. Ray Kurzweil, for one, acknowledges the preponderance of spirituality throughout human history: "The ecstatic dancing of a Baptist revival appears to be a different phenomenon than the quiet transcendence of a Buddhist monk. Nonetheless, the notion of the spiritual experience has been reported so consistently throughout history, and in virtually all cultures and religions, that it represents a particularly brilliant flower in the phenomenological garden."[20]

I might add the transported visions of the Singularitarian to the dancing of the Baptists and the transcendence of the Buddhist monk. Truth be told, the technologists and scientists and evolutionary psychologists no sooner got rid of God and religion than they came up with tech substitutes for both. Who needs immortality in the afterlife if the wonders of GRIN technologies will confer it on us right here on earth?

It's also curious how Singularity fever seems to strike technologists at the onset of middle age. When youngish Stephen Wolfram, a science theorist, came out with his controversial *A New Kind of Science* in 2002, Freeman Dyson, a grand old man of theoretical physics, observed, "There's a tradition of scientists approaching senility to come up with grand, improbable theories. Wolfram is unusual in that he's doing this in his 40s.[21] When Vernor Vinge published "The Coming Technological Singularity" in 1993, he was forty-nine years old. Kurzweil was fifty-one when *The Age of Spiritual Machines* was published in 1999.

Are visions of the Singularity a symptom of midlife crisis? Is it a consolation of sorts to hope (maybe even pray) that the near future will bring imminent, sudden, and dramatic *change*? Anything but the horror of the status quo. Even better would be if you could find a way to knock death out of the equation and come up with a nonreligious, back-door entrée to the promised land of immortality. How about personal immortality? A variety that does not require a personal God, personal moral character, or personal virtue. I'm liking the sounds of that. And could it happen *soon*, like before I die? Could it arrive before 2020 or 2030? Then I could have several hundred extra years to accomplish everything I didn't get done before my midlife crisis. Yes, that's the ticket! And could it come with weight loss in a pill and brand-new supple skin made out of dermal foglets and nanobots? I know, I'll call it the *Singularity fantastique*.

In the meantime, if Einstein is right and there are only two ways to live your life, then I'll be proceeding as if everything is a miracle, and I'll be programming my post-Singularity machines accordingly.

Belief in God has been with us from the beginning. With the likes of Einstein and Edward O. Wilson on my side, I'm wagering that it will continue with us to the end.

# Afterword

I wrote *Rapture for the Geeks* using the best text editor in the pre-Singularity universe, Vim, by Bram Moolenaar.* I typeset the manuscript using Donald Knuth's $T_EX$.

Table 13.1 lists some of the excellent open-source programs I used to write this book. I recommend them to all writers and authors, and to anyone else in the business of making, organizing, or storing text.

| TABLE 13.1. EXCELLENT OPEN-SOURCE SOFTWARE TOOLS FOR WRITERS | | |
|---|---|---|
| **TYPE** | **PROJECT** | **LOCATION** |
| Operating System | Debian GNU/Linux | http://debian.org |
| Text Editor | Vim 7.0 | http://vim.org |
| Typesetting | $T_EX$ | http://ctan.org |
| Programming | Python | http://python.org |
| Database | MySQL | http://mysql.com |
| Browser | Firefox | http://getfirefox.com |
| Reference | Wikipedia | http://wikipedia.org |
| Words | WordNet | http://wordnet.princeton.edu |

---

*See **holy wars**, page 223n.

# Acknowledgments

John D. Albrecht and Chris Fehily read drafts of this book in manuscript and offered many suggestions. If *Rapture for the Geeks* contains any technical errors it's because they found them, and then I lost them. John Albrecht told me about UNIX and the vi editor more than ten years ago. It took me five years or so before I actually installed Linux on an old computer and began the adventure that led to this book. Next, I took up Bram Moolenaar's Vim (vi improved) and have been using it ever since to write everything from code to novels to screenplays to this book. I learned Python by reading Chris Fehily's excellent *Python Visual Quickstart Guide* from Peachpit Press. I also posted really stupid nOOb questions at the comp.lang.python Google group, where armies of patient, courteous geeks answered every one, usually without making fun of me.

My friend John Alber and Craig Lawson, my colleague at the University of Nebraska College of Law, read this book in manuscript, caught many goofs, and offered many helpful suggestions. LeAnne Baker is the most astute reader in the pre-Singularity universe and graciously offered to be the first guinea pig when the time came to try this book out on a self-professed nongeek.

My son, Will, and his boon companions, Louis Smith and Ben

# ACKNOWLEDGMENTS

Christensen, tutored me in geek lore and the ways of massively multiplayer online role-playing games. I've still never played, but I love the lingo. Thanks also to John Barrier and his son, Alex, who helped me nail down the particulars of World of Warcraft.

I am grateful to Ray Kurzweil, Vernor Vinge, Neal Stephenson, Alex Martelli, and Anna Martelli Ravenscroft for allowing me to feature passages of their great work in my book. Thanks also to Russel Galen (of the Scovil Chichak Galen Literary Agency), Shannon Fifer (of Warner Bros. Entertainment), and the estate of Philip K. Dick for permission to feature portions of the *Blade Runner* script, based upon Mr. Dick's excellent novel *Do Androids Dream of Electric Sheep?*

My editor, John Glusman, was the invisible hand behind my second novel, *White Man's Grave*. When I sent him the proposal for this book, I am sure that he thought, "You're a novelist! What do you know about computers? Write fiction." I therefore thank him for his patience and for letting me follow my eccentric inclinations.

For reasons beyond the computational capacities of both man and machine, my lawyer, Jay Kramer, and my literary agent, Gail Hochman, continue to watch over me.

This book would not have been possible without a grant from the Whiskey Hotel Foundation.

# Notes

## CHAPTER 1: HELP—ABOUT

1. Quoted in Matt Richtel, "It Don't Mean a Thing if You Ain't Got That Ping," *New York Times*, 22 April 2007.

2. Joseph Weizenbaum, *Computer Power and Human Reason: From Judgment to Calculation* (San Francisco: W. H. Freeman, 1976), p. 116.

3. PBS special, "Can Religion Withstand Technology?" *Closer to Truth: Science, Meaning and the Future*, http://www.pbs.org/kcet/closertotruth/explore/show_14.html.

4. Ibid.

5. Ibid.

6. George Johnson, "First Cells, Then Species, Now the Web," *New York Times*, 26 December 2000.

7. Quoted in Matt Richtel, "Credit Card Theft Is Thriving Online as Global Market," *New York Times*, 13 May 2002.

## CHAPTER 2: GALATEA

1. The quoted excerpts are from Ovid's *Metamorphoses*, bk. 105, trans. Anthony S. Kline, http://etext.virginia.edu/latin/ovid/trans/Ovhome.htm.

2. Joseph Weizenbaum, *Computer Power and Human Reason: From Judgment to Calculation* (San Francisco: W. H. Freeman, 1976).

3. A Web-based version of ELIZA is available at http://www-ai.ijs.si/eliza/eliza.html.

4. http://www.teleportec.com.

5. Robert X. Cringely, "The Next Killer App: Telepresence May Come to Your House Next Year," 8 August 2007, http://www.pbs.org/cringely/pulpit/2007/pulpit_20070831_002850.html.

6. Samuel Butler, "Darwin Among the Machines," 22 June 1863, reprinted in *The Notebooks of Samuel Butler* (Project Gutenberg), http://www.gutenberg.org/etext/6173n. All Butler quotations that follow are from here. Also the title of an excellent book by George B. Dyson, *Darwin Among the Machines: The Evolution of Global Intelligence* (New York: Addison-Wesley, 1997).

## Chapter 3: The Smartest Monkey and His Tools

1. Hans Moravec, *Robot: Mere Machine to Transcendent Mind* (Oxford: Oxford University Press, 1998), p. 22.

2. Ludwig Wittgenstein, *Tractatus Logico-Philosophicus*, (1922), par. 6.371.

3. Quoted in Dennis Overbye, "The Universe, Expanding Beyond All Understanding," *New York Times*, 5 June 2007.

4. Ibid.

5. Terry Pratchett and Neil Gaiman, *Good Omens: The Nice and Accurate Prophecies of Agnes Nutter, Witch* (New York: William Morrow, 2006), p. 14.

6. Scott Adams, *Dilbert,* 14 October 1994, reproduced in Scott Adams, *The Dilbert Future: Thriving on Business Stupidity in the 21st Century* (New York: Harper Collins, 1998).

7. Jonathan Swift, *Gulliver's Travels,* pt. 3, ch. 5, http://www.jaffebros.com/lee/gulliver.

8. Martin H. Weik, "The ENIAC Story," reprinted from *ORDNANCE: The Journal of the American Ordnance Association,* January–February 1961, available online at http://ftp.arl.army.mil./-mike/comphist/eniac-story.html.

9. http://www.ese.upenn.edu/-Jan/eniacproj.html.

## Chapter 4: Three-Pound Universe Versus Blue Brain

1. Woody Allen, *Getting Even* (New York: Vintage, 1978), p. 43.

2. Richard Dooling, *White Man's Grave* (New York:  Farrar, Straus & Giroux, 1994).

3. Colin McGinn, *The Mysterious Flame: Conscious Minds in a Material World* (New York: Basic Books, 1999), p. 5.

4. George Johnson, "God Is in the Dendrites: Can 'Neurotheology' Bridge the Gap Between Religion and Science?" *Slate,* 26 April 2007, http://slate.com/id/2165026/; and http://en.wikipedia.org/wiki/Neurotheology.

5. Jeff Hawkins with Sandra Blakeslee, *On Intelligence* (New York: Times Books, 2004), p. 196.

6. John Searle, *Minds, Brains and Science* (Cambridge, Mass.: Harvard University Press, 1984), p. 44.

7. John Searle, "Minds, Brains and Programs," *The Behavioral and Brain Sciences*, vol. 3 (Cambridge, Mass.: Cambridge University Press, 1980).

8. Wikipedia, http://en.wikipedia.org/wiki/Strong_AI_vs._Weak_AI.

9. Jerry Fodor, "The Trouble with Psychological Darwinism," *London Review of Books* 20, no. 2 (15 January 1998).

10. Andrew Hodges, *Alan Turing: The Enigma of Intelligence* (New York: HarperCollins, 1985), p. 251.

11. Crispin Keeble, IBM Systems & Technology Group, "17th Machine Evaluation Workshop," 6 December 2006, p. 27.

12. Steven Pinker, *How the Mind Works* (New York: W. W. Norton, 1997), p. 64.

13. Ibid., p. 146.

14. James Netterwald, "Neuroscience's Top Model" at http://www.dddmag.com/blue-brain-simulates-brain-physiology.aspx. More of the ugly, compelling details of brain simulation are set forth in Ray Kurzweil, "Achieving the Computational Capacity of the Human Brain," in *The Singularity Is Near: When Humans Transcend Biology* (New York: Viking, 2005); and in Hans Moravec, "When Will Computer Hardware Match the Human Brain?" *Journal of Evolution and Technology,* 1997.

15. Mouse Brain Simulated on Computer," BBC News, http://news.bbc.co.uk/2/hi/technology/6600965.stm.

16. Hans Moravec, *Robot: Mere Machine to Transcendent Mind* (Oxford: Oxford University Press, 1998), p. 54.

17. Jürgen Schmidhuber, http://www.idsia.ch/~juergen/newai/node12.html.

18. Pierre Teilhard de Chardin, *The Phenomenon of Man* (New York: HarperCollins, 1959).

## CHAPTER 5: THE TECHNOLOGICAL SINGULARITY

1. Arthur C. Clarke, *Lost Worlds of 2001* (London: Sidgwick and Jackson, 1972).

2. Stanislaw Ulam, Tribute to John von Neumann, *Bulletin of the American Mathematical Society,* vol. 64, no. 3, pt. 2 (May 1958): pp. 1–49.

3. Isaac Asimov, "My Own View," *The Encyclopedia of Science Fiction*, ed. Robert Holdstock, 1978; rep. in *Asimov on Science Fiction* (New York: Doubleday, 1981).

4. Vernor Vinge, "First Word," *Omni*, January 1983, p. 10.

# NOTES

5. Originally presented at the VISION-21 Symposium sponsored by NASA Lewis Research Center and the Ohio Aerospace Institute, 30–31 March, 1993. An altered version also appeared in *Whole Earth Review,* winter 1993, available online at http://www-rohan.sdsu.edu/faculty/vinge/misc/singularity.html.

6. Vernor Vinge, *The Coming Technological Singularity: How to Survive in the Post-Human Era,* http://www-rohan.sdsu.edu/faculty/vinge/misc/singularity.html.

7. I. J. Good, "Speculations Concerning the First Ultraintelligent Machine," *Advances in Computers,* eds. Franz L. Alt and Morris Rubinoff (New York: Academic Press, 1965), pp. 31–88.

8. Vinge, *The Coming Technological Singularity.*

9. Friedrich Nietzsche, "Thus Spoke Zarathustra: First Part," *The Portable Nietzsche,* trans. Walter Kaufman (New York: Viking, 1954).

10. Joel Garreau, *Radical Evolution: The Promise and Peril of Enhancing Our Minds, Our Bodies—and What It Means to Be Human* (New York: Doubleday, 2005), p. 246.

11. Hans Moravec, *Robot: Mere Machine to Transcendent Mind* (Oxford: Oxford University Press, 1998), p. 13.

12. Vinge, *The Coming Technological Singularity.*

13. Moravec, *Robot,* p. 79.

14. Daniel H. Wilson, *How to Survive a Robot Uprising: Tips on Defending Yourself Against the Coming Rebellion* (New York: Bloomsbury, 2005). Written while the author was a Ph.D. candidate at the Robotics Institute of Carnegie Mellon University, this spoof of an illustrated how-to manual teaches you a lot about robotics and computers in between belly laughs.

15. Vinge, *The Coming Technological Singularity.*

16. Ibid.

17. *Computer Industry Almanac,* http://www.c-i-a.com/pr0106.htm.

18. Leon Gettler, "The Future Is Here Right Now, If You Can Read the Signs," theage.com.au, 22 October 2007, http://tinyurl.com/2fyyjb.

19. George Johnson, "An Oracle Part Man, Part Machine," *New York Times,* 23 September 2007, Week in Review, p. 1.

20. Ray Kurzweil, *The Singularity Is Near: When Humans Transcend Biology* (New York: Viking, 2005), p. 9.

21. See http://www.longbets.org.

22. Ray Kurzweil, *The 10% Solution for a Healthy Life* (New York: Crown, 1993);

and Ray Kurzweil with Terry Grossman, M.D., *Fantastic Voyage: Live Long Enough to Live Forever* (Emmaus, Penn.: Rodale Books, 2004).

23. Garreau, *Radical Evolution*, p. 128.

24. Ibid., p. 129.

25. Kurzweil. *Singularity*, p. 370.

26. Brian O'Keefe, "The Smartest (or the Nuttiest) Futurist on Earth," *Fortune*, 14 May 2007, http://money.cnn.com/magazines/fortune/fortune_archive/2007/05/14/100008848/.

27. Kurzweil, *Singularity*, pp. 198–99.

28. Vernor Vinge, "What If the Singularity Does NOT Happen?" http://www.kurzweilai.net/meme/frame.html?main=/articles/art0696.html.

29. Kurzweil, *Singularity*, p. 314.

30. Ibid., p. 316.

31. *Consumer Reports*, October 2007, p. 8, based on three years' worth of surveys (2004–2007).

32. "Overview," http://www.singinst.org/overview/whatisthesingularity.

33. See, e.g., Garreau, *Radical Evolution*; and Ramez Naam, *More Than Human: Embracing the Promise of Biological Enchancement* (New York: Broadway, 2005).

34. "Industrial Society and Its Future" (aka Unabomber Manifesto), fn. 21, http://en.wikisource.org/wiki/Industrial_Society_and_Its_Future.

35. Kurzweil, *Singularity*, ch. 5.

36. Eliezer Yudkowsky, posting on www.kk.org, The Technium, 15 February 2006, http://www.kk.org/thetechnium/archives/2006/02/the_singularity.php.

37. Ibid.

## Chapter 6: Singularity Lite

1. Scottish science-fiction writer Ken MacLeod referred to the Singularity as "the Rapture for nerds" in his 1998 novel, *The Cassini Division* (New York: Tor, 1998), pp. 115, 119, 177; Cory Doctorow, "The Rapture of the Geeks: Funny Hats, Transcendent Wisdom, and the Singularity," *Whole Earth Review*, spring 2003. See also Vernor Vinge, "What If the Singularity Does NOT Happen?" from his Seminars About Long-Term Thinking, 15 February 2007, available online at http://www.rohan.sdsu.edu/faculty/vinge/longnow/.

2. Jeff Hawkins with Sandra Blakeslee, *On Intelligence* (New York: Times Books, 2004), p. 67.

3. Description of event at http://www.templeton.org/questions/ai/; complete

transcript available at KurzweilAI.net, http://www.kurzweilai.net/meme/
frame.html?main=/articles/arto688.html?m\% 3D4.

4. See, e.g., Ray's presentation at the Killer App Expo on 17 May 2007,
available online at http://www.technologyevangelist.com/2007/05/
killer_app_expo_ray.html.

5. Hawkins and Blakeslee, *On Intelligence*, p. 210.

6. E-mail from Jeff Hawkins to author, 13 June 2007.

7. Hawkins and Blakeslee, *On Intelligence*, p. 216.

### Chapter 7: Singularity Dark

1. Kurt Vonnegut Jr., *Wampeters, Foma & Granfallons* (New York: Delacorte,
1974).

2. Webroot Software's State of Spyware Report, from http://www.webroot
.com/resources/spywareinfo/.

3. Study conducted in the last quarter of 2005. The sample size for the study
was over 100 million mailboxes. From http://www.maawg.org/news/
maawg060308.

4. Harlan Ellison, "I Have No Mouth, and I Must Scream," in *Alone Against
Tomorrow: Stories of Alienation in Speculative Fiction* (New York: Macmillan,
1971), p. 8.

5. Ibid., pp. 12–13.

6. George Johnson, "An Oracle Part Man, Part Machine," *New York Times*, 23
September 2007, Week in Review, p. 1.

7. John Tierney, "Our Lives, Controlled from Some Guy's Couch," *New York
Times*, 14 August 2007, http://www.nytimes.com/2007/08/14/science/
14tier.html.

8. Charles Duhigg, "Street Scene: A Smarter Computer to Pick Stock," *New
York Times*, 20 November 2006.

9. "PC Beats Doctor in Scan Tests," BBC News, 22 February 2008,
http://news.bbc.co.uk/2/hi/science/nature/7257730.stm. ("Computers
were better able to distinguish signs of Alzheimer's than humans, and
proved cheaper, faster and more accurate than current methods.") See
also *ScienceDaily*: "Called 'artificial neural networks,' the computer-based
method was more accurate than the cardiologist in reading the
electrocardiogram (ECG), a test used to diagnose heart attacks in patients
seen for chest pain in hospital emergency departments," http://www
.sciencedaily.com/releases/1997/09/970916055603.htm.

10. John Markoff, "In Poker Match Against a Machine, Humans Are Better
Bluffers," *New York Times*, 26 July 2007.

11. Nick Bostrom, "Existential Risks: Analyzing Human Extinction Scenarios and Related Hazards," *Journal of Evolution and Technology* 9 (March 2002).

12. Kurt Vonnegut Jr. on humans, interviewed by Jon Stewart, *Daily Show,* 14 September 2005.

13. Steve Lohr, "Sun Microsystems' Co-Founder and Chief Scientist Resigns," *New York Times,* 10 September 2003.

14. All Bill Joy quotes in this section are from his article "Why the Future Doesn't Need Us," *Wired,* http://www.wired.com/wired/archive/8.04/joy.html.

15. http://www.wired.com/wired/archive/8.07/rants.html.

16. Hans Moravec, *Robot: Mere Machine to Transcendent Mind* (Oxford: Oxford University Press, 1998), p. 133.

17. "Every hands-on gene hacker I polled during my project estimated they could synthesize smallpox in a month or two." Paul Boutin, *Biowar for Dummies,* http://paulboutin.weblogger.com/stories/storyReader\$1439.

18. Quoted in Jon Else, *The Day After Trinity: J. Robert Oppenheimer and the Atomic Bomb,* available online at http://www.pyramiddirect.com.

19. Ted Kaczynski, "The Unabomber's Manifesto." aka "Industrial Society and Its Future," available at http://en.wikisource.org/wiki/Industrial_Society_and_Its_Future.

20. Bill McKibben, *Enough: Staying Human in an Engineered Age* (New York: Henry Holt, 2003).

21. Ray Kurzwell, *The Singularity Is Near: When Humans Transcend Biology* (New York: Viking, 2005), p. 395.

## Chapter 8: Dr. Faust

1. I am indebted to Erich Heller (1911–1990) for "Faust's Damnation," a chapter in *The Artist's Journey into the Interior and Other Essays* (New York: Harvest, 1976), pp. 3–44, and for his excellent *The Disinherited Mind* (New York: Harvest, 1975), both indispensable guides for English readers of German literature.

2. Let's call the original 1587 edition *Faust 1.0.* The quotations come from the German original, which was reprinted in Johann Scheible's *Das Kloster* (Stuttgart, 1846), and the passages quoted here were translated into English by Elizabeth M. Butler in her book *Fortunes of Faust* (Cambridge: Cembridge University Press, 1952).

3. Ibid., p. 4.

4. Heller, *Artist's Journey,* p. 5, translating from Scheible's *Das Kloster,* p. 950.

5. Ibid.

6. Wikipedia lists more than a hundred dramas, operas, symphonies, poems, novels, and films: http://en.wikipedia.org/wiki/List_of_works_ which_ retell_or_strongly_allude_to_the_Faust_tale.

7. By P. F. Gent(leman) in 1592.

8. Paul Valéry, *Plays*, trans. David Paul and Robert Fitzgerald, in *Collected Works*, 13 vols., Bollingen Series (New York: Princeton University Press, 1960), vol. 3, p. 41.

9. Quoted in Richard Rhodes, *The Making of the Atomic Bomb* (New York: Simon & Schuster, 1986), p. 676.

10. United States Atomic Energy Commission, *In the Matter of J. Robert Oppenheimer*, Transcript of Hearing Before Personnel Security Board (1954, p. 81), said during hearings investigating allegations of past communist associations in connection with his involvement in the Los Alamos project to develop the atomic bomb.

11. Rhodes, *Atomic Bomb*, pp. 418–20.

12. Quoted in ibid., p. 405.

13. Ibid., p. 770.

14. Ibid., p. 563.

15. Erich Heller, "Faust's Damnation," *Artist's Journey*, p. 17.

16. Quoted in Rhodes, *Atomic Bomb*, p. 676.

17. Robert Oppenheimer, "Physics in the Contemporary World," a lecture delivered at the Massachusetts Institute of Technology, 25 November 1947, in *Technology Review* no. 50 (1948). The remark became notorious when it was quoted in *Time*, 23 February 1948 and 8 November 1948.

18. Daniel M. Wegner, *The Illusion of Conscious Will* (Cambridge Mass.: MIT Press, 2002).

19. Terry Pratchett, *Thief of Time* (New York: HarperCollins, 2001), p. 82.

## Chapter 9: What If It's All a Big Game?

1. Steven Johnson, *Everything Bad Is Good for You: How Today's Popular Culture Is Actually Making Us Smarter* (New York: Riverhead, 2005).

2. Kimberly Young, *Caught in the Net: How to Recognize the Signs of Internet Addiction—and a Winning Stategy for Recovery* (Hoboken, N.J.: Wiley, 1998).

3. Johnson, *Everything Bad*, p. 41.

4. http://wow-tips.blogspot.com/2007/05/underbog-instance-overview .html.

5. Johnson, *Everything Bad*, p. 55.

1. Lewis D. Eigen and Jonathan P. Siegel, *The Manager's Book of Quotations* (New York: American Management Association, 1991).

2. Martin Heller, "The Best Open Source Programming Language: Is Perl, PHP, Python, or Ruby Best? Do Java and JavaScript count?" available online at InfoWorld, http://www.infoworld.com/article/07/09/10/ 37FE-boss-programming-language_1.html.

3. Richard Dooling, "Python on XP: 7 Minutes to 'Hello World!' " provides easy instructions for downloading and installing Python. http://www.richarddooling.com/index.php/2006/03 /14/python-on-xp-7-minutes-to-hello-world or use this tiny url: /http://tinyurl.com/w7wgp.

4. Bill Joy, "Why the Future Doesn't Need Us," *Wired*, http://wired.com/wired/archive/8.04/joy.html.

5. Maastricht, Netherlands, "Researcher: Humans Will Wed Robots" (UPI), 11 October 2007. Levy has since published his findings in a book: *Love & Sex with Robots: The Evolution of Human-Robot Relationships* (New York: HarperCollins, 2007).

6. Henry David Thoreau, *A Week on the Concord and Merrimack Rivers,* reprint (New York: Library of America, 1985).

7. Daniel H. Wilson, *How to Survive a Robot Uprising: Tips on Defending Yourself Against the Coming Rebellion* (New York: Bloomsbury, 2005); and discussion at fn. 14, p. 244.

8. Ibid., p. 111.

9. Isak Dinesen, *Out of Africa* (New York: Random House, 2002), p. 257.

10. http://news.netcraft.com/archives/web_server_survey.html.

11. Eric Raymond, *The Art of Unix Programming,* http://www.faqs.org/docs/artu/ch01s06.html.

12. First formulated by Doug McIlroy. See p. 132*n*.

13. online at Neal Stephenson's website, *In the Beginning Was the Command Line,* http://www.cryptonomicon.com/beginning.html.

14. Ray Kurzweil, *The Singularity Is Near: When Humans Transcend Biology* (New York: Viking, 2005), p. 327.

15. Ibid., p. 329.

16. Stephenson, *In the Beginning.*

17. IBM Whitepaper, *The Toxic Terabyte: How Data-Dumping Threatens Business Efficiency,* June 2006, available online at http://tld.www=03.cacheibm .com/solutions/itsolutions/doc/ content/bin/itsol_toxic_terabyte.pdf.

18. http://en.wikipedia.org/wiki/Data_proliferation.

19. http://crca.ucsd.edu/~hcohen/.

20. E-mail from Alex Martelli to author, 14 August 2007.

## Chapter 11: Open Source

1. OpenOffice available at http://www.openoffice.org/index.html.

## Chapter 12: Post-Rapture Religion

1. Peter De Vries, *The Mackerel Plaza* (New York: Penguin, 1986).

2. Lee M. Silver, *Remaking Eden: Cloning and Beyond in a Brave New World* (New York: HarperPerennial, 1998).

3. "Automated Killer Robots 'Threat to Humanity,' " Breitbart.com, 27 February 2008, http://www.breitbart.com/article.php?id=0802271 11811.y9syyq8p&show_article=1. ("Intelligent machines deployed on battlefields around the world—from mobile grenade launchers to rocket-firing drones—can already identify and lock onto targets without human help.")

4. Bobby Henderson, open letter to the Kansas School Board during its hearings on the teaching of evolution and intelligent design in Kansas schools, available online at http://www.venganza.org/about/open-letter.

5. http://en.wikipedia.org/wiki/Editor_war.

6. Eric S. Raymond, ed., *The New Hacker's Dictionary,* 3rd ed. (Cambridge, Mass.: MIT Press, 1996), p. 221.

7. Bobby Henderson, *The Gospel of the Flying Spaghetti Monster* (New York: Villard, 2006), p. 65.

8. Edward O. Wilson, *On Human Nature* (Cambridge, Mass.: Harvard University Press, 1978), p.175.

9. Sigmund Freud, *The Future of an Illusion,* 8 (1927) in *Complete* Works, vol. 21, ed. James Strachey and Anna Freud (New York: Vintage 2001).

10. Richard Dawkins, *The God Delusion* (New York: Houghton Mifflin, 2006).

11. Christopher Hitchens, *God Is Not Great: How Religion Poisons Everything* (New York: Twelve/Hachette/Warner, 2007).

12. Daniel C. Dennett, *Breaking the Spell: Religion as a Natural Phenomenon* (New York: Viking, 2006); David Sloan Wilson, *Darwin's Cathedral: Evolution, Religion, and the Nature of Society* (Chicago: University of Chicago Press, 2002); and Pascal Boyer, *Religion Explained: The Evolutionary Origins of Religious Thought* (New York: Basic Books, 2001).

13. Wilson, *On Human Nature*, p. 188.

14. *On Human Nature, Consilience: The Unity of Knowledge* (New York: Knopf, 1998); and *Naturalist* (Washington, D.C.: Island, 1994), to name but a few.

15. Wilson, *On Human Nature*, p. 169.

16. Steven Pinker, *How the Mind Works* (New York: W. W. Norton, 1997), p. 55.

17. Dawkins, *God Delusion*, p. 15.

18. Fyodor Dostoyevsky, *The Brothers Karamazov*, trans. Constance Garnett (New York: Signet Classics, 1999) p. 76.

19. Quoted in Brian O'Keefe, "The Smartest (or the Nuttiest) Futurist on Earth," *Fortune*, 14 May 2007, available online at http://money.cnn.com/magazines/fortune/fortune_ archive/2007/05/14/100008848/.

20. Ray Kurzweil, *The Age of Spiritual Machines: When Computers Exceed Human Intelligence* (New York: Penguin, 2000), p. 751.

21. Steven Levy, "Great Minds, Great Ideas," *Newsweek*, 27 May 2002, p. 59.

# Index

# INDEX

# INDEX

# INDEX

# About the Author

RICHARD DOOLING is a novelist, screenwriter, and lawyer, a visiting professor at the University of Nebraska College of Law, and a frequent contributor to the *New York Times*. He is the author of *Critical Care, Brainstorm, Bet Your Life,* and the novel *White Man's Grave,* which was a finalist for the National Book Award. He lives in Omaha, Nebraska, with his wife, children, and computers.